CAMBRIDGE LIBRARY COLLECTION

Books of enduring scholarly value

Naval and Military History

This series includes accounts of sea and land campaigns by eye-witnesses and contemporaries, as well as landmark studies of their social, political and economic impacts. The series focuses mainly on the period from the Renaissance to the end of the Victorian era. It includes major concentrations of material on the American and French revolutions, the British campaigns in South Asia, and nineteenth-century conflicts in Europe, such as the Peninsular and Crimean Wars. Although many of the accounts are semi-official narratives by senior officers and their relatives, the series also includes alternative viewpoints from dissenting leaders, servicemen in the lower ranks, and military wives and civilians caught up in the theatre of war.

Narrative of Services in the Liberation of Chili, Peru, and Brazil, from Spanish and Portuguese Domination

The most renowned naval officer of the mid-nineteenth century, Thomas Cochrane, tenth Earl of Dundonald (1775–1860), led an eventful life. Due to a financial scandal, he left the Royal Navy for a period and became a celebrated mercenary. Volume 1 of this two-volume work, published in 1859, concerns his activity in the wars of independence of Chile and Peru, covering his taking command of the Chilean navy in 1818, his recruitment of British and American officers, attacks on Spanish shipping, littoral warfare on Spanish forts, seizure of booty, and his troubled relationship with the Chilean government. It goes on to recount his command of a Chilean expedition to liberate Peru from the Portuguese in 1820 and his departure from Chile in 1822 before further unrest. Cochrane was the quintessential naval hero of the age, and his memoir remains of interest to both scholars and readers of maritime adventure.

Cambridge University Press has long been a pioneer in the reissuing of out-of-print titles from its own backlist, producing digital reprints of books that are still sought after by scholars and students but could not be reprinted economically using traditional technology. The Cambridge Library Collection extends this activity to a wider range of books which are still of importance to researchers and professionals, either for the source material they contain, or as landmarks in the history of their academic discipline.

Drawing from the world-renowned collections in the Cambridge University Library and other partner libraries, and guided by the advice of experts in each subject area, Cambridge University Press is using state-of-the-art scanning machines in its own Printing House to capture the content of each book selected for inclusion. The files are processed to give a consistently clear, crisp image, and the books finished to the high quality standard for which the Press is recognised around the world. The latest print-on-demand technology ensures that the books will remain available indefinitely, and that orders for single or multiple copies can quickly be supplied.

The Cambridge Library Collection brings back to life books of enduring scholarly value (including out-of-copyright works originally issued by other publishers) across a wide range of disciplines in the humanities and social sciences and in science and technology.

Narrative of Services in the Liberation of Chili, Peru, and Brazil, from Spanish and Portuguese Domination

Volume 1

Thomas Cochrane

CAMBRIDGE UNIVERSITY PRESS

Cambridge, New York, Melbourne, Madrid, Cape Town,
Singapore, São Paolo, Delhi, Mexico City

Published in the United States of America by Cambridge University Press, New York

www.cambridge.org
Information on this title: www.cambridge.org/9781108054034

This edition first published 1859
This digitally printed version 2013

ISBN 978-1-108-05403-4 Paperback

CHILI AND PERU.

NARRATIVE OF SERVICES

IN

THE LIBERATION OF

CHILI, PERU, AND BRAZIL,

FROM

SPANISH AND PORTUGUESE DOMINATION,

BY

THOMAS, EARL OF DUNDONALD, G.C.B.

ADMIRAL OF THE RED; REAR ADMIRAL OF THE FLEET,

ETC. ETC.

VOL. I.

London:

JAMES RIDGWAY, Nº 169, PICCADILLY.

MDCCCLIX.

WESTMINSTER:
PRINTED BY T. BRETTELL, RUPERT STREET, HAYMARKET.

TO THE MOST NOBLE

THE MARQUIS OF LANSDOWNE, K.G.

ETC. ETC.

MY LORD,

I am proud to have been honoured with your Lordship's permission to dedicate to you the following narrative of historical events, respecting which the public has not previously been placed in a position to form a correct judgment. Your Lordship's generous acquiescence enables me to discharge a double debt: First—of thanks to one whose high political character this country will ever warmly cherish;—Secondly—of deep-felt gratitude for the countenance and efficient aid experienced from your Lordship at a period when party faction made me the object of bitter resentment; the injustice of which could in no way be better demonstrated, than by the fact that—in the midst of unmerited obloquy, it was my high privilege to preserve your Lordship's friendship and esteem.

I have the honour to be,

Your Lordship's obliged and faithful Servant,

DUNDONALD.

CONTENTS.

PAGE

CHAPTER VI.

CHAPTER VII.

CHAPTER VIII.

CHAPTER IX.

PREFACE.

THE first of these volumes forms a history of the consolidation of Chilian independence, and of the subsequent liberation of Peru—through the instrumentality of the Chilian squadron under my command; a service which called forth from the Governments and people of the liberated states the warmest expressions of gratitude to the naval service collectively, and to myself personally, as having planned and conducted the operations whereby these results were attained.

It records also the strangely inconsistent fact that—beyond these marks of national approbation—neither Chili nor Peru ever awarded to the squadron or myself any more substantial reward—though, in a pecuniary sense, deeply indebted to us; for, during the greater portion of the war of independence, the subsistence of the crews, and the repairs and equipment of the Chilian squadron were solely provided for by our own exertions, without cost to the Government; since, in addition to the capture of Spanish ships-of-war and merchant vessels—money, provisions, and stores to a great extent fell into our hands; all of which—though our own stipulated right—were voluntarily devoted to state exigencies, in the full conviction that, at the expiration of the war, the value of our sacrifices would, as a point of national honour, be returned to us by Chili. As regards Peru, our still unpaid for captures of ships-of-war formed her first naval force, for which the only requital has been, a vote of her first National Assembly—almost its inaugural act—ascribing to me the double praise of her liberation from the Spanish yoke, and of her subsequent deliverance from an intolerable military tyranny.

The volume contains another point, which forms a yet stranger sequel to my services on the Western shores of South America. After the expiration of thirty years, Chili granted me the absurdly inadequate sum of £.6,000 *in full of all my claims!* And this, with the knowledge that, after my return to England I was involved in litigation on account of the legal seizure of vessels under the orders of her former Government

—by which I was subjected to a loss, directly and indirectly, of *more than three times the amount.* The Chilian portion of this history, therefore, resolves itself into the fact, that not only did I reap no reward whatever, for the liberation of Chili and Peru, but that the independence of both countries was achieved *at a heavy pecuniary sacrifice to myself!* in compensation for which, as well as for my recognised services—Chili has thought its national honour sufficiently vindicated by allotting me *one-third of my losses only,* without other compensation of any kind! I regret to add, that my necessities at the time, arising for the most part from the pecuniary difficulties to which I had been subjected on Chilian account, compelled me to accept the amount tendered.

The second volume is of a character somewhat similar. It narrates the circumstances under which—by promises the most inviting, and stipulations the most binding—I was induced to accept the command, or rather organization of the first Brazilian navy. It details the complete expulsion of all Portuguese armaments, naval and military, from the Eastern shores of the South American Continent, by the squadron alone, wholly unaided by military co-operation; in the course of which arduous service, ships of war, merchant vessels, and valuable property to the extent of several millions of dollars were captured under the Imperial order, and their value —in spite of previous stipulations—*refused to the captors,* on the falsely assumed ground that the provinces liberated were Brazilian—though a Brazilian military force had been recently beaten in an attempt to expel the Portuguese—and though these provinces were, at the period of my assuming the command, in the uninterrupted occupation of the very Portuguese fleets and armies afterwards expelled, it was falsely pretended that the property captured was not enemy's property—though expressly described as such in numerous Imperial decrees—and more especially by the instructions given to me by His Imperial Majesty to seize or destroy it wherever found.

It was, in short, subsequently decided by a Court of Admiralty—for the most part composed of Portuguese members, acting under the influence of a Portuguese faction in the Administration—that neither myself nor the squadron were entitled to the prizes made—though most inconsistently, the same tribunal condemned the ships of war taken—as "*droits*" to the crown—for which, compensation was awarded to the squadron by His Imperial Majesty, but never paid by the ministers to whom the order was directed.

Not to anticipate the contents of the volume devoted to Brazilian affairs. It being found after the expulsion of the enemy, that the stipulations made with myself were too binding to be easily set aside, several futile attempts were made to evade them, but this being found impossible, the unworthy expedient was resorted to of summarily dismissing me from the service, after the establishment of peace with Portugal—an event entirely consequent on my individual services. By this expedient—of the rectitude or otherwise of which the reader will be able to judge from the documentary evidence laid before him—I was got rid of without compensation for my claims, which for thirty years were altogether repudiated; but, at the expiration of that period, fully recognised as *having been due from the beginning!* The Brazilian Government, however, satisfied its own sense of justice by awarding me less than *one-half the simple interest of the amount stipulated in my patents;* thus retaining the whole of the principal admitted to be due.

The preceding remarks form a *synopsis* of my career on both sides of the continent of South America; the narrative, where dispute might arise, being carefully founded on, and in all cases accompanied by documentary evidence, which admits neither dispute nor contradiction.

The trifling amount awarded by Chili, would probably not have been granted at all, but for the earnest remonstrance of Lord Palmerston, warmly seconded by the efforts of the Hon. Mr. Jerningham, British Minister to the Chilian Republic, by whose joint exertions the Government was induced to admit—that national honour was involved in fulfilling national obligations; though an infinitesimal view of either the one or the other was certainly taken when awarding me the insignificant sum previously mentioned.

In Brazil the case was somewhat different. It is to His present Imperial Majesty, Don Pedro II that I owe any investigation of my claims, by the appointment of a Commission (*Secçoes*), which reported that they ought never to have been withheld, as being my stipulated right. But even the limited amount awarded in consequence of this decision, was on the point of being further diminished one half by its projected payment in a depreciated currency—and, had it not been for the intervention of Lord Clarendon, and of the Hon. Mr. Scarlett, British Minister at Rio de Janeiro, of whose zealous exertions in my favour I cannot speak too warmly—this further injustice would have been perpetrated without the knowledge or sanction of His present Imperial Majesty.

It may be asked, why—with the clear documentary evidence in my possession—and now adduced—I have for so many years endured an amount of obloquy and injustice, which might at any time have been set aside by its publication? The reply is obvious. The withholding of my claims by the Governments of both sides the South American Continent, and the ruinous expense to which I was put on account of Chili, entailed upon me many years of pecuniary difficulty. To have told even the truth—unbacked as I then was, by the British Government—would have been to have all my claims set at defiance, so that compulsory discretion was a sufficient reason for my silence. It was long before I could induce a British Minister to satisfy himself of the rectitude of my conduct—the soundness of my claims—or the dishonesty of those who, believing me to be powerless, laughed at reiterated demands for my stipulated rights. Yet more I have never sought from those to whom I gave liberty and dominion.

There is, however, a reason for the present publication, of which I have never lost sight. Amidst all the injustice which it has been my lot to sustain, I have ever determined—for the sake of my family—to whom my character is an heir-loom—that no obloquy shall follow me to the grave, for none have I merited. On the day these volumes see the light, this resolution will be partially fulfilled. On that day I shall have completed the eighty-third year of a career strangely chequered, yet not undistinguished; and, therefore, the opinions of either Chilians or Brazilians are now of small moment to me in comparison with a reputation which has been deemed worthy of belonging to history. None of the present ruling powers in either Chili or Brazil can possibly be offended with me for giving a guardedly temperate documentary narrative of what must hereafter form the basis of their national annals. I do not for a moment contemplate that men of enlightened views such as now direct the affairs of both countries have either part or sympathy with self-interested adventurers who in popular revolutions too often rise to the surface, and for a time make confusion worse confounded; till replaced—as a matter of course, no less than of necessity—by men of greater grasp of mind and more exalted aspirations.

But be this as it may—my reputation as a British seaman is to me of the highest moment, and it shall not be sullied after my death by the aspersions of those who wilfully revenged the thwarting of their anti-Imperial designs, by imputations which can alone enter into the minds of men devoid of generous impulses, and therefore incapable of appreciating higher motives. I have not followed their example, but where it is necessary to bring forward such persons—they will be viewed through the medium of their own documents, which are incontestible and irresistible, and which would as easily convict me of untruth as they convict my maligners of practices unworthy the honour of a nation.

To my own countrymen these volumes can scarcely be matter of indifference; though, perhaps, few reflect that the numerous fleets of British merchantmen which now frequent both shores of South America, are the consequence of the deliverance of these vast territories from an exclusive colonial yoke. It is true that England had previously formed a treaty with Portugal, permitting English vessels to trade to her South American Colonies, but such was the influence of Portuguese merchants with the local governments, that it was nearly inoperative; so that, practically, the Portuguese were in the exclusive possession of that commerce which my expulsion of the fleet and army of the mother country unreservedly threw open to British enterprise. The same, even in a higher degree, may be said with regard to Chili and Peru.

Yet, scarcely had my mission to Chili become known, than the influence of Spain induced the British Ministry to pass a "Foreign Enlistment

" Act," the penal clauses of which were evidently aimed at me, for having entered into the service of unacknowledged governments without permission—though I had shortly before been most unjustly driven from the service of my native country.

In blind animosity towards me, my former English persecutors failed to perceive the advantage to British commerce, of freeing both sides of South America from lingering war and internal dissension. An amusing instance of this occurred on my return to England. Having occasion to wait upon the then Attorney-General relative to a patent which I had in hand, he brusquely inquired "*whether I was not afraid* "*to appear before him?*" On my replying that " I was not aware of having reason to fear " appearing in the presence of any man," he told me the question had been officially put to him, whether I could be punished under the " Foreign " Enlistment Act," for the part I had taken in the liberation of Chili, Peru, and Brazil? To this I replied, that "if Government was " indiscreet enough further to persecute me for " having thrown open to British commerce the " largest field for enterprise of modern times, " they could take what steps they chose, for " that I, having accepted service in South " America before the passing of the Act, was not

" afraid of the consequences of having infringed " its provisions." It is almost needless to say that no such prosecution was instituted, though the will was good, despite the national benefits conferred.

I will not enter farther into the subject in a preface to volumes which themselves form only a summary of events in which I was a principal actor, but at the same time, one, which I hope will prove satisfactory and decisive. It would have been easy to have dilated the narrative, but my object is solely to leave behind me a faithful record of events which must one day become history, and there is no history like documentary history.

To those high personages who have advocated my cause with other nations, the present volume will give satisfaction, as affording additional proof that their advocacy rested upon no visionary basis. To the members of the press, who have adopted the same views, this exposition will be equally satisfactory. To all these I owe the thanks of recognising in me, a love for that service, from which—for a time I was unjustly expelled. It is my intention, if God spare my life, to add to these Memoirs a narrative of my former experience in the British navy, and, what may be of greater utility, an exposition of that which, from jealousy and other causes no less unworthy, *I was not permitted to effect*. To these I shall add a few remarks upon my connexion with the liberation of Greece, developing some remarkable facts, which have as yet escaped the notice of historians. These reminiscences of the past will, at least, be instructive to future generations and if any remarks of mine will conduce to the permanent greatness and security of my country, I shall deem the residue of my life well spent in recording them.

At my advanced age, such a task as that now partially executed, would, perhaps, have presented insuperable difficulties, but for the assistance rendered me by MR. EARP, who, with great perseverance, has unravelled—what, in the lapse of time, had become the almost inextricable confusion of my papers. That, however, has, with his assistance, been accomplished in such a way as to base upon original documents every incident contained in the work—the more important of these documents being adduced, so as to admit of neither doubt nor question. The same course will be pursued in the forthcoming English portion of my career, with a result, I trust, equally clear and convincing.

DUNDONALD.

CHAPTER I.

INVITATION TO TAKE COMMAND OF CHILIAN NAVY—ARRIVAL AT VALPARAISO—FIRST EXPEDITION TO PERU—ATTACK ON SPANISH SHIPPING AT CALLAO—DEPARTURE FOR HUACHO—CAPTURE OF SPANISH CONVOYS OF MONEY—PAITA TAKEN—RETURN TO VALPARAISO TO REORGANIZE THE SQUADRON—OFFER TO GIVE UP MY SHARE OF PRIZEMONEY TO THE REPUBLIC—THIS OFFER DECLINED BY THE SUPREME DIRECTOR—POPULAR CONGRATULATIONS—ATTEMPT ON LADY COCHRANE'S LIFE.

In the year 1817, Don Jose Alvarez, accredited agent of the government of Chili—as yet unacknowledged by European powers—applied to me to undertake the organization of a naval force in that country, capable of contending against the Spaniards; who, notwithstanding the successful revolt of the Chilenos by land, still maintained their predominance on the waters of the Pacific.

Having at that time no professional employment, in consequence of my unjust expulsion from the British naval service, by the machinations of the powerful political party which I had offended—and finding that Chili was making great efforts to create a navy, in furtherance of which object a war steamer had been placed on the stocks in London—I accepted the invitation, engaging to superintend her building and equipment, and to take her to Valparaiso when completed.

Meanwhile, Alvarez received orders from his Government, that, if his proposals had been accepted, no time must be lost in my departure, as the position of Chili was critical, the Spaniards threatening Valparaiso by sea, and being still in possession of the continent from Conception to Chiloe, where they were organizing the savage Indian tribes to carry desolation into the newly emancipated provinces. Reliable information had also been received, that the Court of Madrid was making strenuous efforts to recover its lost possessions by a powerful reinforcement to its Pacific squadron, against which the Chileno ships of war, in their present state, were not in a condition to contend.

Alvarez therefore begged me not to wait for the steamer, the completion and equipment of which he would hasten, but at once to sail for Chili in the *Rose* merchantman, then on the eve of departure. Knowing that the whole of Peru was in the hands of the Spaniards, and that they were also in possession of Valdivia, the strongest fortified harbour to the southward—from both of which there would be considerable difficulty in dislodging them after the arrival of the anticipated reinforcements—I embarked without delay; and on the 28th of November, 1818, landed at Valparaiso, accompanied by Lady Cochrane and our two children.

Our reception, both from the authorities and the people, was enthusiastic, the Supreme Director, General O'Higgins, coming from the seat of Government, Santiago, to welcome us. This excellent man was the son of an Irish gentleman of distinction in the Spanish service, who had occupied the important position of Viceroy of Peru. The son had, however, joined the patriots, and whilst second in command had not long before inflicted a signal defeat upon the Spaniards in the interior; in reward for which service the gratitude of the nation had elevated him to the Supreme Directorate.

A variety of *fêtes* was given at Valparaiso in honour of our arrival, these being prolonged for so many days as to amount to a waste of time. The same scenes were, however, re-enacted at the distant capital, whither the Supreme Director insisted on taking us, till I had to remind His Excellency that our purpose was rather fighting than feasting. Nevertheless, the reception we had met impressed me with so high a sense of Chilian hospitality, that, heartbroken as I had been by the infamous persecution which had driven me from the British navy, I decided upon Chili as my future home; this decision, however, being only an exemplification of the proverb "*L'homme* "*propose—Dieu dispose.*"

The Chilian squadron had just returned from a successful cruise, the gallant Admiral Blanco Encalada, who commanded it, having captured a noble Spanish 50-gun frigate, the *Maria Isabel*, in the bay of Talcahuano.

The squadron consisted of the recently captured Spanish frigate, now named the *O'Higgins*, in honour of the Supreme Director; the *San Martin*, 56 guns, formerly the *Cumberland* Indiaman, which had been bought into the service; the *Lautaro*, 44 guns, also a purchased Indiaman; the *Galvarino*, 18 guns, recently the British sloop of war *Hecate;* the *Chacabuco*, 20 guns; and the *Aracauno*, 16 guns; a force which, though deficient in organization and equipment, was very creditable to the energy of a newly emancipated people.

A few days after my arrival a commission was issued, conferring upon me the title of "Vice-Admiral "of Chili, Admiral and Commander in Chief of the "Naval Forces of the Republic." Admiral Blanco, with patriotic liberality, relinquishing his position in my favour, though, from his recent achievement, justly entitled to retain it; paying me also the additional compliment of personally announcing to the ships' companies the change which had been effected.

My advent was regarded by the captains of the squadron with great jealousy, the more so, as I had brought with me from England officers upon whom I could place implicit reliance. It so happened that two of the Chilian commanders, Captains Guise and Spry, had shortly before arrived from England with the *Hecate*, which had been sold out of the British navy, and bought by them on speculation. The Buenos Ayrean Government having declined to purchase her, they had brought her on to Chili, where the Government took her and received her former owners into its service. These officers, together with Captain Worcester, a North American, got up a cabal, the object of which was to bring about a divided command between myself and Admiral Blanco, or, as they expressed it—" two commodores and no Cochrane." Finding that Admiral Blanco would not listen to this, they persuaded one or two of the inferior ministers—whose jealousy it was not difficult to excite—that it was dangerous and discreditable to a republican Government to allow a nobleman and a foreigner to command its navy, and still more so, to allow him to retain his title; the object being to place Admiral Blanco in the chief command, with myself as his second—by which arrangement, as he had not been accustomed to manage British seamen, they expected to control him as they pleased. Admiral Blanco, however, insisted on reversing our positions, offering his services as second in command, in which arrangement I gladly acquiesced. This insignificant squabble would not be worth narrating, but for its bearing on subsequent events; as well as enabling me to confer a pleasing testimony to the patriotic disinterestedness of Admiral Blanco, who is still one of the brightest ornaments of the Republic which he so eminently aided to establish.

On the 22nd of December my flag was hoisted on board the *O'Higgins*, after which the greatest despatch was used to get the squadron ready for sea. Anxious to avoid delay, on the 16th of January I sailed with four ships only, the *O'Higgins*, *San Martin*, *Lautaro*, and *Chacabuco;* leaving Admiral Blanco to follow with the *Galvarino*, *Aracauno*, and *Puyrredon*. A mutiny having broken out on board the *Chacabuco*, it became necessary to enter Coquimbo, where the leading mutineers were landed, tried, and punished.

I shall here narrate an incident which occurred on our departure. Lady Cochrane, with her children, had returned from Santiago to Valparaiso, to take leave of me on embarkation. She had just gone ashore, and the last gun had been fired to summon all hands on board, when, hearing a loud *hurrah* near the house where she resided, she went to the window, and saw our little boy—now Lord Cochrane, but then scarcely more than five years old—mounted on the shoulders of my flag-lieutenant, waving his tiny cap over the heads of the people, and crying out with all his might, "*Viva la patria!*" the mob being in a frenzied state of excitement.

The child had slipped out of Lady Cochrane's house with the officer, insisting on being carried to his father; with which request the lieutenant, nothing loth, complied. To the horror of Lady Cochrane, she saw her boy hurried down to the beach amidst the shouts of the multitude, and, before she could interfere, placed in a boat and rowed off to the flag-ship, which was at the time under weigh, so that he could not be sent ashore again; there being no alternative but to take him with us, though without clothes—which were afterwards made for him by the sailors—and with no other attendance save that which their rough but kindly natures could administer.

On our way along the coast we received information that the *Antonio* was about to sail from Callao for

Cadiz, with a considerable amount of treasure, so that, in the hope of intercepting her, we cruized just out of sight of the port till the 21st of February. As she did not make her appearance, preparations were made to put in execution a plan which had been formed to attack the Spanish shipping during the Carnival, when, in the height of that festival, less vigilance than ordinary might reasonably be expected. We had previously ascertained that the naval force in the harbour consisted of the frigates *Esmeralda* and *Venganza*, a corvette, three brigs of war, a schooner, twenty-eight gun-boats, and six heavily-armed merchantmen; the whole being moored close in under the batteries, which mounted upwards of 160 guns, whilst the aggregate force of the shipping was 350 guns, as appeared from an official account of their armament.

A direct attack with our small force seemed, therefore, a thing not at present to be attempted; but in its place I had formed the design to cut out the frigates during the carnival, which terminated on the 23rd. Knowing that two North American ships of war were daily expected at Callao, it was arranged to take in the *O'Higgins* and *Lautaro*, under American colours, leaving the *San Martin* out of sight behind San Lorenzo, and if the *ruse* were successful, to make a feint of sending a boat ashore with despatches, and in the meantime suddenly to dash at the frigates, and cut them out. Unfortunately, one of those thick fogs, so common on the Peruvian coast, arose, in which the *Lautaro* parted company, and did not rejoin the flag-ship for four days afterwards, when the carnival being at an end, our plan was rendered abortive.

The fog, which in the climate of Peru often continues for a considerable length of time, lasted till the 29th, when hearing heavy firing, and imagining that one of the ships was engaged with the enemy, I stood with the flag-ship into the bay; the other ships, imagining the same thing, also steered in the direction of the firing, when the fog clearing for a moment, we discovered each other, as well as a strange sail near us; which, when taken possession of by the flag-ship, proved to be a Spanish gunboat, with a lieutenant and twenty men, who, on being made prisoners, informed us that the firing was a salute in honour of the Viceroy, who had that morning been on a visit of inspection to the batteries and shipping, and was then on board the brig of war *Pezuela*, which we saw crowding sail in the direction of the batteries.

The fog again coming on, suggested to me the possibility of a direct attack, which, if not altogether successful, would give the Spaniards such an idea of our determination of purpose, as would inspire them with respect for the Chilian squadron, and might induce their ships to refrain from the protection of their commerce; in which case a blockade would prevent the necessity of separating our small force in chase of them, should they evince a desire of getting to sea.

Accordingly, still maintaining our disguise under American colours, the *O'Higgins* and *Lautaro* stood towards the batteries, narrowly escaping going ashore in the fog. The Viceroy having no doubt witnessed the capture of the gun-boat, had, however, provided for our reception, the garrison being at their guns, and the crews of the ships of war at their quarters. Notwithstanding the great odds, I determined to persist in an attack, as our withdrawing without firing a shot, would produce an effect upon the minds of the Spaniards the reverse of that intended; having sufficient experience in war to know that moral effect, even if the result of a degree of temerity, will not unfrequently supply the place of superior force.

The wind falling light, I did not venture on laying the flag-ship and the *Lautaro* alongside the Spanish frigates, as at first intended, but anchored with springs on our cables, abreast of the shipping, which was arranged in a half-moon of two lines, the rear rank being judiciously disposed so as to cover the intervals of the ships in the front line. A dead calm succeeding, we were for two hours exposed to a heavy fire from the batteries, in addition to that from the two frigates, the brigs *Pezuela* and *Maypeu*, and seven or eight gun-boats; nevertheless, the northern angle of one of the principal forts was silenced by our fire.

A breeze springing up, we weighed anchor, standing to and fro in front of the batteries, and returning their fire; when Captain Guise, who commanded the *Lautaro*, being severely wounded, that ship sheered off, and never again came within range. As from want of wind, or doubt of the result, neither the *San Martin* nor *Chacabuco* had ever got within fire, the flag-ship was thus left alone to continue the action; but as this, from want of co-operation on the part of the other ships, was useless, I was reluctantly compelled to relinquish the attack, and withdrew to the island of San Lorenzo, about three miles distant from the forts; the Spaniards, though nearly quadruple our numbers, exclusive of their gun-boats, not venturing to follow us.

The annexed was the Spanish naval force present:

Frigates.—Esmeralda, 44 guns; Venganza, 42 guns; Sebastiana, 28 guns.

Brigs.—Maypeu, 18 guns; Pezuela, 22 guns; Potrilla, 18 guns; and one, name unknown, 18 guns.

Schooner, name unknown, one long 24, and 20 culverins.

Armed Merchantmen.—Resolution, 36 guns; Cleopatra, 28 guns; La Focha, 20 guns; Guarmey, 18 guns; Fernando, 26 guns; San Antonio, 18 guns.

Total, fourteen vessels, of which ten were ready for sea; and twenty-seven gun-boats.

In this action my little boy had a narrow escape. As the story has been told by several Chilian writers somewhat incorrectly, I will recapitulate the circumstances.

When the firing commenced, I had placed the boy in my after-cabin, locking the door upon him; but not liking the restriction, he contrived to get through the quarter gallery window, and joined me on deck, refusing to go down again. As I could not attend to him, he was permitted to remain, and, in a miniature midshipman's uniform, which the seamen had made for him, was busying himself in handing powder to the gunners.

Whilst thus employed, a round shot took off the head of a marine close to him, scattering the unlucky man's brains in his face. Instantly recovering his self-possession, to my great relief, for believing him killed, I was spell-bound with agony, he ran up to me exclaiming, "I am not hurt, papa: the shot did not "touch me; Jack says, the ball is not made that can "kill mamma's boy." I ordered him to be carried below; but, resisting with all his might, he was permitted to remain on deck during the action.

Our loss in this affair was trifling, considering that we were under the fire of more than two hundred guns; but the ships were so placed that the enemy's frigates lay between us and the fortress, so that the shot of the latter only told upon our rigging, which was considerably damaged.

The action having been commenced in a fog, the Spaniards imagined that all the Chilian vessels were engaged, and were not a little surprised, as it again cleared, to find that their own frigate, the quondam *Maria Isabella*, was their only opponent. So much were they dispirited by this discovery, that as soon as possible after the close of the contest, their ships of war were dismantled, the top masts and spars being formed into a double boom across the anchorage so as to prevent approach. The Spaniards were also previously unaware of my being in command of the Chilian squadron, but on becoming acquainted with this fact, bestowed upon me the not very complimentary title of "El Diablo," by which I was afterwards known amongst them. The title might have been rendered more appropriate, had my efforts been better seconded by the other vessels.

On the following day, having repaired damages, the flag-ship and *Lautaro* again went in and commenced a destructive fire upon the Spanish gun-boats, the neutral vessels in the harbour removing out of the line of shot. As the gun-boats withdrew to a position closer under the batteries, where we could make little impression upon them without getting severely punished by the fire of the fortress, we contented ourselves with the demonstration made.

On the 2nd of March, I despatched Capt. Foster with the gun-boat captured from the Spaniards, and the launches of the *O'Higgins* and *Lautaro*—to take possession of the island of San Lorenzo, when an unworthy instance of Spanish cruelty presented itself in the spectacle of thirty-seven Chilian soldiers taken prisoners eight years before. The unhappy men had ever since been forced to work in chains under the supervision of a military guard—now prisoners in turn; their sleeping place during the whole of this period being a filthy shed, in which they were every night chained by one leg to an iron bar. The joy of the poor fellows at their deliverance, after all hope had fled, can scarcely be conceived.

From the liberated patriots and the Spanish prisoners, I learned that in Lima there were a number of Chilian officers and seamen taken on board the *Maypeu*, whose condition was even more deplorable than their own, the fetters on their legs having worn their ancles to the bone, whilst their commander, by a refinement of cruelty, had for more than a year been lying under sentence of death as a rebel. Upon this, I sent a flag of truce to the viceroy, Don Joaquim de la Pezuela, requesting him to permit the prisoners to return to their families, in exchange for the Spanish prisoners on board the squadron, and others in Chili— where there were great numbers, who were comparatively well treated. The Viceroy denied the charge of ill-treatment—asserted his right, if he thought proper, to regard his prisoners as pirates; retorting that after the battle of Maypeu, General San Martin had treated the Spanish Commissioner as a spy, and had repeatedly threatened him with death. The exchange of prisoners was uncourteously refused, the Viceroy concluding his reply with an expression of surprise that a British nobleman should command the maritime forces of a Government "unacknow-" ledged by all the Powers of the globe." To this latter observation, I considered it incumbent upon me to reply that "a British nobleman was a free " man, and therefore had a right to adopt any " country which was endeavouring to re-establish " the rights of aggrieved humanity; and that I " had hence adopted the cause of Chili, with the " same freedom of judgment that I had previously " exercised when refusing the offer of an Admiral's " rank in Spain, made to me not long before, by the " Spanish Ambassador in London;" this offer having been made by the Duke de San Carlos, in the name of Ferdinand the Seventh.

Our means being clearly inadequate to any decisive attack on the Spanish ships of war, I resolved to try the effect of an explosion vessel, and accordingly established a laboratory on the island of San Lorenzo, under the superintendence of Major Miller, the Commandant of Marines. Whilst engaged in this duty, that able and gallant officer was so severely burned by an accidental explosion, as to render his further services on this occasion unavailable.

On the 22nd of March—our preparations being completed—we again stood towards the batteries, the flag-ship going close in under the combined fire of the forts and shipping, in order to divert the attention of the enemy from the explosion vessel, which was set adrift in the direction of the frigates, but, unfortunately, when within musket shot of them, she was struck by a round shot and foundered, causing complete failure in our object. The *San Martin* and the *Lautaro* keeping far astern, there was no alternative but to withdraw from further attack, leaving the explosion vessel to her fate.

As other attempts, with our want of means, would answer no better purpose than useless demonstration, and as the ships were now destitute of water and provisions, we were obliged to fall back upon Huacho, leaving the *Chacabuco* to watch the movements of the enemy.

The inhabitants of Huacho, who were well disposed to co-operate in any effort for the emancipation of

Peru, afforded us every assistance in provisioning and watering the ships, for which the commandant, Cevallos, shot two influential persons who had been foremost in aiding us, and severely punished others; at the same time seizing our water casks, and sending me an insolent letter of defiance, on which a party of seamen and marines was landed and put the garrison to flight; the officer commanding the party however withdrew from pursuit at hearing salutes fired on the arrival of Admiral Blanco with the *Galvarino* and *Puyrredon*, mistaking this for an engagement with a newly-arrived enemy. The whole of the Government property found in the Spanish custom-house was captured.

The people of Huacho having volunteered information that a quantity of specie belonging to the Philippine Company had been placed for safety on board a vessel in the river Barrança, she was forthwith overhauled, and the treasure transferred to the flagship.

Leaving Admiral Blanco at Huacho with the *San Martin* and *Puyrredon*, on the 4th of April we sailed for Supe, with the *O'Higgins* and *Galvarino*, having previously ascertained that a sum of money destined for the payment of Spanish troops was on its way from Lima to Guambucho; on the following day a party of marines being landed at Patavilca, captured the treasure, amounting to 70,000 dollars, together with a quantity of military stores. On the 7th, having received further information that the Philippine Company had placed other treasure on board the French brig, *Gazelle*, at Guambucho, we sailed for that place, and, on the 10th, the seamen of the *O'Higgins* examined her, and brought off an additional sum of 60,000 dollars.

The secret of our obtaining possession of these and other convoys of Spanish money along the coast, was, that I paid the inhabitants highly for information relative to their transmission, and was thus enabled to seize the treasure even in the interior of the country. As the Chilian Ministry subsequently refused to allow me " secret service money," these disbursements were actually made at my own expense.

It was also my object to make friends of the Peruvian people, by adopting towards them a conciliatory course, and by strict care that none but Spanish property should be taken, whilst their own was in all cases respected. Confidence was thus inspired, and the universal dissatisfaction with Spanish colonial rule speedily became changed into an earnest desire to be freed from it. Had it not been for this good understanding with the inhabitants, I should scarcely have ventured to detach marines and seamen for operations at a distance into the country, as was subsequently the case; the people giving me the most reliable information of every movement of the enemy.

On the 13th, we arrived at Paita, where the Spaniards had established a garrison. A party of marines and seamen was again landed, on which the enemy fled from the fort, and a quantity of brass ordnance, spirits, and military stores, was captured.

Contrary to strict orders, some marines stole a

number of valuable church ornaments, but on the complaint of the authorities I caused them to be restored, punishing the offenders, and at the same time presenting the priests with a thousand dollars to repair the damage done in their churches; this act, though far from conciliating the priests—who dreaded Chilian success—adding greatly to our popularity amongst the inhabitants, which was my object in bestowing the amount. Our thus refraining from plunder was almost beyond the comprehension of a people who had bitter experience of Spanish rapacity, whilst the undisciplined Chilenos, who formed the greater portion of the squadron, as little comprehended why their plundering propensities should be restrained.

On the 5th of May, I proceeded with the flag-ship alone to reconnoitre Callao, having learned that the *Chacabuco* and *Puyrredon* had been chased off the port by the Spanish frigates. Finding that these were again moored under shelter of the batteries, we returned to Supe, convinced that our previous visit to Callao had proved sufficient to deter them from putting to sea for the protection of their own coasts; this, indeed, forming my chief reason for having persisted in attacks which, with our small force, could answer no other purpose; but this alone was an advantage gained, as it enabled us to communicate freely with the inhabitants on the coast, and to ascertain their sentiments, which—from our forbearance, no less than command of the sea—were almost uniformly in favour of co-operation with Chili for their emancipation.

Both at Lima and on the coast, the best effect was produced by the circulation of the following proclamation :—

" Compatriots ! The repeated echoes of liberty in South America have been heard with pleasure in every part of enlightened Europe, more especially in Great Britain, where I, unable to resist the desire of joining in such a cause, determined to take part in it. The Republic of Chili has confided to me the command of her naval forces. To these must the dominion of the Pacific be consigned. By their co-operation must your chains be broken. Doubt not but that the day is at hand on which, with the annihilation of despotism and your now degraded condition, you will rise to the rank of a free nation, to which your geographical position and the course of events naturally call you.

" But it is your duty to co-operate in preparing for this success, and to remove obstacles, under the assurance that you will receive the most efficacious assistance from the government of Chili, and your true friend, COCHRANE."

This proclamation was accompanied by another from the Chilian government, declaratory of the sincerity of its intentions, so that these combined caused us to be everywhere received as liberators.

On the 8th, we returned to Supe, and having learned that a Spanish force was in the vicinity, a detachment of marines and seamen was, after dark, pushed through a heavy surf, and landed, in the hope of taking them by surprise. But the enemy was on the alert, and on the following morning our little party fell into an ambuscade, which would have proved serious, had not Major Miller, who commanded the marines, promptly formed his men, who, attacking in turn, soon put the enemy to flight at the point of the bayonet, capturing their colours, and the greater portion of their arms. On the 13th, a detachment of Spanish troops arrived from Lima under Major Camba, who, notwithstanding his superiority of numbers, did not venture to attack our small party, which withdrew to the ships with a number of cattle taken from the Spaniards; Camba writing to the Viceroy so effective a description of his having "driven "the enemy into the sea," that he was immediately promoted.

Not to enter into further details of our visits to other parts of the coast, where similar captures of provisions and military stores, &c. were effected—it being my practice to compel the Spaniards to supply all the wants of the squadron, nothing being ever taken from the natives without payment,—I resolved—as our means were clearly incommensurate with our main object—to return to Valparaiso, for the purpose of organizing a more effective force, and on the 16th of June reached that port, where we found Admiral Blanco with the *San Martin* and *Chacabuco*, he having been obliged to raise the blockade of Callao for want of provisions; a step with which the Government was highly displeased, though with more reason to blame its own negligence or want of foresight in not providing them. Admiral Blanco was nevertheless put under arrest, but a court of inquiry being held, he was honourably acquitted.

The objects of the first expedition had been fully accomplished, viz. to reconnoitre, with a view to future operations, when the squadron should be rendered efficient; but more especially to ascertain the inclinations of the Peruvians with regard to their desire for emancipation—a point of the first importance to Chili, as being obliged to be constantly on the alert for her own newly-acquired liberties, so long as the Spaniards were in undisturbed possession of Peru. To the accomplishment of these objects had been superadded the restriction of the Spanish naval force to the shelter of the forts, the defeat of their military forces wherever encountered, and the capture of no inconsiderable amount of treasure.

It had, however, become evident to me that the passive system of defence which the Spaniards adopted in Callao, would render it a difficult matter to get at them without more effective means than the guns of the ships, which were greatly inferior in number to those of the enemy's fortress and shipping combined, whilst their experience in the use of artillery was greater than that of our crews. The Supreme Director having paid a visit to the squadron—on the 21st of June I addressed to him a letter, stating my apprehension that the finances of the Government might be limited, and that I would gladly give up to the exigencies of the Republic the whole of my share of prize-money taken during our recent cruize, provided it were applied to the manufacture of rockets. This offer was declined, with a compliment from the Supreme Director, on the advantage already gained, by compelling the Spaniards "ignominiously to shut " themselves up in their port, in spite of their " numerical superiority."

Complimentary addresses from the Chilian people

were also presented to me in profusion, and a public panegyric was pronounced at the National Institute of the capital, upon the service rendered; but as this was only a recapitulation of what has been already narrated—conveyed in flowery rhetorical phrases—in the use of which the Occidentals are almost as expert, and often as exaggerated, as are the Orientals—I shall refrain from giving it. Suffice it to say, that the people were not a little delighted with the plain facts, that whereas only a few months before theirs had been the blockaded port, they were now able to beard the enemy in his stronghold, till then believed—both by Spaniards and Chilians—to be inviolable; and that, with only four ships on our part, the Spanish Viceroy had been shut up in his capital, and his convoys, both by sea and land, intercepted, whilst his ships of war did not venture to emerge from their shelter under the batteries of Callao.

The manufacture of rockets was now carried on in earnest, under the superintendence of Mr. Goldsack, an eminent engineer, who had been engaged in England for the purpose. From a mistaken notion of parsimony, the labour of constructing and filling them was allotted to a number of Spanish prisoners, with what result will appear in the sequel.

In these and other preparations two months were consumed, in the course of which another vessel—an American built corvette—was added to the squadron, and named by the Supreme Director the *Independencia.*

During my absence Lady Cochrane chiefly resided

at Valparaiso, where she diligently employed herself in promoting objects essential to the welfare of the squadron; after a time removing to a delightful country house at Quillota, where her life was endangered by a ruffian in the interest of the Spanish faction.

This man, having gained admission to her private apartment, threatened her with instant death if she would not divulge the secret orders which had been given to me. On her declaring firmly that she would not divulge anything, a struggle took place for a paper which she picked off a table; and before her attendants could come to her assistance she received a severe cut from a stiletto. The assassin was seized, condemned, and ordered for execution, without the last offices of the Catholic religion.

In the dead of the night preceding the day fixed for his execution, Lady Cochrane was awoke by loud lamentations beneath her window. On sending to ascertain the cause, the wretched wife of the criminal was found imploring her Ladyship's intercession that her husband should not be deprived of the benefits of confession and absolution. Forgiving the atrocity of the act, Lady Cochrane, on the following morning, used all her influence with the authorities, not for this alone, but to save the man's life, and at length wrung from them a reluctant consent to commute his punishment to banishment for life.

CHAPTER II.

SECOND EXPEDITION TO PERU—DISAPPOINTMENT AT NOT BEING PROVIDED WITH TROOPS—FAILURE OF ROCKETS—DEPARTURE FOR ARICA—CAPTURE OF PISCO—CAPTURE OF SPANISH SHIPS AT PUNA—DETERMINE TO MAKE AN ATTEMPT ON VALDIVIA—ARRIVAL OFF THAT PORT, AND CAPTURE OF SPANISH BRIG OF WAR POTRILLO—TROOPS OBTAINED FROM CONCEPTION—FLAG-SHIP NEARLY WRECKED—ATTACK ON FORTS, AND CONQUEST OF VALDIVIA.

On the 12th of September, 1819, I again sailed for the Peruvian coast, with Admiral Blanco as second in command. The squadron consisted of the *O'Higgins*, *San Martin*, *Lautaro*, *Independencia*, and *Puyrredon*, the *Galvarino* and *Araucano* not being in readiness. Two vessels accompanied the squadron, to be afterwards fitted up as fire-ships.

The Government was exceedingly anxious that some decisive blow should be at once struck. With the exception of the rockets, the squadron was in little better condition than before, a loan having failed, whilst 4,000 dollars only were subscribed by the merchants. The crews for the most part consisted of *cholos*, or native peasants, whom it was difficult to shape into good seamen, though they fought gallantly when well led. The officers were nearly all English or North American, this being a redeeming feature, but very few of them possessed the tact to bring up the men to anything like a seaman-like standard; a by no means easy task however, as a considerable portion of those embarked did duty both as marines and seamen.

I begged of the Government to supply me with 1,000 troops, asserting that even with that number of men it would be possible to take the castles of Callao, and destroy the whole of the Spanish shipping in the harbour. I was assured that this force had been provided, and was in readiness to embark at Coquimbo, where, on my arrival on the 16th, in place of 1,000 troops I found only 90!—and these in so ragged a condition, that a subscription of 400 dollars was raised by the inhabitants, and given to Major Miller to buy clothing for them.

I was so much annoyed at this, as to be on the point of returning to Valparaiso to throw up my commission; but, reflecting that the squadron was in possession of rockets, and that the Government might even yet forward a military force, I made up my mind to proceed, and on the 29th the squadron again came to an anchor in Callao roads.

The two following days were occupied in making rocket rafts, and in getting ready life-preservers for the men, in case of their falling from the rafts. On the 1st of October the *Galvarino*, *Puyrredon*, and *Araucano*, stood into the bay to reconnoitre, and sustained a heavy fire from the shore, upon which I ordered the *Independencia* to their aid; but that vessel was brought to an anchor when at the distance of several miles from them. On the same day Lieutenant-Colonel Charles, a most able and gallant officer, reconnoitred in a boat, and made trial of some rockets, upon which he reported unfavourably.

In this affair the mast of the *Araucano* was struck by a round shot, and severely damaged—the circumstance being merely mentioned to shew the state in which the squadron was equipped; the only means of repairing the damage being by fishing the mast with an anchor-stock taken from the *Lautaro*, whilst an axe had to be borrowed for the purpose from the flag-ship!

On the 2nd, the *Araucano* again went in, accompanied by a squadron of boats under the command of Captain Guise, and fired several rockets, but with no perceptible effect—the Spaniards having unrigged their ships; the brig sustained considerable damage from the firing of the forts and shipping.

After dark, an attack by rockets and shells was arranged, the *Galvarino* taking in tow a mortar raft, under the command of Major Miller, and placing it, under a heavy fire, within half a mile of the enemy's batteries. The *Puyrredon* followed with another raft, carrying the shells and magazine; the *Araucano* took charge of a rocket-raft, under Captain Hind, whilst the *Independencia* towed in a second rocket-raft, under Lieut.-Colonel Charles, the rest of the squadron remaining at anchor.

Great expectations were formed, as well by myself as the whole squadron, as to the effect to be produced by these destructive missiles, but they were doomed to disappointment, the rockets turning out utterly useless. Some, in consequence of the badness of the solder used, bursting from the expansive force of the charge before they left the raft, and setting fire to others—Captain Hind's raft being blown up from this cause, thus rendering it useless, besides severely burning him and thirteen men: others took a wrong direction in consequence of the sticks not having been formed of proper wood, whilst the greater portion would not ignite at all from a cause which was only discovered when too late. It has been stated in the last chapter that the filling of the tubes was, from motives of parsimony, entrusted to Spanish prisoners, who, as was found on examination, had embraced every opportunity of inserting handfulls of sand, sawdust, and even manure, at intervals in the tubes, thus impeding the progress of combustion, whilst in the majority of instances they had so thoroughly mixed the neutralizing matter with the ingredients supplied, that the charge would not ignite at all, the result being complete failure in the object of the expedition. It was impossible to blame the Spanish prisoners in the Chilian arsenal for their loyalty, but to me their ingenuity was a bitter ground for disappointment, as with useless rockets we were no better off than in the first expedition; nor indeed so well off, for in the interval the Spaniards had so strengthened their booms at the anchorage, as to render it impossible for the ships to get at them—whilst, by constant practice, their fire had acquired a precision which our crews could not equal.

The only damage effected was by Major Miller's

mortar, the shells sinking a gun-boat, and doing some execution in the forts and amongst the shipping. As daylight appeared, I ordered the whole of the rafts to be towed off, there being no further use in their remaining exposed to the heavy fire of the batteries. As it was, our loss was trifling, only about twenty being killed and wounded; but amongst these I had to regret the death of a promising young officer, Lieut. Bealey, who was cut in two by a round shot.

The failure of the rockets was very unfairly attributed by the Chilian Government to Mr. Goldsack, whereas the fault lay in itself for having neither supplied him with proper workmen nor materials. From the scarcity and high price of spelter, he had also been compelled to make use of an inferior solder for the tubes, and thus the saving of a few hundred dollars frustrated the success of a great object. The consequence to poor Goldsack was utter ruin, though of his capability there could be no question, he having for many years been one of the principal assistants of Sir W. Congreve at Woolwich.

By the 5th, one of the explosion vessels was completed, and I resolved to try her effect on the booms and shipping, for which purpose she was placed in charge of Lieut. Morgell, who carried her in gallant style towards the enemy's shipping; but the wind falling calm, she became a target for their really excellent practice, and was in a short time riddled through and through. As the Spaniards began to fire red-hot shot, Lieut. Morgell was compelled to abandon her, first setting fire to the train, then turning her adrift, thus causing her to explode, though at a distance which did no damage to the enemy.

Whilst this was going on, a strange sail was reported off the bay, and the *Araucano* went in chase, Captain Crosbie returning the next morning with the intelligence that she was a frigate. Upon this, the squadron got under weigh, in pursuit, when she made all sail, and as I did not deem it expedient to quit the bay of Callao, the chase was given up, and we returned in the evening to our former anchorage. It was afterwards learned that she was the *Prueba*, of 50 guns, just arrived from Cadiz; whence she had convoyed another ship, with a cargo valued at half a million of dollars; this ship contriving to slip into Callao during the short absence of the squadron in pursuit of the frigate, so that we lost both prizes.

It was useless to remain any longer at Callao, as my instructions peremptorily commanded me not to approach with the ships within range of the enemy's batteries, nor to make any attempt on their squadron, except with the rockets and fire-ships. I was moreover ordered to return within a given time to Valparaiso, these restrictions being insisted on by the Minister of Marine, ostensibly from what he considered my temerity in having attacked the forts and shipping at Callao on the first expedition—but really, from his own narrow-minded jealousy, that I, a foreigner, should effect anything which might give me undue prominence in the estimation of the Chilian people.

I had, however, other reasons for quitting Callao. The newly-arrived Spanish frigate *Prueba*, was at large, and as I had reason to believe, was sheltering at Guayaquil, from which port I made up my mind to dislodge her. The Government had not sent any of the promised supplies for the squadron, which was running short of provisions, so that it was necessary to resort to my former practice of compelling the Spaniards to furnish them; whilst as no troops had been supplied, it was clear that there had never been an intention of sending any; the assurance of the Minister of Marine that they were waiting for me at Coquimbo being only a *ruse* on his part to get me to sea without a military force.

We now received intelligence that the *Prueba* had been accompanied from Spain by two line of battle ships, and that these were daily expected at Arica, whither I proceeded in quest of them, but was disappointed in not finding them. It was subsequently learned, that although they had sailed from Cadiz, in company with the *Prueba*, they never reached the Pacific, one of them, the *Europe*, being pronounced unseaworthy on crossing the line; and the other, the *St. Elmo*, foundering on the passage round Cape Horn!

On the 5th of November, three hundred and fifty troops—now brought by the experience and zeal of Lieut.-Col. Charles into a tolerably soldier-like condition—were distributed on board the *Lautaro*, *Galvarino*, and the remaining fire-ship, and were despatched to Pisco, under the command of Captain

Guise, for supplies to be taken from the Spaniards, the troops being under the orders of Lieut.-Col. Charles, and the marines under the direction of Major Miller.

As it was not improbable that the expected Spanish ships would make for Callao, whilst it was more than probable that the *Prueba* would again attempt to run in, I therefore proceeded towards that port, and on the 8th anchored at San Lorenzo, the United States frigate *Macedonia* being also at anchor there. The presence of the latter put the Spaniards on their mettle, for shortly after our arrival, they made a show of sending twenty-seven gun-boats to attack us, not however, venturing to get their frigates under weigh. Preparations being made on our part to cut off the gun-boats, they quickly retreated, to the no small amusement of the North Americans, for whose edification the spectacle had been exhibited.

I was not mistaken in the expectation that the *Prueba* might again attempt to take shelter under the forts of Callao. On her appearance, we immediately gave chase, but she once more escaped in the night. On my return, I fell in with, and captured her boat, which had been sent ashore with despatches to the Viceroy, and from the information gained from the crew, I now felt certain that she would take refuge in Guayaquil, whither I determined to follow her.

Before doing so in the narrative, the success of the expedition despatched to Pisco must be mentioned. It was the intention of the officers commanding to land in the night, and thus take the garrison by surprise; but this plan was frustrated by the wind dying away, so that the landing could not be effected till broad daylight, when the garrison, supported by field artillery and cavalry, were prepared to receive them. Nothing daunted, the patriot troops landed without firing a shot, through the fire of the guns, whilst the Spanish infantry from house tops, and the church tower, thinned their ranks at every step. At length it came to the bayonet, for which the Spaniards did not wait, but rushed into the square of the town, after having mortally wounded the brave Col. Charles. Major Miller instantly followed, when their last volley in the square, before flying in all directions, brought down him also, with three bullets in his body, so that his life was despaired of. The ships remained for four days, during which they obtained all they wanted; but 200,000 gallons of spirits, placed on the beach for shipment, was destroyed by order of Captain Guise, in consequence of his not being able to control the men, who, from the facility of obtaining liquor, were becoming unmanageable.

On the 16th, the *Galvarino* and *Lautaro* rejoined me at Santa, which place had previously been taken possession of by the marines left on board the flag-ship. On the 21st, I despatched the *San Martin*, *Independencia*, and *Araucano* to Valparaiso, together with a transport filled with sick—an epidemic of a destructive nature having broken out on board the squadron. This disease, which carried off many men, had been introduced on board by the Minister of Marine's army of ninety men, shipped at Coquimbo.

I now proceeded in search of the *Prueba*, with the

flag-ship, *Lautaro*, *Galvarino*, and *Puyrredon*. On the 27th, we entered the river Guayaquil, and leaving the *Lautaro* and the brigs outside, the flag-ship crowded all sail during the night—though without a pilot—arriving next morning at the island of Puna, under which two large vessels were anchored, and instantly attacked, when, after a brisk fire of twenty minutes, they struck, proving to be the *Aguila*, of 20 guns, and *Vigonia*, of 16 guns, both laden with timber, destined for Lima. The village of Puna was also taken possession of. On rejoining the other vessels with the prizes, they were found ready to sail, imagining from the firing that I had fallen in with the *Prueba*, and might possibly get the worst of the contest.

The *Prueba* was at Guayaquil as had been anticipated, but having been lightened of her guns and stores she had been towed up the river, where, from the shallowness of the water, it was impossible to get at her; whilst, as she lay under the protection of the batteries, I did not deem it practicable to cut her out with the boats.

A circumstance here occurred which would not be worth mentioning, did it not bear upon future matters. Captains Guise and Spry—imagining that I should now return to Valparaiso, and that the comparative failure of the expedition would be attributed to me, instead of to the worthless rockets, and to my instructions not to attempt anything beyond their use—endeavoured to get up a mutiny, by circulating a report that I did not intend to permit the ships left outside to share in the prizes, and had indeed left them behind for this purpose; having also permitted my officers to plunder the prizes *ad libitum*, before leaving the river—further declaring, that I intended to claim a double share, from having acted in the capacity of admiral and captain.

As there was not the slightest doubt of their having sedulously circulated these reports, with the object of entering the port of Valparaiso with the squadron in a discontented condition, I determined to take serious notice of their conduct. On the necessary steps being taken, they both pledged their honour that they had not made or even heard of such a report!

But I had no intention to return to Valparaiso, and still less to make officers so inimical to me acquainted with my future plans.

On the 13th of December, Major Miller was so far recovered as to be removed on board the flag-ship, after which I despatched the *Lautaro* to Valparaiso with the two prizes, first transferring to her armament the beautiful brass guns taken in the *Vigonia;* leaving the *Galvarino* and *Puyrredon* to watch the movements of the Spanish frigate.

As the reader may suppose, I was greatly annoyed at having been foiled at Callao, from causes altogether beyond my control, for the bad rockets, and worse faith of the Minister of Marine in not supplying me with the promised troops, were no faults of mine. My instructions, as has been said, were carefully drawn up to prevent my doing anything rash—as the first trip to Callao had been represented by certain officers under my command, who had no great relish for fighting. At the same time the Chilian people expected impossibilities; and I had, for some time, been revolving in my mind a plan to achieve one which should gratify them, and allay my own wounded feelings. I had now only one ship, so that there were no other inclinations to consult; and felt quite sure of Major Miller's concurrence where there was any fighting to be done, though a ball in the arm, another through the chest, passing out at his back, and a left hand shattered for life, were not very promising fighting incentives as far as physical force was concerned, yet the moral courage of my gallant guest was untouched, and his capacity to carry out my plans was greater than before, as being more matured by sharp experience.

My design was, with the flagship alone, to capture by a *coup de main* the numerous forts and garrison of Valdivia, a fortress previously deemed impregnable, and thus to counteract the disappointment which would ensue in Chili from our want of success before Callao. The enterprise was a desperate one; nevertheless, I was not about to do anything desperate, having resolved that, unless fully satisfied as to its practicability, I would not attempt it. Rashness, though often imputed to me, forms no part of my composition. There is a rashness without calculation of consequences; but with that calculation, well-founded, it is no longer rashness. And thus, now that I was unfettered by people who did not second my operations as they ought to have done, I made up my mind to take Valdivia, if the attempt came within the scope of my calculations.

The first step clearly was to reconnoitre the place, where the flagship arrived on the 18th of January, 1820, under Spanish colours, and made a signal for a pilot, who—as the Spaniards mistook the *O'Higgins* for the long-expected *Prueba*—promptly came off, together with a complimentary retinue of an officer and four soldiers, all of whom were made prisoners as soon as they came on board. The pilot was ordered to take us into the channels leading to the forts, whilst the officer and his men, knowing there was little chance of finding their way on shore again, thought it most conducive to their interests to supply all the information demanded, the result being increased confidence on my part as to the possibility of a successful attack. Amongst other information obtained was the expected arrival of the Spanish brig of war *Potrillo*, with money on board for the payment of the garrison.

As we were busily employing ourselves in inspecting the channels, the officer commanding the garrison began to suspect that our object might not altogether be pacific, this suspicion being confirmed by the detention of his officer. Suddenly a heavy fire was opened upon us from the various forts, to which we did not reply, but, our reconnoissance being now completed, withdrew beyond its reach. Having occupied two days in reconnoitring—on the third the *Potrillo* hove in sight; and being also deceived by our Spanish colours was captured without a shot—20,000 dollars and some important despatches being found on board.

As nothing could be done without troops, with which the Chilian ministers had been careful not to supply me, I determined to sail to Conception, where Governor Freire had a considerable force to keep in check the savage tribes of Indians whom the Spaniards employed, under the monster Benavides and his brother, to murder the defenceless patriots. On the 22nd of January we anchored in Talcahuano bay, where we found the Buenos Ayrean brig *Intrepido* and the Chilian schooner *Montezuma.*

Governor Freire received us with great hospitality; and after explanation of my plans, placed two hundred and fifty men at my disposal, under the command of a gallant Frenchman, Major Beauchef; notwithstanding that Freire was on the eve of attacking Benavides, and by thus weakening his division might incur the displeasure of the Government. No time was lost in embarking the men in the three vessels, the *Montezuma* being taken into the service, and the Buenos Ayrean brig volunteering to accompany us.

It was highly praiseworthy on the part of General Freire to place these troops under my orders, inasmuch as they were destined for a service in the praise of which, even if successful, he could not participate; whilst, if unsuccessful, he would certainly have incurred great blame. He knew, moreover, that the Ministry had refrained from supplying me with regular troops; yet he not only generously contributed them, but pledged himself not to communicate my plans to the Government; our destination being even kept secret from the officers, who were told not to encumber themselves with baggage, as we were only going to Tucapel, in order to harass the enemy at Arauco, thus making it appear that we were about to aid General Freire against Benavides, instead of his aiding us to capture Valdivia.

But our difficulties, though we had obtained the troops, were not at an end. The flagship had only two naval officers on board, one of these being under arrest for disobedience of orders, whilst the other was incapable of performing the duty of lieutenant; so that I had to act as admiral, captain, and lieutenant, taking my turn in the watch—or rather being constantly on the watch—as the only available officer was so incompetent.

We sailed from Talcahuano on the 25th of January, when I communicated my intentions to the military officers, who displayed great eagerness in the cause—alone questioning their success from motives of prudence. On explaining to them that if unexpected projects are energetically put in execution they almost invariably succeed, in spite of odds, they willingly entered into my plans; and Major Miller's health being now sufficiently re-established, his value as a commander was as great as ever.

On the night of the 29th, we were off the island of Quiriquina, in a dead calm. From excessive fatigue in the execution of subordinate duties, I had laid down to rest, leaving the ship in charge of the lieutenant, who took advantage of my absence to retire also, surrendering the watch to the care of a midshipman, who fell asleep. Knowing our dangerous position, I had left strict orders to be called the moment a breeze sprang up, but these orders were neglected, and a sudden wind taking the ship unawares, the midshipman, in attempting to bring her round, ran her upon the sharp edge of a rock, where she lay beating, suspended, as it were, upon her keel, and had the swell increased, she must inevitably have gone to pieces.

We were forty miles from the mainland, the brig and schooner being both out of sight. The first impulse both of officers and crew was to abandon the ship, but as we had six hundred men on board, whilst not more than a hundred and fifty could have entered the boats, this would have been but a scramble for life. Pointing out to the men that those who escaped could only reach the coast of Arauco, where they would meet nothing but torture and inevitable death at the hands of the Indians, I with some difficulty got them to adopt the alternative of attempting to save the ship.

The first sounding gave five feet water in the hold, and the pumps were entirely out of order. Our carpenter, who was only one by name, was incompetent to repair them; but having myself some skill in carpentry I took off my coat, and by midnight got them into working order, the water meanwhile gaining on us, though the whole crew were engaged in bailing it out with buckets.

To our great delight the leak did not increase,

upon which I got out the stream anchor, and commenced heaving off the ship, the officers clamouring first to ascertain the extent of the leak. This I expressly forbade, as calculated to damp the energy of the men, whilst as we now gained on the leak, there was no doubt the ship would swim as far as Valdivia, which was the chief point to be regarded, the capture of the fortress being my object, after which the ship might be repaired at leisure. As there was no lack of physical force on board, she was at length floated; but the powder magazine having been under water, the ammunition of every kind—except a little upon deck and in the cartouch boxes of the troops—was rendered unserviceable; though about this I cared little, as it involved the necessity of using the bayonet in our anticipated attack, and to facing this weapon the Spaniards had, in every case, evinced a rooted aversion.

Before making the land to the southward of Punta Galera, the troops in the *O'Higgins* as well as the marines, were, in a high sea, removed into the *Intrepido* and *Montezuma*, to which I shifted my flag, ordering the *O'Higgins* to stand off and on out of sight of land, to avoid creating suspicion. We then made for the harbour, intending to land the same evening and take the Spaniards by surprise, but, as it fell calm, this plan was frustrated.

The fortifications of Valdivia are placed on both sides of a channel three quarters of a mile in width, and command the entrance, anchorage, and river leading to the town, crossing their fire in all directions so effectually, that with proper caution on the part of the garrison no ship could enter without suffering severely, while she would be equally exposed at anchor. The principal forts on the western shore are placed in the following order:—El Ingles, San Carlos, Amargos, Chorocomayo Alto, and Corral Castle. Those on the eastern side are Niebla, directly opposite Amargos, and Piojo; whilst on the island of Manzanera is a strong fort mounted with guns of large calibre, commanding the whole range of the entrance channel. These forts, with a few others, amounted in the whole to fifteen, and in the hands of a skilful garrison would render the place almost impregnable, the shores on which they stand being almost inaccesible by reason of the surf, with the exception of a small landing place at the Aguada del Ingles.

It was to this landing-place that we first directed our attention, anchoring the brig and schooner off the guns of Fort Ingles, on the afternooon of Feb. 3rd, amidst a swell which rendered immediate disembarkation impracticable. The troops were carefully kept below; and to avert the suspicion of the Spaniards, we had trumped up a story of our having just arrived from Cadiz, and being in want of a pilot: upon which they told us to send a boat for one. To this we replied, that our boats had been washed away in the passage round Cape Horn. Not being quite satisfied, they began to assemble troops at the landing-place, firing alarm guns, and rapidly bringing up the garrisons of the western forts to Fort Ingles, but not molesting us.

Unfortunately for the credit of the story about the loss of the boats, which were at the time carefully concealed under the lee of the vessels, one drifted astern, so that our object became apparent, and the guns of Fort Ingles, under which we lay, forthwith opened upon us, the first shots passing through the sides of the *Intrepido*, and killing two men, so that it became necessary to land in spite of the swell. We had only two launches and a gig, into which I entered to direct the operation, Major Miller, with forty-four marines, pushing off in the first launch, under the fire of the party at the landing place, by which the coxswain being wounded, the Major had to take the helm, and whilst doing this, received a ball through his hat, grazing the crown of his head. Ordering a few only of his party to fire, the whole leaped ashore at the landing place, driving the Spaniards before them at the point of the bayonet. The second launch now pushed off from the *Intrepido*, and, in this way, in less than an hour, three hundred men had made good their footing on shore.

The most difficult task—the capture of the forts—was to come; the only way in which the first, Fort Ingles, could be approached being by a precipitous path, along which the men could only pass in single file; the fort itself being inaccessible except by a ladder, which the enemy, after being routed by Major Miller, had drawn up.

As soon as it was dark, a picked party, under the guidance of one of the Spanish prisoners, silently advanced to the attack, expecting to fall in with a body of the enemy outside the fort, but all having re-entered, our men were unopposed.

This party having taken up its position, the main body moved forward, cheering and firing in the air, to intimate to the Spaniards that their chief reliance was on the bayonet. The enemy, meanwhile, kept up an incessant fire of artillery and musketry in the direction of the shouts, but without effect, as no aim could be taken in the dark. Whilst the patriots were thus noisily advancing, a gallant young officer, Ensign Vidal—who had previously distinguished himself at Santa—got under the inland flank of the fort, and with a few men, contrived unperceived to tear up some pallisades, by which a bridge was made across the ditch, whereby he and his small party entered, and formed noiselessly under cover of some branches of trees which overhung it, the garrison directing their whole attention to the shouting patriots in an opposite direction.

A volley from Vidal's party convinced the Spaniards that they had been taken in flank. Without waiting to ascertain the number of those who had outflanked them, they instantly took to flight, filling with a like panic a column of three hundred men, drawn up behind the fort. The Chilians, who were now well up, bayoneted them by dozens, in their efforts to gain the other forts, which were opened to receive them; the patriots thus entering at the same time, and driving them from fort to fort into the Castle of Corral, together with two hundred more, who had abandoned some guns advantageously placed on a height at Fort Chorocomayo. The Corral was stormed with equal rapidity, a number of the enemy escaping in boats to Valdivia, others plunging into the forest; whilst upwards of a hundred, besides officers, fell into our hands, the like number being found bayoneted on the following morning. Our loss was seven men killed, and nineteen wounded.

The Spaniards had, no doubt, regarded their position as impregnable, which, considering its difficulty of access and almost natural impenetrability, it ought to have been, if properly defended. They had only found out their error when too late, thus justifying my former remark to the military officers, that an attack where least expected is almost invariably crowned with success. Much less had the Spaniards calculated on a night attack, the most favourable of all to the attacking party, as necessitating unity of action—and the least favourable of all to the party attacked, as inspiring doubt and panic, almost certain to end in irresolution and defeat. The garrison consisted of the Cantabria regiment of the line, numbering about eight hundred, with whom was associated a militia of upwards of a thousand.

On the 5th, the *Intrepido* and *Montezuma*, which had been left at the Aguada Inglesa, entered the harbour, being fired at in their passage by Fort Niebla on the eastern shore. On their coming to an anchor at the Corral, two hundred men were again embarked to attack Forts Niebla, Carbonero, and Piojo. The *O'Higgins* now appearing in sight off the mouth of the harbour, the Spaniards abandoned the forts on the eastern side, no doubt judging that as the western forts had been captured without the aid of the frigate, they had—now that she had arrived—no chance of successfully defending them; the patriot troops were therefore disembarked at Fort Niebla till the tide served to take them to the town of Valdivia.

In crossing the harbour, the *Intrepido*, from want of precaution in taking soundings, grounded on a bank in the channel, where, bilged by the surf, she finally became a wreck. Nor was the *O'Higgins* in a much better condition, as, from the injury sustained at Quiriquina, it became necessary to put her ashore on a mud bank, as the sole means of saving her from going down in deep water, so that the only vessel left was the little schooner *Montezuma*.

On the 6th, the troops were again embarked to pursue the flying garrison up the river, when we received a flag of truce informing us that the enemy had abandoned the town, after plundering the private houses and magazines; and, together with the Governor, Colonel Montoya, had fled in the direction of Chiloe. From the disorders which were committed by the Spaniards, previous to their retreat, the town was in great consternation, many of the inhabitants having also fled; a proclamation issued by me, to the effect that no one should be molested in person or property, had, however, the effect of inducing them to return; and an additional order immediately to choose for themselves a Governor, at once restored peace and tranquillity—the disposition of the people being for the most part good, whilst any leaning which might have existed in favour of Spanish rule was dissipated by the excesses which, previous to their flight, the royalist troops had committed.

The fortifications were so numerous, that at first it was my intention to destroy them and embark the artillery, as the Spaniards who had escaped to Chiloe—where another Spanish regiment was stationed—might return after my departure and recover them, the force which could be spared to garrison them being insignificant when distributed amongst fifteen forts. On further reflection, I could not make up my mind to destroy fortresses, the erection of which had cost upwards of a million of dollars, and which Chili would find it difficult to replace; and therefore determined on leaving them intact, with their artillery and ammunition, intending, before my return to Valparaiso, to render the rout of the Spaniards who had escaped, yet more complete.

The booty which fell into our hands, exclusive of the value of the forts and public buildings, was considerable, Valdivia being the chief military depôt in the southern part of the continent. Amongst the military stores, were upwards of 1,000 cwt. of gunpowder, 10,000 cannon shot, of which 2,500 were brass, 170,000 musket cartridges, a large quantity of small arms, 128 guns, of which 53 were brass, and the remainder iron; the ship *Dolores*, afterwards sold at Valparaiso for 20,000 dollars, with public stores, also sold for the like value; and plate, of which General Sanchez had previously stripped the churches of Conception, valued at 16,000 dollars.

From correspondence found in the archives of Valdivia, it was clear that Quintanilla, the Governor of Chiloe, had serious apprehensions of a revolt at San Carlos, so that, in place of returning to Valpaparaiso, I resolved to see what could be effected there. The loss of the *Intrepido* was a serious drawback to our means of transporting troops, and the flag-ship would no longer float; as, however, we had possession of the *Dolores*, it was resolved to crowd into her and the *Montezuma* all the troops that could be spared, leaving Major Beauchef the whole of those brought from Conception.

Meanwhile, I despatched a *piragua* to Valparaiso with the intelligence of our success; the unexpected news, as was afterwards learned, creating such an amount of popular enthusiasm as had never before been witnessed in Chili. The most amusing part of the affair was, that by the time my despatches announcing our victory reached Vaparaiso, the other ships of the squadron had also arrived, when Captain Guise and his officers had attributed our rocket failure at Callao to my want of skill in their use; the inference desired, being my want of capability to command a squadron. Not a word of blame was then attributed to poor Goldsack, who had superintended their manufacture, as indeed none was deserved, though the blame afterwards attributed to him ended as before stated in his ruin.

To this alleged want of professional skill on my part, Zenteno had drawn up an elaborate accusation against me of disobedience to orders, in not having returned, according to my instructions; the whole *clique* felicitating themselves on my dismissal with disgrace. Even the people did not know what judgment to form, as all materials for forming an opinion were kept from them, whilst every pretence tending to my discredit was carefully made known. On news of the victory, all this was immediately hushed up—the ministers, to retrieve their own credit, joined in the popular enthusiasm, which it would have been unavailing to thwart—and poor Goldsack was overwhelmed with reproach for the failure of his rockets, though the whole blame rested with the Government in having employed Spanish prisoners as his workmen.

CHAPTER III.

DEPARTURE FOR CHILOE—PREPARATIONS OF THE ENEMY—CAPTURE OF FORT CORONA—FAILURE AT FORT AGUY, AND SUBSEQUENT RETREAT—RETURN TO VALDIVIA—CAPTURE OF OSORIO—RETURN TO VALPARAISO—ENTHUSIASTIC RECEPTION—CHAGRIN OF THE MINISTRY—IMPORTANCE OF CONQUEST OF VALDIVIA IN A POLITICAL POINT OF VIEW—PROMOTION OF OFFICERS UNDER ARREST—EMPLOYMENT OF INDIANS BY THE SPANIARDS—CAREER OF BENAVIDES—MUTINOUS SPIRIT OF THE SEAMEN IN CONSEQUENCE OF THEIR CAPTURES BEING APPROPRIATED BY GOVERNMENT—RESIGNATION OF MY COMMISSION—REFUSAL THEREOF—RENEWED OFFER OF AN ESTATE—THIS AGAIN DECLINED—SEAMEN OBTAIN THEIR WAGES—PRIVATE PURCHASE OF AN ESTATE—GOVERNMENT GIVES NOTICE OF TAKING IT—APPOINTMENT OF FLAG CAPTAIN AGAINST MY WISHES—ANNOYANCE GIVEN TO ME BY MINISTER OF MARINE—RENEWED RESIGNATION OF THE COMMAND—OFFICERS OF THE SQUADRON RESIGN IN A BODY—GOVERNMENT BEGS OF ME TO RETAIN THE COMMAND—MY CONSENT—GENERAL SAN MARTIN—THE SENATE—ZENTENO—CORRUPTION OF PARTIES IN THE ADMINISTRATION.

HAVING provided for the safety of the city and province of Valdivia, by establishing a provisional government, and left Major Beauchef with his own troops to maintain order—on the 16th of February, I sailed with the *Montezuma* schooner, and our prize the *Dolores*, for the island of Chiloe, taking with me two hundred men, under the command of Major Miller, my object being to wrest Chiloe from Spain, as I had done Valdivia. Unfortunately, the services of the flag-ship, the *O'Higgins*, were not available, there being no way of rendering her seaworthy, without tedious repairs, for which there was no time, as our success depended on attacking Chiloe before the Governor had leisure to prepare for defence. Neither of our vessels being armed for fighting, I depended altogether upon Major Miller and our handful of soldiers to oppose a thousand regular troops, besides a numerous militia; but having been informed that the garrison was in a mutinous state, I calculated that by judicious management, they might be induced to join the patriot cause.

Unluckily, our design had got wind, and the Spanish Governor, Quintanilla, a judicious officer, had managed to conciliate them. On coming to an anchor on the 17th, at Huechucucay, we found a body of infantry and cavalry, with a field-piece, ready to dispute our landing; but drawing off their attention by a feigned attack upon a distant spot, and thus dividing them into two parties, Major Miller got on shore, and soon routed them, capturing their field-piece

A night attack being decided upon, the troops, a hundred and seventy in number, moved on under the direction of a guide, who, wilfully or treacherously, misled them, the men thus wandering about in the dark throughout the whole night. At dawn, they found their way to Fort Corona, which, with a detached battery, was taken without loss. Halting for a short time to refresh the men, Major Miller bravely, but too precipitately, moved on Fort Aguy, in broad daylight; this fort being the stronghold of the enemy, mounting twelve guns, with others flanking the only accessible path by which entrance could be gained, and being garrisoned by three companies of regulars, two companies of militia, and a full proportion of artillerymen. The fort stood on a hill, washed on one side by the sea, and having on the other an impenetrable forest, the only access being by a narrow path, whilst the means of retreat for the garrison was by the same path, so that the attack became for the latter a matter of life and death, since, in case of defeat, there was no mode of escape, as at Valdivia.

In spite of these odds, and the spectacle of two fanatical friars on the ramparts, with lance in one hand, and crucifix in the other, urging on the garrison to resist to the death the handful of aggressors—the indomitable courage of Miller did not allow him to remain in the forts he had already taken till nightfall, when he would have been comparatively safe by attacking in the dark. Choosing out of his small band a forlorn hope of sixty men, he perilled his own safety, upon which so much depended, by leading them in person; every gun and musket of the enemy being concentrated on a particular angle of the path which he must needs pass. As the detachment reached the spot, a shower of grape and musketry mowed down the whole, twenty out of the sixty being killed outright, whilst nearly all the rest were mortally wounded. Seeing their gallant Commander fall, the marines, who were waiting to follow, dashed through the fire, and brought him off, with a grape-shot through his thigh, and the bones of his right foot crushed by a round shot. Another dash by the force which remained brought off the whole of the wounded, though adding fearfully to their numbers. This having been accomplished, Captain Erescano, who succeeded to the command, ordered a retreat; the Spaniards, animated by success, and urged on by the friars, following just within musket-shot, and making three separate attacks, which were on each occasion repelled, though from the killed and wounded, the pursuers were now fully six times their number. Nevertheless one-half of the diminished band kept the enemy at bay, whilst the other half spiked the guns, broke up the gun-carriages, and destroyed the military stores in the forts captured in the morning, when they resumed their march to the beach, followed by the Spaniards as before.

The marines who, with affectionate fidelity, had borne off Major Miller, had been careful to protect him from fire, though two out of the three who carried him were wounded in the act; and when, on arriving at the beach, they were invited by him to enter the boat, one of them, a gallant fellow named Roxas, of whom I had spoken highly in my despatches from Valdivia, on account of his distinguished bravery, refused, saying, "No, Sir, I was the first "to land, and I mean to be the last to go on board." He kept his word; for on his Commander being placed in safety, he hastened back to the little band, now nearly cut up, and took his share in the retreat, being the last to get into the boats. Such were the Chilenos, of whom the mean jealousy of the Minister of Marine, Zenteno, refused to allow me a thousand for operations at Callao—which could have been conducted with ease, as Valdivia had been captured with less than a third of that number.

Our force being now seriously diminished, and feeling convinced that the fanatics of Chiloe were devoted to the cause of Spain, there was nothing left but to return to Valdivia, where, finding that the Spaniards who had been dispersed in the neighbourhood were committing excesses, I despatched Major Beauchef with 100 men to Osorio to secure that town, the relief being accepted with great joy even by the Indians, of whom, wrote Major Beauchef to me, "I have embraced more than a thousand "Caciques and their followers. They have all "offered their services to fight in the patriotic "cause; but as circumstances do not require this, I "have invited them to return to their own lands, "and have received their promises to be ready if the "country should call for their services." The Spaniards being driven from Osorio, the flag of Chili was, on the 26th of February, hoisted on the castle by Major Beauchef, who returned to Valdivia.

There being nothing further to require my presence, I placed the *O'Higgins* under the orders of my secretary, Mr. Bennet, to superintend her repairs, and embarked in the *Montezuma*, for Valparaiso, taking with me five Spanish officers who had been made prisoners, amongst whom was Colonel Fausto De Hoyos, the Commandant of the Cantabria regiment.

On my departure, the Spaniards, elated by their success at Chiloe, combined with those who had been driven from Valdivia, in an attempt to recover their lost possessions, but Major Beauchef, having timely intelligence of their intention, set out to meet them. A number of volunteers having joined the patriot force, Major Beauchef on the 6th of March encountered the enemy on the river Toro, and instantly attacked them, when, in about an hour, the Spanish officers mounted their horses and fled in a body, leaving the men to their fate. Nearly three hundred of these immediately surrendered, and Major Beauchef—having captured the whole of the arms and baggage—returned in triumph to Valdivia.

On the 27th of February, I arrived at Valparaiso, in the *Montezuma*, amidst the most lively demonstrations of enthusiasm on the part of the populace, and warm expressions of gratitude from the Supreme Director. But my reception by his ministers was wholly different. Zenteno, through whose orders I had broken, declared, that the conquest of Valdivia "was the act of a madman! that I deserved to have "lost my life in the attempt; and even now ought "to lose my head for daring to attack such a place "*without instructions*, and for exposing the patriot "troops to such hazard;" afterwards setting on foot a series of intrigues, having for their object the depreciation of the service which had been rendered, so that I found myself exposed to the greatest possible vexation and annoyance, with not the slightest indication of national acknowledgment or reward to myself, officers, or men.

The chagrin of Zenteno and the bad passions of his adherents were further enhanced by the congratulatory addresses which poured in on both the

Supreme Director and myself from all parts, the people declaring, contrary to the assertions of Zenteno, that I had acted, not from any feeling of personal vanity, but from a conviction of the national utility of the act; and that by its accomplishment the valour of the Chilenos had been so displayed as to shew that they had the utmost confidence in their officers, and hence possessed the moral as well as physical courage necessary for further achievements.

Notwithstanding the envious dissatisfaction of Zenteno, the government was compelled, in deference to the popular voice, to award medals to the captors, the decree for this stating that "the capture of "Valdivia was the happy result of the devising of "an admirably arranged plan, and of the most "daring and valorous execution." The decree further conferred on me an estate of 4,000 quadras from the confiscated lands of Conception, which I refused, as no vote of thanks was given by the legislature; this vote I finally obtained as an indemnification to myself for having exceeded my orders; such being necessary after Zenteno's expressions of ill-will towards me on account of breaking through instructions.

Situated as Chili then was, it is impossible to over-rate the importance of this acquisition—the capture of a noble harbour protected by fifteen forts, and the magazines with their vast amount of military stores, being even secondary to the political advantages gained by the Republic.

The annexation of this province, at one blow

conferred on Chili complete independence, averting the contemplated necessity for fitting out a powerful military expedition for the attainment of that object, vitally essential to her very existence as an independent state; because, so long as Valdivia remained in the hands of the Spaniards, Chili was, in her moments of unguardedness or disunion, in constant danger of losing the liberties she had, as yet, but partially acquired.

The resources of the province of Valdivia, together with those of Conception, had contributed the means whereby the Spaniards maintained their hold upon the Chilian territory. Not only were they deprived of these resources—now added to those of Chili—but a great saving was effected by exonerating the Republic from the necessity of maintaining a military force in the southern provinces, as a check upon both Spaniards and Indians, who, at the moment of our conquest of Valdivia, were being let loose in all directions against the Chilian patriots.

Setting aside, therefore, the removal of danger, and the complete establishment of independence, the money value alone of the conquest was, to a Government of very limited means, of the first importance, as doing away with the necessity of military expenditure, estimated by competent judges at a million of dollars, merely to attempt the accomplishment of an object, which, without any additional cost, I had effected with a single ship, so unseaworthy that she had to be left behind.

But the advantage of the conquest did not end

here. Had it not been for this capture, the Spanish power in Chili, aided by the Indians, would have found it easy to maintain itself in such a country for a protracted period, despite any military force Chili was in a condition to bring against it; so that no effective co-operation with the people of Peru could have been undertaken—as common prudence would have deterred them from entering into distant revolutionary projects, so long as the Spaniards were in possession of any part of the Chilian territory; whilst the necessity of defending herself through a protracted civil war, would have prevented Chili from aiding in the liberation of Peru, which would thus have remained a permanent base of operations for the Spaniards to annoy, if not again to recover, the Chilian provinces.

A further advantage was the successful negociation of a loan of one million sterling in England, which was accomplished solely on account of what had been achieved, every attempt at this having failed so long as the Spaniards were in possession of the most important harbour and fortress in the country, from which, as a basis, they might organize future attempts to recover the revolted provinces.

Notwithstanding these advantages, not a penny in the shape of reward, either for this or any previous service, was paid to myself, the officers, or seamen, nevertheless the Government appropriated the money arising from the sale of the *Dolores*, and the stores with which she was loaded; neither was there any account taken of the value of the guns and the enormous amount of ammunition left in the forts at Valdivia. The men who performed this achievement were literally in rags, and destitute of everything, no attempt being made by the department of Marine to lessen their sufferings—for to this extent was their condition reduced.

In place of reward, every encouragement was offered to the officers to disobey my orders. Two of these I had marked for punishment, for deliberate murder. Ensign Vidal having captured two Spanish officers in Fort Ingles, they surrendered their swords, receiving the gallant youth's pledge of safety; but Captain Erescano coming up, immediately butchered them. Another case was even worse: Ensign Latapia, who had been left in command of the castle of Corral, after my departure to Chiloe, ordered two of his prisoners to be shot; and four officers would have met the same fate, had not my secretary, Mr. Bennet, taken them on board the *O'Higgins*. For this I placed Latapia under arrest, making the necessary declarations for a court-martial, and conveyed him as a prisoner to Valparaiso, where, in place of being punished, both he and Erescano were promoted, and taken into the liberating army of General San Martin.

I have spoken of the aid afforded to the Spaniards by the Indians. On the 10th of March General Freire, afterwards Supreme Director, wrote me a letter congratulatory of my success against Valdivia, which he concluded by informing me that its capture had already caused the Indians of Angol, and their

Cacique, Benavente, to declare in favour of Chili, and that he did not doubt but that this would shortly be followed by a similar declaration on the part of the Indians throughout the province; General Freire not being aware that I had already produced this effect by distributing amongst them an immense quantity of trumpery stores and gewgaws, accumulated by the Spaniards in the magazines at Valdivia, for the purpose of rewarding murderous inroads into the Chilian territory.

It will be interesting briefly to note the employment of Indians by the Spaniards. Their agent, or leader, in this horrible warfare, was a wretch named Benavides, who may fairly lay claim to the distinction of being the most perfect monster who ever disgraced humanity. He had originally been a common soldier in the Buenos Ayrean army, and, together with his brother, had *carte blanche* from the Spaniards to commit the most fearful atrocities on the Chilian patriots, who could not defend themselves against the stealthy cowardice of Indian warfare. His invariable practice was, whenever a village or estate could be surprised, to sew up the leading inhabitants as tightly as possible in raw ox-hides stripped from their own cattle, when, being laid in the burning sun, the contraction of the hides as they dried caused a slow and lingering death of perfect agony, which it was the amusement of himself and the savages whom he led to enjoy whilst smoking their cigars. When any persons of influence fell into his hands, he cut out their tongues, and otherwise horribly mutilated them—a bishop and several other gentlemen surviving as witnesses of his atrocities.

Valdivia was this man's *point d'appui*, whence he drew his supplies, and when we took the place a small vessel fell into our hands, laden with arms and ammunition for his disposal amongst the Indians. She was destined for Arauco, and had on board two Spanish officers and four non-commissioned officers, sent for the purpose of rendering the Indians still more formidable by indoctrinating them into European modes of warfare.

The wretch Benavides was afterwards bought over by General San Martin, and sent to Conception for the orders of General Freire, who told him to his face that he would have nothing to do with such a monster; whereupon Benavides left Conception, and commenced a desolating warfare upon the inhabitants of the coast, even refining upon his former barbarities. The country getting too hot for him, he again offered his services to the Spaniards, and was on his way to Peru in a small vessel, when, being compelled to go ashore for water, in the vicinity of Valparaiso, one of his men betrayed him, and he was sent to Santiago, where he was hung.

The seamen were becoming mutinous, in consequence of neither receiving pay nor prize-money, every promise given being broken, as well to them as to myself. As they looked to me for the vindication of their rights, and, indeed, had only been kept from open outbreak by my assurance that they should be paid, I addressed a letter of expostulation to the Supreme Director, recounting their services and the ill-merited harshness to which they were exposed at the hands of his Ministers, notwithstanding that since their return they had aided the Government in the construction of wharves and other conveniences necessary for the embarkation of troops and stores to Peru—a military expedition to that country being now decided on.

The fact was, that the proceeds of the captures were appropriated by the Government, which, to avoid repayment, declared that the conquest of Valdivia was a *restoration!* though the place had never been in possession of Chili. On my refusing to allow the stores I had brought from thence to be disembarked, unless as a compensation to the seamen, it was alleged as a reason for the course pursued that even if Valdivia had not belonged to the Republic, Chili did not make war on every section of America. It was therefore put to my liberality and honourable character whether I would not give up to the Government all that the squadron had acquired?

These views were written by Monteagudo, afterwards the willing instrument of General San Martin in Peru. I asked him, "Whether he considered that "which had been advanced as just, or according to "law?" The reply was, "*Certainly not, but I was* "*ordered to write so!*" Finding that I would surrender nothing, it was next debated in the Council whether I ought not to be brought to a court martial for having delayed and diverted the naval forces of Chili to the reduction of Valdivia, without the orders of Government!

No doubt this course would have been decided on but from the unsettled condition of the Republic and fear of the populace, who denounced the views of the Ministry as heartily as they advocated my proceedings.

As nothing in the shape of justice could be obtained for the squadron, on the 14th of May, I begged His Excellency the Supreme Director to accept the resignation of my Commission, as, by retaining it, I should only be instrumental in promoting the ruin which must follow the conduct of his advisers; at the same time telling him I had not accepted it to have my motives misconstrued, and my services degraded as they had been on account of objects which I was unable to divine, unless, indeed, a narrow-minded jealousy, such as that which designated the capture of Valdivia, its "*restoration*," though it had never before passed from under the dominion of the Spaniards.

This course had not been anticipated, though it was not adopted in any spirit of intimidation, but from repugnance to the heartless ingratitude with which important national services had been met. The Ministers were, however, thus brought for a time to their senses, the justice of my complaints being acknowledged, and every assurance given that for the future the Government would observe good faith towards the squadron. An estate, as has been said, had been offered to me as a reward for my services, which was declined for reasons already adduced. The offer was now renewed, but again declined, as nothing but promises were as yet forthcoming to the service, and the only hold upon the seamen was my personal influence with them, in consequence of my unyielding advocacy of their rights—a hold which I was not likely to forego for a grant to myself. In place, therefore, of accepting the estate, I returned the document conveying the grant, with a request that it might be sold, and the proceeds applied to the payment of the squadron; but the requisition was not complied with.

Seeing that I was determined not to be trifled with, and shamed by my offer of applying the estate to the payment of the men, General San Martin, who was appointed to command the military portion of the expedition to Peru, came to Valparaiso in June, and on the 13th of July, the squadron was paid wages in part only, but as I insisted on the whole being liquidated, this was done on the 16th; but without any portion of their prize-money. My share alone of the value of captures made at and previous to the capture of Valdivia was 67,000 dollars, and for this I received the assurance of the Supreme Director that it should be paid to me at the earliest possible moment; upon which I accepted the estate which continued to be pressed upon me, the grant expressing the purpose for which it was given, adding as a reason that "my "name should never cease from the land." This estate, situated at Rio Clara, was, after my departure from Chili, forcibly resumed by the succeeding Government; and the bailiff, whom I had placed upon it for the purpose of seeing how it could be improved by culture and the introduction of valuable European seeds, was forcibly expelled from its supervision.

On my first refusal to accept the estate—for the reason before assigned—in order to convince the Chilians how great was my desire to be enrolled amongst the number of their citizens, I purchased a *hacienda* at Herradura, about eight miles from Valparaiso. The effect produced by this upon the Ministry was almost ludicrous. It was gravely argued amongst them as to what I, a foreigner, could intend by purchasing an estate in Chili? The conclusion to which they came being, as I was credibly informed, that as the whole population was with me, I must intend, when opportunity served, to set myself up as the ruler of the Republic, relying upon the people for support! Such was statesmanship at that day in Chili.

It so happened, that soon after purchasing this property I pointed out to the Government how much better the Bay of Herradura was calculated for a naval arsenal, than the ill-protected Bay of Valparaiso; offering at the same time to make them a gratuitous present of all the land required for the establishment of a naval arsenal and marine *depôt.* This offer was, no doubt, construed into an act, on my part, to gain additional popularity—though this, perhaps, would have been no easy matter; and a notice was served upon me not to make any improvements, as the

Government intended to appropriate the estate—but would not reimburse any outlay, though they would repay me the purchase money, and also for any improvements that had already have been effected!

I instantly solicited an explanation of the Supreme Director, and received an apology, attributing the whole affair to the officiousness of the Attorney-General, who had founded his proceeding on an old Spanish law; and there, for a time, the matter dropped, but for a time only—viz. so long as the necessities of the state required my services.

A new source of annoyance now arose, in all kinds of attempts to lessen my authority in the navy, but as I was always on the alert to maintain my position, these resulted in nothing but defeat to their concoctors. At length an overt act was committed in the appointment of Captain Spry as my flag captain on board the *O'Higgins*, which had been repaired at Valdivia, and was now come down to Valparaiso. An order to this effect was sent to me, which I promptly refused to obey, adding that Captain Spry should never tread my quarter-deck as flag captain, and that if my privilege as an admiral were not admitted, the Government might consider my command as at an end, for so long as I continued in command of the squadron, I would not permit an executor of my orders to be forced upon me. The point was immediately conceded, and Captain Crosbie was appointed flag captain.

The nomination of Spry was, no doubt, meant to control my efforts in the future expedition to Peru, the credit of which, if any, was to be reserved for the army. As far as I knew anything of Captain Spry, I had no personal objections to him, but, restricted as I had been by the Minister of Marine Zenteno, I had great doubts as to the motives for appointments of his making, being convinced that his principal aim was to prevent me from doing anything beyond keeping the Spaniards in check, an operation to which I was by no means inclined to accede, as had been evinced by the recent conquest of Valdivia, in excess of his instructions.

Encouraged by the annoyance given to me by the Minister of Marine and his party, one or two of my captains thought themselves at liberty to manifest a disregard to my authority, which, as their admiral, I did not choose to tolerate. The most influential of these was Captain Guise, who, having been guilty of several acts of direct disobedience and neglect of duty, was, by my orders, put in arrest, pending a demand made by me that the Government should institute a court martial for the investigation of his conduct. This act greatly irritated Zenteno, who desired to support him, and refused consent to the inquiry; thus establishing a precedent for the captain of any ship to consider himself independent of the admiral.

Such an act of folly in violation of the discipline of the navy, no less than of personal insult to myself, determined me to have nothing more to do with the Chilian administration, and on July 16th, I once more transmitted to the Government my resignation, at the same time demanding my passport to quit the

F

country, notifying to the officers of the squadron that on the receipt of the same I should cease to command. A meeting was immediately held amongst them, and on the same day, I received—not a valedictory address, as might have been expected—but two letters, one signed by five captains, and the other by twenty-three commissioned officers, containing resolutions of abandoning the service also, at the same time handing in their commissions. To this proof of attachment, I replied, by requesting that they would not sacrifice their own positions on my account, and recommended them not to make their resolutions public till they had further considered the matter, as it might be seriously detrimental to the interests of the country.

The following letter was addressed to me on this occasion by the officers of the squadron:—

"On board the *Independencia*, July 18, 1820.

"My Lord,

"The general discontent and anxiety which your Lordship's resignation has occasioned amongst the officers and others of the squadron, afford a strong proof how much the ungrateful conduct of the Government is felt by those serving under your command.

"The officers whose names are subscribed to the enclosed resolutions, disdaining longer to serve under a Government which can so soon have forgotten the important services rendered to the State, beg leave to put in your hands their commissions, and to request you will be kind enough to forward them to the Minister of Marine. At the same time that we are thus forced to withdraw ourselves from the service, our warmest wishes will be offered up for the prosperity and liberty of the country.

"Signed by 23 Commissioned Officers."

The following resolutions accompanied this letter:—

"RESOLVED—1. That the honour, safety, and interest of the Chilian navy entirely rest on the abilities and experience of the present Commander-in-Chief.

"2. That, as the feelings of unbounded confidence and respect which we entertain for him cannot be transferred to another, we have come to the resolution of resigning our commissions, and of transmitting them to Government, through the hands of our admiral.

"3. That our commissions shall be accompanied by a letter expressive of our sentiments, signed by all whose commissions are enclosed.

"Signed by 23 Officers."

Pending the acceptance of my resignation by the Government, the equipment of the squadron was carried on with the greatest alacrity, so that there might be no ground for complaint that the termination of my command had caused any remissness in our duties. I, however, withheld the commissions which had been enclosed to me by the officers of the squadron, lest the measure should excite popular dissatisfaction, and thus cause a danger for which the Government was unprepared.

The only captains who did not sign the resolutions were Guise and Spry, the former being in arrest, and the latter being offended with me on account of my refusal to accept him as flag captain. There is no doubt but that he immediately communicated to Zenteno the resolutions of the officers, for on the 20th I received from him the following letter:—

"Valparaiso, July 20th, 1820.

"My Lord,

"At a moment when the services of the naval forces of the State are of the highest importance, and the personal services of your Lordship indispensable, the Supremacy, with the most profound sentiments of regret, has received your resignation, which, should it be admitted, would involve the future operations of the arms of liberty in the New World in certain ruin; and ultimately replace in Chili, your adopted home, that tyranny which your Lordship abhors, and to the annihilation of which your heroism has so greatly contributed.

"His Excellency the Supreme Director commands me to inform your Lordship that should you persist in resigning the command of the squadron which has been honoured by bearing your flag—the cause of terror and dismay to our enemies, and of glory to all true Americans; or should the Government unwisely admit it, this would indeed be a day of universal mourning in the New World. The Government, therefore, in the name of the nation returns you your commission, soliciting your re-acceptance of it, for the furtherance of that sacred cause to which your whole soul is devoted.

"The Supremacy is convinced of the necessity which obliges your Lordship to adopt the measures which placed Captain Guise, of the *Lantaro*, in arrest, and of the justice of the charges exhibited against this officer; but being desirous of preventing any delay in the important services in which the ships of war are about to proceed, it is the request of His Excellency the Supreme Director that his trial be postponed to the first opportunity which does not interfere with the service of the squadron, so important at the present epoch.

"(Signed) JOSE IGNACIO ZENTENO."

In addition to this communication from the Minister of Marine, I received private letters from the Supreme Director and General San Martin, begging me to continue in command of the naval forces, and assuring me that there should be no further cause for complaint.

On receipt of these letters I withdrew my resignation, and returned to the officers of the squadron their commissions, at the same time setting Captain Guise at liberty, and reinstating him in the command of his ship. I would not have done this but from a feeling of attachment to the Supreme Director, General O'Higgins, whose amiable disposition—too easy to contend with the machinations of those around him,—was a sufficient assurance that he was neither an actor in, nor even privy to the system of annoyance pursued towards me by a clique of whom Zenteno was the agent. Like many other good commanders, O'Higgins did not display that tact in the cabinet which had so signally served his country in the field, in which,—though General San Martin, by his unquestionable powers of turning the achievements of others to his own account, contrived to gain the credit —the praise was really due to General O'Higgins. The same easy disposition, after the elevation of the latter to the Supreme Directorate, induced him to consent to the establishment of a senatorial court of consultation, conceding to it privileges altogether incompatible with his own supremacy; and it was with this body that all the vexations directed against me originated—as has been asserted by writers on Chili, at the instigation of General San Martin; but having no documentary evidence to prove this, I shall not take upon myself to assert the fact, notwithstanding that the subsequent conduct of the General gave more than probability to the generally received opinion.

There was, however, no doubt but that General San Martin had been privy to much of the annoyance given to the squadron and myself, as, upon my accusing him of this, he replied that he only "wanted "to see how far the Supreme Director would allow a "party spirit to oppose the welfare of the expedition;" adding, "Never mind, my lord, I am general of "the army, and you shall be admiral of the "squadron." "*Bien, milord, yo soy General del* "*exercito, y V. sara Almirante de la esquadra.*" His allusion to the complicity of the Supreme Director I knew to be false, as His Excellency was anxious to do all in his power both for the squadron and his country; had not the Senate, on which he had conferred such extraordinary powers, thwarted all his endeavours.

General San Martin was, however, much surprised when I shewed him the letters and returned commissions of the officers, he having no conception of their determination not to serve under any command but my own; this step on their part being fraught with the greatest danger to the equipment of the contemplated expedition.

The Senate just noticed was an anomaly in state government. It consisted of five members, whose functions were to remain only during the first struggles of the country for independence; but this body had now assumed a permanent right to dictatorial control, whilst there was no appeal from their arbitrary conduct, except to themselves. They arrogated the title of "Most Excellent," whilst the Supreme Director was simply "His Excellency;" his position, though nominally head of the executive, being really that of mouth-piece to the Senate, which, assuming all power, deprived the Executive Government of its legitimate influence, so that no armament could be equipped, no public work undertaken, no troops raised, and no taxes levied, except by the consent of this irresponsible body. For such a clique, the plain, simple good sense, and thorough good feeling of the Supreme Director was no match; as, being himself above meanness, he was led to rely on the honesty of others from the uprightness of his own motives. Though in every way disposed to believe, with Burke, that "what is morally wrong "can never be politically right," he was led to believe that a crooked policy was a necessary evil of Government; and as such a policy was adverse to his own nature, he was the more easily induced to surrender its administration to others who were free from his conscientious principles.

Of these the most unscrupulous was Zenteno, who, previous to the revolution, had been an attorney at Conception, and was a *protégé* of General San Martin —carrying with him into State Administration the practical cunning of his profession, with more than its usual proportion of chicanery. As he was my bitter opponent, obstructing my plans for the interests of Chili in every possible way, it might ill become me to speak of him as I then felt, and to this day feel. I will therefore adduce the opinion of Mrs. Graham, the first historian of the Republic, as to the estimation in which he was generally held:— "Zenteno has read more than usual among his

" countrymen, and thinks that little much. Like
" San Martin, he dignifies scepticism in religion,
" laxity of morals, and coldness of heart, if not
" cruelty, with the name of philosophy; and while
" he could shew creditable sensibility for the fate
" of a worm, would think the death or torture of a
" political opponent matter for congratulation." I was his political opponent, as wishing to uphold the authority of the Supreme Director, and hence, no doubt, his enmity to me; his influence even extending so far as to prevent the Supreme Director from visiting me whilst in Santiago, on the ground that such a course on his part would be undignified!

At this distance of time—now that Chili is in possession of a Government acting on more enlightened principles—there is no necessity for withholding these remarks, without which the subsequent acts of the Chilian Government towards me might be liable to misconstruction as to my representations of them. So long as Chili was in a transition state from a corrupt and selfish Government to one acting in accordance with the true interests of the country, I forbore to make known these and other circumstances, which, having now become matters of history, need not any longer be withheld.

Writing in this spirit, I may mention a reason, notorious enough at the time, why the squadron was not paid even its wages. The Government *had* provided the means, but those to whom the distribution was entrusted retained the money during their pleasure, employing it for their own advantage in trading speculations or in usury, only applying it to a legitimate purpose when further delay became dangerous to themselves. One great cause of the hatred displayed towards me by these people, was my incessant demands that the claims of the squadron should be satisfied as regarded wages. As to prize-money, not a dollar was ever conceded by the Government either to myself, officers, or men, so long as I remained in Chili; but I had the satisfaction to see that the constant watch which I kept on those financial disorders, was the means of ameliorating the system, though with the additional dislike to myself of those whose short-sighted policy I was thwarting, and whose avaricious speculations were thus curtailed.

In spite of his enmity, the Minister of Marine had been officially compelled to write me the following letter:—

"My Lord,

"If victories over an enemy are to be estimated according to the resistance offered, or the national advantages obtained, the conquest of Valdivia is, in both senses, inestimable; encountering, as you did, the natural and artificial strength of that impregnable fortress which, till now, had obstinately defended itself by means of those combined advantages. The memory of that glorious day will occupy the first pages of Chilian history, and the name of Your Excellency will be transmitted from generation to generation by the gratitude of our descendants.

"His Excellency the Supreme Director, highly gratified by that noble conquest, orders me to inform you (as I have now the satisfaction of doing), that he experiences, in his own name, and in that of the nation, the most heartfelt gratification at that signal achievement. The meritorious officers, Beauchef, Miller, Erescano, Carter, and Vidal, and all the other officers and soldiers who, in imitation of your Excellency, encountered such vast dangers, will be brought to the notice of Government, in order to receive a decorative medal, in gratitude for their gallantry, and in proof that Chili rewards the heroes who advocate her cause.

Our national flag has been displayed amidst the most festive public demonstrations, above those of Valdivia and Cantabria, in proof of the subjection of our enemies.

" I beg, with the greatest gratification, the honour to announce to you your letter of the 3rd instant, transmitting those of Major Beauchef and Major Miller.

" God preserve your Excellency many years.

(Signed) JOSE IGNACIO ZENTENO."

" The Vice-Admiral commanding the Chilian Squadron."

It is difficult to see how a man who could have written the above letter, even officially, could have become my worst enemy; the reasons for which will, however, develop themselves as we proceed.

As the estate which was conferred upon me at Rio Clara was afterwards taken from me, without reason assigned, I will here give the letter conveying it, as this will again have to be alluded to. The attorney-like cunning of Zenteno prevented its conveyance by any more formal document than the decree conferring it.

" My Lord,

" A Decree of this date has been issued by His Excellency the Supreme Director, of which the annexed is a copy :—

" ' Desirous to expedite, without loss of time, the gift of 4000 *quadras* of land, which, by decree of the Senate, was assigned to the Commander-in-Chief of the Squadron, Vice-Admiral Lord Cochrane, as a demonstration of public appreciation for his distinguished services in the " *Restoration* " of the important fortress of Valdivia ;

the said 4000 *quadras* are assigned on the lands of Rio Clara, in the province of Conception, being part of the confiscated estate of Pablo Furtado, a fugitive Spaniard.

" 'The present deed shall serve as a sufficient title to the property in favour of the Vice-Admiral, being communicated to the Minister of Finance, in order to the accustomed formalities, to receive possession and enjoy the benefits.'

" I have the honour to communicate the above, by Supreme orders, for your information.

" God preserve your Excellency many years.

" (Signed) JOSE IGNACIO ZENTENO.

" Administration of Marine,

" Valparaiso, *August* 20, 1820.

" Published by order of His Excellency."

CHAPTER IV.

OBSTACLES TO EQUIPPING THE SQUADRON—SAILING OF THE LIBERATING EXPEDITION—DEBARCATION AT PISCO—LONG INACTION OF THE ARMY—GENERAL SAN MARTIN REMOVES TO ANCON—CAPTURE OF THE ESMERALDA—EXCHANGE OF PRISONERS—ACKNOWLEDGMENT OF THE SERVICE BY GENERAL SAN MARTIN—LADY COCHRANE'S VISIT TO MENDOZA.

The difficulties which attended the equipment of the squadron and troops destined for the liberation of Peru were very great, the Government being without credit, whilst its treasury had been completely exhausted by efforts to organise an army—a loan being impossible, and indeed refused. By my influence with the British merchants, I managed to obtain considerable quantities of naval and military stores, and in addition, a contribution to a subscription which was set on foot, in place of a forced loan, upon which the Government hesitated to venture.

The greatest difficulty was, however, with regard to the foreign seamen, who, disgusted with the want of faith towards them, refused to re-enter the service. The Government, upon this, requested me to resort to impressment, which I declined, telling them, moreover, that the captain of the British frigate then in port would not permit his countrymen to be impressed.

The alternative proposed was to use my influence with the men, by issuing such a proclamation, dictated by myself, as would render them dependent for their pay and prize-money upon General San Martin, and on the success of the expedition; it being evident that they would not place further confidence in the promises of the Government.

A joint proclamation was therefore issued by Gen. San Martin and myself, my signature being added as a guarantee, whilst his bore the authority of Commander-in-Chief. The following extract will shew the nature of this proclamation:—

"On my entry into Lima, I will punctually pay to all foreign seamen who shall voluntarily enlist into the Chilian service, the whole arrears of their pay, to which, I will also add to each individual, according to his rank, one year's pay over and above his arrears, as a premium or reward for his services, if he continue to fulfil his duty to the day of the surrender of that city, and its occupation by the liberating forces.

(Signed) "JOSE DE SAN MARTIN.
"COCHRANE."

This proclamation had the desired effect, and the crews of the ships were immediately completed.

The Chilian force amounted to 4200 men, General San Martin, to the great disappointment of General Freire, being nominated Captain-General — the force under his command was designated the "liberating army" (*Exercito Libertador*). Whilst the expedition was in process of formation, the Supreme Director had apprised the Peruvian people of its object, and lest they should entertain any jealousy of its presence uninvited, had declared his views in a general proclamation, from which the following is an extract:—

"Peruvians—Do not think we shall pretend to treat you as a conquered people? such a desire could have entered into the heads of none but those who are inimical to our common happiness. We only aspire to see you free and happy; *yourselves will frame your own government*, choosing that form which is most consistent with your customs, your situation, and your wishes. Consequently, *you will constitute a nation as free and independent as ourselves.*"

This, and subsequent proclamations, will require to be borne in mind, as the result by no means corresponded with the intentions of the Supreme Director, whose honesty of purpose was afterwards set at nought by those in whose estimation Peru was only a field for the furtherance of their own ambition. The Chileno officers, both native and foreign, certainly believed in the sincerity of their leaders, but were subsequently doomed to be miserably disappointed as regarded the chief of them.

On the 21st of August, 1820, the squadron sailed amidst the enthusiastic plaudits of the people, who felt proud that in so short a time the power of Spain had not only been humbled, but that they were enabled to despatch an army to liberate her principal remaining State.

On the 25th, the squadron hove to off Coquimbo, taking on board another battalion of troops. On the 26th we again sailed, when General San Martin made known to me his intention of proceeding with the main body of the army to Truxillo, a place four degrees to leeward of Lima, where the army could have gained no advantage, nor, indeed, have found anything to do, except to remain there safe from any attack by the Spaniards, who could not approach it by land, whilst the squadron could protect it by sea.

By representing to General San Martin that this course would cause great dissatisfaction amongst the Chileno officers and men, who expected to be landed and led at once against Lima, for the immediate conquest of which they were amply sufficient, he consented to give up his plan of proceeding to Truxillo, but firmly refused to disembark his men in the vicinity of Lima; for what reason I could not then divine. My own plan was to land the force at Chilca, the nearest point to Callao, and forthwith to obtain possession of the capital; an object by no means difficult of execution, and certain of success.

Finding all argument unavailing, we sailed for Pisco, where the expedition arrived on the 7th of September, and on the 8th, to my great chagrin, the troops were disembarked, and for fifty days remained in total inaction! with the exception of despatching Colonel Arenales into the interior with a detachment, which, after defeating a body of Spaniards, took up a position to the eastward of Lima.

Even on arriving at Pisco, General San Martin declined to enter the town, though the Spanish forces consisted of less than three hundred men. Landing the troops under Major-General Las Heras, he went down the coast in the schooner *Montezuma*, the inhabitants meanwhile retiring into the interior, taking with them their cattle, slaves, and even the furniture of their houses. This excess of caution excited great discontent in the army and the squadron, as contrasting strangely with the previous capture of the place, in the preceding year, by Lieut.-Colonel Charles and Major Miller, with their handful of men.

On the return of General San Martin, he professed to be greatly chagrined at the departure of the inhabitants, and the consequent loss of supplies. Instead of attributing this to his own tardy movements, he declared his disbelief in the accounts he had received from Peru as to the friendly disposition of the inhabitants, even throwing out doubts as to the success of the expedition in consequence. It was of the first importance to have taken the place immediately, and to have conciliated the inhabitants, as the ships were scantily provisioned, and all but destitute of other necessary supplies. A detailed account, however, of the capture of the place was transmitted to Santiago, where it was duly recorded in the official organ as the first feat of the great expedition.

During these fifty days the squadron was also necessarily kept in inaction, having achieved nothing beyond the capture of a few merchantmen along the coast, and a fruitless chase of two Spanish frigates, the *Prueba* and *Venganza*, which I did not follow up, as involving risk to the transports during my absence.

This delay was productive of the worst disasters which could have befallen the expedition. The people were eager to receive us, and not calculating on such tardiness on the part of General Martin—were everywhere declaring in our favour; but being unsupported, were fined, imprisoned, and subjected to corporal punishment by the Viceroy. Rendered cautious by this, they naturally distrusted the force idling away its time at Pisco, manifesting reluctance to bring forward the requisite supplies, upon which they were treated, by order of General San Martin, with military rigour; being thus harassed, the Peruvians began to look upon the Chilenos as oppressors in common with the Spaniards, to the no small danger of losing every desire for national independence.

Nevertheless, on reaching Pisco, Gen. San Martin had promulgated a proclamation from the Supreme Director full of fervent appeals to God and man as regarded the good intentions of the Chilian Government: the following are extracts:—

"Peruvians, here are the engagements under which Chili—before the Supreme Being—and calling all nations to witness as avengers of any violation of the compact, engages to aid you—setting death and toil at defiance. You shall be free and independent. You shall choose your own government and laws, by the spontaneous will of your representatives. No military or civil influence, direct or indirect, shall your brethren use to influence your social dispositions. You shall dismiss the armed force sent to your assistance the moment you judge proper, without regard to our opinion of your danger or security. Never shall any military division occupy the soil of a free people, unless called for by your lawful magistrate. Neither by ourselves, nor by our aid, shall party opinions which may have preceded your liberty be punished. Ready to overthrow any armed force which may resist your rights, we beseech you to forget all grievances antecedent to the day of your glory, so as to reserve the most severe justice to obstinacy and oppression."

Such were the inducements held out to the Peruvian people, and such was their first experience with regard to their liberators.

Yet even amidst inaction the fruits of demonstration early became manifest, a vessel arriving on the 4th of October, from Guayaquil, with the intelligence that on receiving news of the sailing of the expedition, that province had declared itself independent. Upon the arrival of this welcome news, I again begged of General San Martin to reimbark the troops and move on Lima, and at length succeeded in inducing him to make a move.

Previous to our departure, General San Martin issued the following proclamation, here given to shew how promises solemnly entered into could afterwards be broken.

> "Peruvians! I have paid the tribute which, as a public man, I owe to the opinion of others, and have shewn what is my object and mission towards you. I come to fulfil the expectations of all those who wish to belong to the country which gave them birth, and who desire to be governed by their own laws. On the day when Peru shall freely pronounce as to the form of her institutions, be they whatever they may, *my functions shall cease*, and I shall have the glory of announcing to the Government of Chili, of which I am a subject, that their heroic efforts have at last received the consolation of giving liberty to Peru, and peace to the neighbouring states."

The troops being reimbarked—on the 28th we sailed from Pisco, and on the following day anchored before Callao. After having reconnoitred the fortifications, I again urged on General San Martin an immediate disembarcation of the force, but to this he once more strenuously objected, to the great disappointment of the whole expedition ; insisting on going to Ancon, a place at some distance to the northward of Callao. Having no control over the disposition of the troops, I was obliged to submit; and on the 30th, detached the *San Martin*, *Galvarino*, and *Araucano*, to convoy the transports to Ancon, retaining the *O'Higgins*, *Independencia*, and *Lautaro*, as if for the purpose of blockade.

The fact was, that—annoyed in common with the whole expedition—at this irresolution on the part of General San Martin, I determined that the means of Chili, furnished with great difficulty, should not be wholly wasted, without some attempt at accomplishing the objects of the expedition; and accordingly formed a plan of attack with the three ships which I had kept back—though being apprehensive that my design would be opposed by General San Martin, I had not even mentioned to him my intentions.

This design was to cut out the *Esmeralda* frigate from under the fortifications, and also to get possession of another ship, on board of which we had learned that a million of dollars was embarked for flight, if it became necessary; my opinion being that if such display of power were manifested, the Spaniards would either surrender the capital or abandon it.

The enterprise was hazardous, for since my former visit the enemy's position had been much strengthened, no less than 300 pieces of artillery being mounted on shore, whilst the *Esmeralda* was crowded with the best sailors and marines that could be procured, these sleeping every night at quarters. She was, moreover, defended by a strong boom with chain moorings, and by armed blockships; the whole being surrounded by twenty-seven gun-boats; so that no ship could possibly get at her.

For three days we occupied ourselves in preparations, still keeping secret the purpose for which they were intended. On the evening of 5th of November, this was communicated to the ships by the following proclamation:—

"Marines and Seamen,

"This night we are going to give the enemy a mortal blow. To-morrow you will present yourselves proudly before Callao, and all your comrades will envy your good fortune. One hour of courage and resolution is all that is required of you to triumph. Remember, that you have conquered in Valdivia, and be not afraid of those who have hitherto fled from you.

"The value of all the vessels captured in Callao will be yours, and the same reward in money will be distributed amongst you as has been offered by the Spaniards in Lima to those who should capture any of the Chilian squadron. The moment of glory is approaching, and I hope that the Chilenos will fight as they have been accustomed to do, and that the English will act as they have ever done at home and abroad.

"COCHRANE."

On issuing this proclamation, it was stated that I should lead the attack in person, volunteers being requested to come forward, on which the whole of the marines and seamen on board the three ships offered to accompany me. As this could not be permitted, a hundred and sixty seamen and eighty marines were selected, and after dark were placed in fourteen boats alongside the flag-ship, each man armed with cutlass and pistol, being, for distinction's sake, dressed in white, with a blue band on the left arm. The Spaniards I expected would be off their guard, as, by way of *ruse*, the other ships had been sent out of the bay under the charge of Captain Foster, as though in pursuit of some vessels in the offing—so that the Spaniards would consider themselves safe from attack for that night.

At ten o'clock all was in readiness, the boats being formed in two divisions, the first commanded by my flag-captain Crosbie, and the second by Captain Guise, —my boat leading. The strictest silence, and the exclusive use of cutlasses were enjoined; so that, as the oars were muffled, and the night dark, the enemy had not the least suspicion of the impending attack.

It was just upon midnight when we neared the small opening left in the boom, our plan being well-nigh frustrated by the vigilance of a guard-boat, upon which my launch had luckily stumbled. The challenge was given, upon which, in an under-tone, I threatened the occupants of the boat with instant death if they made the least alarm. No reply was made to the threat, and in a few minutes our gallant fellows were alongside the frigate in line, boarding at several points simultaneously.

The Spaniards were completely taken by surprise—the whole, with the exception of the sentries, being asleep at their quarters—and great was the havoc made amongst them by the Chileno cutlasses whilst they were recovering themselves. Retreating to the forecastle, they there made a gallant stand, and it was not until the third charge that the position was carried. The fight was for a short time renewed on the quarter-deck, where the Spanish marines fell to a man, the rest of the enemy leaping overboard and into the hold to escape slaughter.

On boarding the ship by the main chains, I was knocked back by the butt end of the sentry's musket, and falling on a thole pin of the boat, it entered my back near the spine, inflicting a severe injury, which caused me many years of subsequent suffering. Immediately regaining my footing, I reascended the side, and when on deck, was shot through the thigh, but binding a handkerchief tightly round the wound, managed, though with great difficulty, to direct the contest to its close.

The whole affair, from beginning to end, occupied only a quarter of an hour, our loss being eleven killed and thirty wounded, whilst that of the Spaniards was a hundred and sixty, many of whom fell under the cutlasses of the Chilenos before they could stand to their arms. Greater bravery I never saw displayed than that of our gallant fellows. Before boarding, the duties of all had been appointed, and a party was told off to take possession of the tops. We had not been on deck a minute, when I hailed the foretop, and was instantly answered by our own men, an equally prompt answer being returned from the frigate's maintop. No British man-of-war's crew could have excelled this minute attention to orders.

The uproar speedily alarmed the garrison, who, hastening to their guns, opened fire on their own frigate, thus paying us the compliment of having taken it; though, even in this case, their own men must still have been on board, so that firing on them was a wanton proceeding, as several Spaniards were killed or wounded by the shot of the fortress, and amongst the wounded was Captain Coig, the commander of the *Esmeralda*—who, after he was made prisoner, received a severe contusion by a shot from his own party.

The fire from the fortress was, however, neutralised by a successful expedient. There were two foreign ships of war present during the contest—the United States frigate *Macedonian*, and the British frigate *Hyperion;* and these, as previously agreed on with the Spanish authorities in case of a night attack—hoisted peculiar lights as signals, to prevent being fired upon. This contingency being provided for by us—as soon as the fortress commenced its fire on the *Esmeralda*, we also ran up similar lights, so that the garrison became puzzled which vessel to fire at; the intended mischief thus involving the *Hyperion* and *Macedonian*, which were several times struck, the *Esmeralda* being comparatively untouched. Upon this the neutral frigates cut their cables and moved away; whilst Captain Guise, contrary to my orders, cut the *Esmeralda*'s cables also, so that there was nothing to be done but to loose her top-sails and follow; the fortress then ceasing its fire.

My orders were *not* to cut the cables of the *Esmeralda;* but after taking her to capture the *Maypu*, a brig of war previously taken from Chili—and then to attack and cut adrift every ship near, there being plenty of time before us; no doubt existing but that when the *Esmeralda* was taken, the Spaniards would desert the other ships as fast as their boats would permit them, so that the whole might either have been captured or burned. To this end all my previous plans had been arranged; but on being placed *hors de combat* by my wounds, Captain Guise, on whom the command of the prize devolved, chose to interpose his own judgment, and content himself with the *Esmeralda* alone, cutting her cables without my orders; the reason assigned being, that the English had broken into her spirit-room and were getting drunk, whilst the Chilenos were disorganized by plundering. It was a great mistake, for if we could capture the *Esmeralda*, with her picked and well-appointed crew, there would have been little or no difficulty in cutting the other ships adrift in succession. It would only have been the rout of Valdivia over again, chasing the enemy, without loss, from ship after ship, instead of from fort to fort.

The following extract, from the order issued preparatory to the attack, will clearly shew the plan frustrated by cutting the *Esmeralda* adrift:—

"On securing the frigate, the Chilian seamen and marines are not to give the Chilian cheer, but to deceive the enemy, and give time for completing the work: they are to cheer "*Viva el Rey*."

"The two brigs of war are to be fired on by the musketry *from the Esmeralda*, and are to be taken possession of by Lieutenants Esmonde and Morgell, in the boats they command; which, being done, they are to cut adrift, run out, and anchor in the offing as quickly as possible. The boats of the *Independencia* are to turn adrift all the outward Spanish merchant ships; and the boats of the *O'Higgins* and *Lantaro*, under Lieutenants Bell and Robertson, are to set fire to one or more of the headmost hulks; but these are not to be cut adrift, so as to fall down upon the rest.

(Signed) "COCHRANE."

By the cutting of the *Esmeralda*'s cables, not one of these objects was effected. The captured frigate was ready for sea, with three months' provisions on board, and with stores sufficient for two years. She was, no doubt, if opportunity offered, intended to convoy the treasure-ship, which, by the precipitancy of Captain Guise, we had missed; indeed the Spanish Admiral being on board at the time, with his flag flying, was a pretty clear proof that she was on the point of departure; instead of which, the Admiral, his officers, and 200 seamen were made prisoners, the remainder of the crew, originally 370 in number, being killed, wounded, or drowned.

An incident occurred during the contest which, at this distance of time, I shall not refrain from mentioning. His Britannic Majesty's ship *Hyperion* was so close to the *Esmeralda*, as to be a witness of the whole proceeding. A midshipman was standing at the gangway looking on, amongst others, when his truly English nature, unable to restrain itself as our gallant fellows cleared the forecastle of the enemy, gave vent to its expression by clapping his hands in approbation. It was afterwards reported that he was immediately ordered below by his commander, Captain Searle, who threatened to put him under arrest. Such was the feeling of an English commander towards me. I should not have condescended to notice this occurrence but for the bravado shown by the same officer on a previous occasion, by casting loose his guns, with their tompions out, when my flag-ship entered the roads; thereby either intimating that he considered me a pirate, or that he would so treat me, if he had an opportunity.

When approaching the *Esmeralda*, the British frigate also hailed each boat separately, with the evident intention of alarming the enemy; which would no doubt have been the case, had not the Spaniards been thrown off their guard by the before-mentioned *ruse* of sending the ships out of the bay.

Far different was the conduct of the commander of the United States frigate *Macedonian*—whose sentinels did not hail the boats—the officers in an under-tone wishing us success; and still more honourable was the subsequent testimony of that talented officer, Captain Basil Hall, who commanded His Britannic Majesty's ship *Conway*, then in the Pacific. This testimony, though in some degree a recapitulation of the events already related, but slightly inaccurate as regards the number of men employed, I feel proud to adduce:—

"While the liberating army, under General San Martin, was removing to Ancon, Lord Cochrane, with part of his squadron, anchored in the outer roads of Callao. The inner harbour was guarded by an extensive system of batteries, admirably constructed, and bearing the general name of the 'Castles of Callao.' The merchant ships, as well as the men of war, consisting of the

Esmeralda, a large 40-gun frigate, and two sloops of war, were moored under the guns of the castle, within a semicircle of fourteen gun-boats, and a boom made of spars chained together.

" Lord Cochrane, having previously reconnoitred these formidable defences in person, undertook, on the 5th of November, 1820, the desperate enterprise of cutting out the Spanish frigate, although she was known to be fully prepared for an attack. His Lordship proceeded in fourteen boats, containing 240 men—all volunteers from the different ships of the squadron—in two divisions, one under the orders of Captain Crosby, and the other under Captain Guise, both officers commanding the Chileno squadron.

" At midnight, the boats having forced their way across the boom, Lord Cochrane, who was leading, rowed alongside the first gun-boat, and taking the officer by surprise, proposed to him, with a pistol at his head, the alternative of silence or death. No reply being made, the boats pushed on unobserved, and Lord Cochrane, mounting the *Esmeralda*'s side, was the first to give the alarm. The sentinel on the gangway levelled his piece and fired, but was instantly cut down by the coxwain, and his Lordship, though wounded in the thigh, at the same moment stepped on the deck, the frigate being boarded with no less gallantry on the opposite side by Captain Guise, who met Lord Cochrane midway on the quarter-deck, as also Captain Crosby, and the afterpart of the ship was soon carried, sword in hand. The Spaniards rallied on the forecastle, where they made a desperate resistance, till overpowered by a fresh party of seamen and marines, headed by Lord Cochrane. A gallant stand was again made on the main deck, but before one o'clock the ship was captured, her cables cut, and she was steered triumphantly out of the harbour.

" This loss was a death-blow to the Spanish naval force in that quarter of the world; for, although there were still two Spanish frigates and some smaller vessels in the Pacific, they never afterwards ventured to shew themselves, but left Lord Cochrane undisputed master of the coast."

On the morning of the 6th a horrible massacre was committed on shore. The market-boat of the

United States frigate was, as usual, sent for provisions, when the mob took it into their heads that the *Esmeralda* could not have been cut out without the assistance of the *Macedonian*, and, falling upon the boat's crew, murdered the whole of them.

The wounded amongst the *Esmeralda*'s crew were sent on shore under a flag of truce, a letter from me to the Viceroy proposing an exchange of prisoners being at the same time transmitted. The proposal was this time civilly acceded to, and the whole were sent on shore; the Chilian prisoners, who had long languished in the dungeons of the fortress, being returned, and ordered to join the army of General San Martin.

On transmitting the intelligence of our success to General San Martin, I received from him the following acknowledgment of the achievement:—

10th November, 1820.

"My Lord,

"The importance of the service you have rendered to the country by the capture of the frigate *Esmeralda*, and the brilliant manner in which you conducted the gallant officers and seamen under your orders to accomplish that noble enterprise, on the night of the memorable 5th of November, have augmented the gratitude due to your former services by the Government, as well as that of all interested in the public cause, and in your fame.

"All those who participated in the risks and glory of the deed, also deserve well of their countrymen, and I have the satisfaction to be the medium of transmitting the sentiments of admiration which such transcendent success has excited in the chiefs of the army under my command. Permit me to express them to you, in order that they may be communicated to the meritorious officers, seamen, and marines of the squadron, to whom will be religiously fulfilled *the promises you made.*

" It is grievous that, connected with the memory of so glorious a deed, regret for those who shed their blood in its achievement should enter ; but let us hope that such thoughts will be dissipated, by your adding further deeds of glory to the country, and to your name.

" God preserve you many years.

" JOSE DE SAN MARTIN."

San Martin's expression of "religiously fulfilling the " promises I made," is in allusion to the promise, signed by himself, which had been exacted previous to the departure of the squadron from Valparaiso, that the men should have a year's pay given to them. With the preceding letter General San Martin voluntarily sent another promise to the captors, of 50,000 dollars, to be paid on gaining possession of Lima. Neither the one promise nor the other were ever fulfilled, nor did they ever obtain any prize-money.

To the Administration in Chili General San Martin wrote as follows:—

" Head Quarters, Supe, Dec. 1, 1820.

" Senor Minister,

" I have the honour of forwarding to you the despatches of the Right Hon. Lord Cochrane, Vice-Admiral of the squadron, relative to the heroic capture of the frigate *Esmeralda*, by boarding her under the batteries of Callao.

" It is impossible for me to eulogise in proper language the daring enterprise of the 5th of November, by which Lord Cochrane has decided the superiority of our naval forces—augmented the splendour and power of Chili—and secured the success of this campaign.

" I doubt not that His Excellency the Supreme Director will render the justice due to the worthy chief, his officers, and other individuals who have had a share in that successful action.

" I beg you will honour me by congratulating His Excellency on this important success, and principally on account of the influence it will have on the great object which occupies his attention.

"JOSE DE SAN MARTIN."

"To Don Jose Ignaccia Zenteno,
Minister of Marine."

Soon after my departure for Peru, Lady Cochrane undertook a journey across the *Cordillera*, to Mendoza, the passes being, at that season, often blocked up with snow. Having been entrusted with some despatches of importance, she pushed on rapidly, and on the 12th of October arrived at the celebrated *Ponte del Inca*, 15,000 feet above the level of the sea. Here the snow had increased to such an extent as to render farther progress impossible, and her ladyship was obliged to remain at a *Casucha*, or strong house, built above the snow for the safety of travellers; the intense cold arising from the rarity of the atmosphere, and the absence of all comfort—there being no better couch than a dried bullock's hide—producing a degree of suffering which few ladies would be willing to encounter.

Whilst proceeding on her mule up a precipitous path in the vicinity, a Royalist, who had intruded himself on the party, rode up in an opposite direction and disputed the path with her, at a place where the slightest false step would have precipitated her into the abyss below. One of her attendants, a tried and devoted soldier, named Pedro Flores, seeing the movement, and guessing the man's intention, galloped up to him at a critical moment, striking him a violent blow across the face, and thus arresting his murderous design. The ruffian finding himself vigorously attacked, made off, without resenting the blow, and so, no doubt, another premeditated attempt on Lady Cochrane's life was averted.

CHAPTER V.

SAN MARTIN'S VIOLATION OF TRUTH—REMOVAL OF BLOCKADE—SPANISH DEPRESSION—TROOPS DYING OF FEVER—SAN MARTIN'S DESIGNS ON GUAYAQUIL—MUTINOUS CONDUCT OF OFFICERS—REFUSAL TO OBEY ORDERS—DEPOSITION OF VICEROY—SAN MARTIN GIVES ME TROOPS—JEALOUSY OF SAN MARTIN—ATTACK ON ARICA—CAPTURE OF TACNA—CAPTURE OF MOQUEGA—REFUSAL OF MORE MEN—AN ARMISTICE RATIFIED—DISTRESS OF LIMA—DISSATISFACTION OF THE ARMY—LADY COCHRANE—GOES INTO THE INTERIOR—DANGEROUS POSITION—LADY COCHRANE IN ACTION—DEVOTION OF SEAMEN.

On the 8th of November I went to Ancon with our prize, this being hailed with great enthusiasm by the army, which—now that the Spanish naval force had received, what even the Spaniards themselves considered its death blow—made certain that it would be at once led against Lima, before the authorities recovered from their consternation. To their mortification—no less than my own—General San Martin, in defiance of all argument to the contrary, ordered the troops on board the transports, having decided on *retreating to Huacho!* whither the *O'Higgins* and *Esmeralda*, abandoning the blockade, had to convoy them. In place of prompt action—or rather demonstration, for the occupation of the city would have amounted to little more—he issued a proclamation, promising, as before, the most perfect freedom to the Peruvian people if they would join him:—

"Spaniards, your destiny is in your own hands. I come not to declare war against the fortunes and persons of individuals. The enemy of the liberty and independence of America alone is the object of the vengeance of the arms of the PATRIA. I promise you in the most positive manner, that your property and persons shall be inviolable, and that you shall be treated as respectable citizens, if you co-operate in the great cause," &c. &c.

By the 12th the army was again disembarked, amidst evident manifestations of dissatisfaction on the part of the officers, who were naturally jealous of the achievements of the squadron, from being themselves restrained from enterprise of any kind. To allay this feeling General San Martin had recourse to an almost incredible violation of truth, intended to impress upon the Chilian people, that the army, and not the squadron, had captured the *Esmeralda!*—indeed stating as much in words, and declaring that the whole affair was the result of his own plans, to which I had agreed! though the truth is, that doubting his confidants, I had concealed from him my intentions of making the attack. The following is an extract from the bulletin issued to the army:—

"Before the General-in-Chief left the Vice-Admiral of the Squadron, *they agreed on the execution of a memorable project, sufficient to astound intrepidity itself!* and to make the history of the liberating expedition of Peru eternal!

"Those valiant soldiers who for a length of time have suffered with the most heroic constancy the severest oppression, and the most inhuman treatment in the dungeons of Casas-matas, have just arrived at our head-quarters. Flattering promises of liberty, and the threats of death, were not sufficient to destroy their loyalty to their country; they have waited with firmness the day on which their companions in arms should rescue them from their misery, and revenge the insults which humanity has received in their persons. This glory was reserved *to the liberating army, whose efforts have snatched from the hands of tyranny these respectable victims.* Let this be published for the satisfaction of these individuals, *and that of the army, to whose arms they owe their liberty.*"

It thus went forth to the people of Chili, that the army captured the frigate, and subsequently released the prisoners, though not a man in the whole force had the most distant idea that an attack was even contemplated, much less could it have co-operated, seeing that it was far away in cantonments! This bulletin excited the astonishment of the troops; but as it contributed to their *amour propre*, by representing to the Chilian people that the achievement which had been effected was due to them, they accepted it; whilst I thought it beneath me to refute a falsehood palpable to the whole expedition. It had, however, as General San Martin no doubt calculated, the effect of allaying, for the moment, a dissatisfaction which foreboded serious consequences.

On the 15th we again sailed from Huacho, to renew the blockade at Callao, beyond which nothing could be done; though even this was of importance, as cutting off supplies from the capital, the inhabitants of which, in consequence of the privations they were subjected to, caused great uneasiness to the Viceregal Government.

Several attempts were now made to entice the remaining Spanish naval force from their shelter under the batteries, by placing the *Esmeralda* apparently within reach, and the flag-ship herself in situations of some danger. One day I carried her through an intricate strait called the Boqueron, in which nothing beyond a fifty-ton schooner was ever seen. The Spaniards, expecting every moment to see the ship strike, manned their gun-boats, ready to attack as soon as she was aground, of which there was little danger, for we had found, and buoyed off with small bits of wood invisible to the enemy, a channel through which a vessel could pass without much difficulty.

On the 2nd of December the *Esmeralda*, being in a more than usually tempting position, the Spanish gun-boats ventured out in the hope of recapturing her, and for an hour maintained a smart fire; but on seeing the *O'Higgins* manœuvring to cut them off, they precipitately retreated.

The preceeding successes caused great depression amongst the Spanish troops, and on the following day the battalion of Numantia, numbering 650 disciplined men, deserted in a body, and joined the Chilian forces at Chancay. On the 8th, forty Spanish officers followed their example; and every day afterwards, officers, privates, and civilians of respectability, joined the patriot army, which thus became considerably reinforced; the defection of so large a portion of his troops being a severe loss to the Viceroy.

On the 6th, Colonel Arenales, who, after his previous success, had marched into the interior, defeated a division of the royalist army at Pasco. On his proceeding to Huamanga, the authorities fled, and the inhabitants declared themselves independent. Tarma was next abandoned, and followed the same example, as did Huanuco, Cueñca, and Loxa; whilst, on the news of the capture of the *Esmeralda* arriving at Truxillo, that important province also revolted, under the direction of the Spanish governor, the Marquis of Torre Tagle.

Notwithstanding this succession of favourable events, General San Martin still declined to march on Lima, remaining inactive at Haura, though the unhealthy situation of the place was such, that nearly one-third of his troops died of intermittent fever, during the many months they remained there. In place of securing the capital, where the army would have now been welcomed, he proposed to send half the army to Guayaquil, in order to annex that province, this being the first manifestation on the part of General San Martin to found a dominion of his own—for to nothing less did he afterwards aspire, though the declared object of the expedition was to enable the South Pacific provinces to emancipate themselves from Spain, leaving them free to choose their own governments, as had been repeatedly and solemnly declared, both by the Chilian Government and himself.

Finding that I would not consent to avert the naval force from the purposes to which it was destined, the project was abandoned; but the troops which had advanced to Chancay were ordered to fall back on Haura, this step being actually a further retreat as regarded the position of the Spanish forces, which thus managed to check further desertion by apprehending and shooting all who attempted it.

Still General San Martin was determined, if possible, to accomplish his views on Guayaquil. Two deputies, Tomas Guido and Colonel Luzuriago, were despatched with complimentary messages to Torre Tagle and others, warning them against the designs of Bolivar, whose success in the north led San Martin to fear that he might have designs on Peru. The deputies were strictly enjoined to represent that if such were Bolivar's intention, Guayaquil would only be regarded as a conquered province; whilst, if the people of that place would adhere to him, he would, on the fall of Lima, make it *the principal port of a great empire*; and that the establishment of the docks and arsenals which *his navy* would require, would enrich the city beyond measure. They were at the same time exhorted to form a militia, in order to keep out Bolivar.

By way of conciliating me, General San Martin proposed in a flattering way to call the captured frigate the "*Cochrane*," as two vessels before had been named the "*San Martin*," and "*O'Higgins*;" but to this I demurred, as acquiescence in such a proceeding might in the estimation of others have identified me with any course the general might be inclined to pursue, and I had already formed my conjectures as to what were evidently his future purposes. Finding me firm in declining the proffered honour, he told me to give her what name I thought proper; but this was also refused, when he said, "Let her be called the '*Valdivia*,' in memory of your conquest of that place;"

her name was accordingly changed from the *Esmeralda* to the *Valdivia.*

The command of the frigate had been given to Captain Guise; and after her change of name, his officers wrote to him a letter deprecating the name, and alleging, that as they had nothing to do with the conquest of Valdivia, it ought to be withdrawn, and one more consonant with their feelings substituted. This letter was followed by marked personal disrespect towards myself, from the officers who had signed it, who made it no secret that the name of Guise was the one sought to be substituted.

As the conversations held by these officers with the rest of the squadron were of such a derogatory nature as regarded my character and authority, as might lead to serious disorganization, I brought the whole of the officers who had signed the letter to a court-martial, two being dismissed the service, the remainder being dismissed the ship, with a recommendation to General San Martin for other appointments.

During the arrest of these officers, I had determined upon an attack upon the fortifications of Callao, intending to carry them by a *coup de main*, similar to that which had succeeded at Valdivia, and having, on the 18th, taken soundings in the *Potrillo*, was convinced of the feasibility of the plan.

On the 20th, this intention was notified by an order, stating that on the following day I should make the attack with the boats of the squadron and the *San*

Martin, the crew of which received the order with loud cheers, volunteers for the boats eagerly pressing forward from all quarters.

In place of preparing to second the operations, Captain Guise sent me a note refusing to serve with any other but the officers under arrest—stating that unless they were restored, he must resign his command. My reply was that I would neither restore them nor accept his resignation, without some better reason for it than the one alleged. Captain Guise answered, that my refusal to restore his officers was a sufficient reason for his resignation, whereupon I ordered him to weigh anchor on a service of importance; the order being disobeyed on the ground that he could no longer act, having given over the command of the ship to Lieutenant Shepherd.

Feeling that something like a mutiny was being excited, and knowing that Guise and his colleague, Spry, were at the bottom of the matter, I ordered the latter to proceed with the *Galvarino* to Chorillos, when he also requested leave to resign, as "his friend Captain Guise had been compelled so to "do, and he had entered the Chilian navy condition-"ally to serve only with Captain Guise, under whose "patronage he had left England." Such was the state of mutiny on board the *Galvarino*, that I deputed my flag-captain, Crosbie, to restore order, when Spry affected to consider himself superseded, and claimed exemption from martial law. I therefore tried him by court-martial, and dismissed him from the ship.

The two officers now made their way to head-quarters, where General San Martin immediately made Spry his naval *aide-de-camp*, thus promoting him in the most public manner for disobedience to orders, and in defiance of the sentence of the court-martial; this being pretty conclusive proof that they had been acting under the instructions of General San Martin himself, for what purpose will appear in the course of the narrative. The course now pursued by General San Martin sufficiently shewed that the disturbance previously made at Valparaiso emanated also from himself, and that in both cases the mutinous officers felt quite secure in his protection; though I will do both the credit of supposing them ignorant at the time of the treacherous purposes of which they were afterwards the instruments.

Knowing that I should take their punishment into my own hands if they returned to the squadron, General San Martin kept both about his own person at head-quarters, where they remained.

So dissatisfied were the Spanish troops at Lima with the government of their Viceroy, Pezuela, to whose want of military capacity they absurdly attributed our successes, that they forcibly deposed him, after compelling him to appoint General Lacerna as his successor. The deposed Viceroy wishing to send his lady and family to Europe, applied to General San Martin for a passport, to avoid capture by the Chilian squadron. This was refused; but Lady Cochrane having arrived at Callao in the British frigate *Andromache*, to take leave of me previous to her departure for England, the Viceroy's lady, Donna Angela, begged of her Ladyship to use her influence with the General to obtain leave for her departure for Europe. Lady Cochrane immediately proceeded to Haura, and effected the object; after which she remained for a month at head-quarters, residing at the house of a Peruvian lady, Donna Josefa Monteblanco.

A passage was also, by Lady Cochrane's influence, procured for the lady in the *Andromache*, on board which ship Captain Sherriff politely invited me to meet her. At this interview the ex-Vicequeen expressed her surprise at finding me "a gentleman and *rational* "*being* and not the *ferocious brute* she had been "taught to consider me!" A declaration which, from the unsophisticated manner in which it was made, caused no small merriment in the party assembled.

As I was determined not to be idle, General San Martin was with some difficulty prevailed upon to give me a division of 600 troops, under the command of Lieutenant-Colonel Miller. On the 13th of March we sailed for Pisco, of which, on its previous abandonment by the army, after a useless sojourn of fifty days, the enemy had again taken possession. On the 20th it was retaken, when it was found that the Spaniards had severely punished the alleged defection of the inhabitants for contributing to the supplies of the patriot force during its stay. Not imagining that we should return, the Spanish proprietors of estates had brought back their cattle, of which we managed to seize some 500 head, besides 300 horses for the use of the Chilian forces, the squadron thus supplying their wants instead of remaining in total inaction.

Previous to going to Pisco, I had again urged on General San Martin to advance on Lima, so convinced was I of the goodwill of the inhabitants. On his refusal, I begged him to give me 2,000 men, with whom I offered to take the capital, but this was also declined. I then offered to undertake the capture of Lima with 1,000 men, but even this was refused, and the detachment under Colonel Miller was only given to me to get rid of my importunity. Of this detachment I however determined to make the most before our return.

The only way of accounting for this indisposition on the part of General San Martin to place an adequate military force at my disposal, was the reason current amongst the officers of the army, who were all eager to place themselves under my orders; viz. the violent jealousy which caused him to look upon me as a rival, though without reason, as I should certainly not have attempted to interfere with him in the government of Peru when its reduction was complete. Suspicious himself he could not trust me, employing every effort to lessen my reputation amongst his officers, and endeavouring to the utmost to prevent the squadron from gathering fresh laurels; even sacrificing his own reputation to this insane jealousy, by preventing anything being done in which I could take part.

On the 18th I shifted my flag into the *San Martin*, and leaving the *O'Higgins* and *Valdivia* at Pisco to protect the troops, sailed for Callao, where we arrived on the 2nd of April. On the 6th, we again attacked the enemy's shipping under the batteries, and did them considerable damage, but made no further attempt to gain possession of them, as I had other aims in view. After this demonstration, the object of which was to deter them from quitting their shelter, we returned to Pisco.

General San Martin having now given me discretionary power to do what I pleased with the few troops placed at my disposal, I determined on attacking Arica, the southernmost port of Peru. Reimbarking the troops, and abandoning Pisco, we sailed on the 21st, and on the 1st of May arrived off Arica, to the Governor of which I sent a summons to surrender, promising to respect persons and personal property. As this was not complied with, an immediate bombardment took place, but without any great effect, as, from the difficulties of the port, it was impracticable to get sufficiently near to the fortifications.

After a careful survey, the *San Martin* was on the 6th, hauled nearer in shore, and some shells were thrown over the town by way of intimidation. As this had not the desired effect, a portion of the troops was landed at Sama, to the northward of the town, being followed by Colonel Miller with the remainder, and Captain Wilkinson with the marines of the *San Martin*; when the enemy fled, and the patriot flag was hoisted on the batteries. We took here a considerable quantity of stores, and four Spanish brigs, besides the guns of the fort and other detached artillery. A quantity of European goods, belonging to the Spaniards at Lima, was also seized and put on board the *San Martin*.

On the 14th Colonel Miller, with the troops and marines, advanced to Tacna, and by my directions took possession of the town, which was effected without opposition, two companies of infantry deserting the royalist cause and joining his force. These I ordered to form the nucleus of a new regiment, to be called the "Tacna Independents."

Learning that the Spanish General Ramirez had ordered three detachments from Arequipa, Puno, and La Paz, to form a junction at Tacna, to execute the usual Spanish order—to "drive the insurgents into "the sea"—Miller determined on attacking them separately. The Arequipa detachment, under Colonel Hera, was fallen in with at Maribe, and immediately routed, the result being that nearly the whole were killed or taken prisoners, together with four hundred mules and their baggage. In this affair we lost a valued officer, Mr. Welsh, an assistant surgeon, who had volunteered to accompany the detachment. This gentleman was sincerely mourned by all, and his early death was a great loss to the patriot service.

This action was fought none too soon, for before it was over the other detachments from Puno and La Plaz appeared in sight, so that the patriots had to face a fresh enemy. With his usual promptness Miller despatched Captain Hind, with a rocket party, to oppose their passage of a river; when, finding that the Arequipa detachment had been cut up, the royalists remounted their mules and decamped, in the direction of Moquega.

On the 22nd Miller pursued the runaway royalists, and, on the 24th, entered Moquega, by a forced march of nearly a hundred miles, where he found the enemy, deserted by their colonel. Notwithstanding the fatigue of the Chilenos, an instant attack was made, when the whole, with the exception of about twenty killed, were made prisoners. The inhabitants at once gave in their adherence to the cause of independence, their Governor, Colonel Portocarrera, being the first to set the example.

On the 25th Colonel Miller learned that a Spanish force was passing Torata, about fifteen miles distant, when, coming up with them on the following day, they were all taken prisoners or dispersed, as were also those who had fled from Arica, numbering four hundred men; so that in less than a fortnight after landing at Arica, the patriot forces had killed and made prisoners upwards of one thousand of the royalist army, by a series of difficult forced marches, and amidst hunger and privations of every kind, which were cheerfully borne by the Chilenos, who were no less inspired by a love of country than with attachment to their commander. The result was the complete submission of the Spaniards from the sea to the Cordilleras, Arica forming the key to the whole country.

Having ascertained that Colonel Miller was at Moquega, I took the *San Martin* to Ilo, from which anchorage the patriot force was supplied with every thing requisite. The sick were taken on board the brigs captured at Arica, as were also the Spanish colonels, Sierra and Suares, who had been taken prisoners, but whom I liberated on their *parole*, not to serve again until regularly exchanged.

It has been said that, before sailing to Arica, I had procured from General San Martin discretionary powers to do as I pleased with the troops placed at my disposal. My object was believed to be to create a diversion in favour of the general, but this was the least part of my intention; for, as the army had remained inactive from its first landing in Peru—with the exception of the detachment under Colonel Arenales,—no diversion would have been of much use. I wrote to the Government at Santiago for 1,000 men, or, if these could not be sent, for 500, and also for 1,000 stand of arms, of which there was abundance in the arsenal to equip recruits, who would have been forthcoming; and with these we could, with the greatest ease, have secured the whole of the southern provinces of Peru, the people being warmly disposed in our favour. I therefore told the Government that with such a force, we could hold the whole of Lower Peru, and gain eventual possession of Upper Peru. My request was refused, on the false ground that the Government had no means to equip such an expedition, and thus the good will manifested by the natives was thrown away.

In spite of this neglect, I determined to persevere, relying upon sacrifices made by the Peruvians themselves in our favour. General Ramirez was actively engaged in drawing men from distant garrisons to act against our small force, which was suffering severely from ague. Nevertheless, every effort was made again to advance into the interior—a number of recruits from the adjacent provinces having been enrolled—and everything promised a general revolt in favour of independence, when the Governor of Arequipa communicated to us intelligence that an armistice had been agreed upon for twenty days, between General San Martin and the Viceroy Lacerna. This happening just at the moment when hostilities could have been carried on with the greatest effect, and we were preparing to attack Arequipa itself—was annoying in the extreme; the more so, as the application had come from the Viceroy, who, being the first to receive intelligence of our success, had, no doubt, deceived General San Martin into the arrangement, in order to check our operations in the South.

This armistice was ratified on the 23rd of May, and sent by express to the Governor of Arequipa, the unusual haste proving the object of the Viceroy in persuading General San Martin to its ratification. To have regarded the armistice as a preliminary to the independence of Peru was a great mistake on the part of General San Martin, as the Viceroy Lacerna had no more power to acknowledge the absolute independence of the Colonists, than had his predecessor; and therefore the object of the armistice could have been none other than to put a stop to our progress, thereby giving the Spanish generals time to collect their scattered forces, without any corresponding advantage to the patriot cause.

Being thus reluctantly reduced to inaction, I dropped down to Mollendo, where we found a neutral vessel taking in corn for supplying the city of Lima, which city, from the vigilance of the squadron, was reduced to great straits, as shewn in an address from the *Cabildo* to the Viceroy:—"The richest and most opulent "of our provinces has succumbed to the unopposable "force of the enemy, and the remaining provinces "are threatened with the same fate; whilst this "suffering capital of Lima is undergoing the horrible "effects of a rigorous blockade, hunger, robberies, "and death. Our soldiers pay no respect to "the last remains of our property, even our oxen, "indispensable for the cultivation of the land, being "slain. If this plague continues, what will be our "lot—our miserable condition?" From this extract it is plain that Lima was on the point of being starved out by the squadron, whilst the inhabitants foresaw that, although the army of General San Martin was inactive, our little band in the south would speedily overrun the provinces, which were willing to second our efforts in favour of independence.

To return to the shipment of wheat for the relief of Lima. On ascertaining the fact, I wrote to the Governor of Arequipa, expressing my surprise that neutrals should be allowed to embark provisions during an armistice; the reply being that the most positive orders should be given to put a stop to it, upon which I retired from Mollendo, but leaving an officer to keep watch, and finding that the embarkation was persisted in, I returned and shipped all the wheat found on shore. The consequence of this was that Colonel La Hera, with 1,000 royalists, took possession of Moquega, on pretence that I had broken the armistice.

My private advices from head quarters informed me that the dissatisfaction of the Chilian army was daily increasing, on account of their continued inaction, and from jealousy at our success; knowing also, that the capital of Peru was, from the straits to which it was reduced, as well as from inclination, eager to receive them. General San Martin nevertheless declined to take advantage of the circumstances in his favour, till dissension began to assume the character of insubordination. A daily toast at the tables of the officers was, "to those who fight for the liberties of Peru, not "those who write." "*A los que pelean por la* "*libertad del Peru, no los que escriven.*" General San Martin, aware of the state of feeling in the army, went on board the schooner *Montezuma*, for the re-establishment of his health."

I was further informed that the Viceroy was negociating with General San Martin for the prolongation of the armistice to *sixteen months*, in order to give time for communication with the Court of Madrid, to ascertain whether the parent state would consent to the independence of Peru! At the same time official information was forwarded to me that a further prolongation of twelve days had been conceded.

Feeling certain that there was something wrong

at head-quarters, I determined to proceed to Callao for the purpose of learning the true state of affairs, leaving Colonel Miller to return to Arica, and in case of emergency, victualling and equipping the prizes, so as to be in readiness, if necessary, for the reception of his troops.

During my absence Lady Cochrane sailed for England, partly for the sake of her health, but more for the purpose of obtaining justice for me, for in addition to the persecution which I had undergone, a "Foreign Enlistment Bill" had been passed, the enactments of which were especially aimed at my having engaged in a service which had for its object the expulsion of Spain, then in alliance with England, from her Colonies in the Pacific.

As an incident relating to her Ladyship has been mentioned in the "Memoirs of General Miller," I may be pardoned for giving it as narrated in that work.

"On the 25th, six hundred infantry and sixty cavalry, all picked men, were placed under the command of Lieutenant-Colonel Miller, who received directions to embark on a secret service under the orders of Lord Cochrane, and proceeded to Huacho. On the day after his arrival there, and whilst he was inspecting the detachments in the Plaza, Lady Cochrane galloped on to the parade to speak to him. The sudden appearance of youth and beauty on a fiery horse, managed with skill and elegance, absolutely electrified the men, who had never before seen an English lady. "*Que hermosa! Que graciosa! Que linda! Que airosa! Es un angel del cielo!*" were exclamations which escaped from one end of the line to the other. Colonel Miller, not displeased at this involuntary homage to the beauty of his countrywoman, said to the men, "This "is our *generala*;" on which her Ladyship, turning to the line, bowed to the troops, who no longer confining their expressions of admiration to suppressed interjections, loud *vivas* burst from officers and men, to which Lady Cochrane, smiling her acknowledgments, cantered off the ground like a fairy."

In the month of February, during my absence, Lady Cochrane, tired of the crowded villages occupied by the liberating army, undertook a journey into the interior, in the hope that change of air might prove advantageous to our infant child, which was in a precarious state of health. She performed the journey on horseback, under the intense heat of a vertical sun, across a desert, impeded by the precipitous beds of torrents which intersect the country in every direction. On her arrival at Quilca, she was most hospitably received by the Marchioness de la Pracer, who placed her palace and every luxury at Lady Cochrane's disposal.

In the midst of the festivities which followed, her child was taken dangerously ill, whilst no medical assistance of any kind was at hand. On this she determined to return to the coast, and seek the aid of an English or Spanish physician, but as the Royalist army was advancing towards the direction necessary to be taken, this was judged impracticable till they had passed.

Whilst her Ladyship was in this state of suspense, information was received that the Royalists, having gained intelligence that she was at Quilca, had determined to seize her and her infant that very evening, and to detain them as hostages. This intelligence arrived just as a large party was assembled in the ball-room, when, with a decision which is one of her chief characteristics, Lady Cochrane ordered a *palanquin*—presented to her by the Marquis of Torre Tagle—to be got ready instantly, and placing the child and its nurse in it, she despatched them under the protection of a guard. Leaving the ball-room secretly, she changed her dress, immediately following on horseback with relays of her best horses.

Travelling all night and the following day without intermission, the party came to one of those swollen torrents which can only be crossed by a frail bridge made of cane-rope, a proceeding of extreme danger to those who are not well accustomed to the motion produced by its elasticity. Whilst the party was debating as to how to get the palanquin over, the sound of a Royalist bugle was heard close at hand. Lady Cochrane sprang to the palanquin, and taking out her suffering infant, rushed on to the bridge, but when near the centre, the vibration became so great that she was compelled to lie down, pressing the child to her bosom—being thus suspended over the foaming torrent beneath, whilst in its state of vibration no one could venture on the bridge. In this perilous situation, Pedro, the faithful soldier of whom mention has been previously made, seeing the imminent danger of her Ladyship, begged of her to lie still, and as the vibration ceased, crept on his hands and knees towards her Ladyship, taking from her the child, and imploring her to remain motionless, when he would bring her over in the same way; but no sooner had he taken the child, than she followed, and happily succeeded in crossing, when the ropes being cut, the torrent was interposed between her and her pursuers.

All travellers agree in describing these torrent bridges as most perilous. They are constructed of six elastic cane or hide ropes, four of which, with some sticks laid across, form the floor, and two the parapet. Only one person can pass at a time, and as the weight of the passenger causes the bridge to belly downwards, he remains suspended as it were in an elastic bag, from which it requires considerable skill to extricate himself with safety. Mules and horses cannot go over at all, but are hauled through the torrent with ropes.

Having reached the coast in safety, Lady Cochrane came down to me at Callao. Whilst she was on board, I received private information that a ship of war laden with treasure was about to make her escape in the night. There was no time to be lost, as the enemy's vessel was such an excellent sailer that, if once under weigh, beyond the reach of shot, there was no chance of capturing her. I therefore determined to attack her, so that Lady Cochrane had only escaped one peril ashore to be exposed to another afloat. Having beat to quarters, we opened fire upon the treasure-ship and other hostile vessels in the anchorage, the batteries and gun-boats returning our fire, Lady Cochrane remaining on deck during the conflict. Seeing a gunner hesitate to fire his gun, close to which she was standing, and imagining that his hesitation from her proximity might, if observed, expose him to punishment, she seized the man's arm, and directing the match fired the gun. The effort was, however, too much for her, as she immediately fainted, and was carried below.

The treasure-vessel having been crippled, and the gun-boats beaten off, we left off firing and returned to our former anchorage, Lady Cochrane again coming on deck. As soon as the sails were furled, the men in the tops, and the whole crew on deck, no doubt by preconcerted arrangement, spontaneously burst forth with the inspiring strains of their national anthem, some poet amongst them having extemporized an alteration of the words into a prayer for the blessing of Divine providence on me and my devoted wife; the effect of this unexpected mark of attachment from five hundred manly voices being so overwhelming as to affect her Ladyship more than had the din of cannon.

CHAPTER VI.

RETURN TO CALLAO—LIMA ABANDONED—HESITATION OF GEN. SAN MARTIN TO OCCUPY THE CITY—LOSS OF THE SAN MARTIN—EXCESSES OF THE SPANIARDS—PROCLAMATION OF INDEPENDENCE—SAN MARTIN ASSUMES AUTOCRATIC POWER UNDER THE TITLE OF PROTECTOR—MY REMONSTRANCE —HIS REPLY—MUTINOUS STATE OF THE SQUADRON FROM NEGLECT.

WE arrived at Callao on the 2nd of July, when learning that Lima was no longer tenable from want of provisions, and that an intention existed on the part of the Viceroy to abandon it, I forebore to make any hostile demonstration which might interfere with such decision, and withdrew to a distance from the port, awaiting the result, which could not be far distant, as the people had become clamorous, and all hope of assistance from Spain was abandoned.

Having, however, learned, on the 5th of July, that an attempt was being made by the Viceroy to obtain a still further prolongation of the armistice, I again entered the bay with the *San Martin*—my former flagship, the *O'Higgins*, being absent on the coast.

On the 6th the Viceroy abandoned the city, retaining, however, the fortresses at Callao, the garrison of which was reinforced from the troops which had evacuated Lima; a large quantity of warlike stores being also deposited in the forts, thus securing greater efficiency than before.

To the astonishment of the Peruvians and Chilenos, no movement was made by the liberating army to take possession of the Capital; and as the Spanish troops were withdrawn, whilst no government existed, serious disorders were anticipated, so that the *Cabildo* applied to Capt. Basil Hall, then in command of the British ship of war *Conway*, for his assistance to maintain tranquillity and protect public and private property. Captain Hall immediately despatched a party of marines, who contributed to maintain order.

General San Martin having been apprised by the Viceroy of his intention to abandon the capital, had entered the harbour in the schooner *Sacramento*, but nevertheless gave no orders for its occupation. On the 7th a detachment of cavalry, *without orders*, entered Lima, and those on the 8th were followed by another detachment of infantry.

On working up to the port on the 8th, I was surprised to find General San Martin still afloat in his schooner, though the liberating army was now entering the city in a body, and the occupation was complete; General San Martin remained on board till the evening of the 10th, when he privately landed.

As the forts at Callao were still in the possession of the enemy, I made preparations to attack them, and to destroy the shipping still sheltered under them. Aware of my intentions, the garrison, on the 11th, sank the *San Sebastian*, the only frigate left in the harbour, in order to prevent her falling into our hands On the following day, the *O'Higgins*, *Lautaro*, *Puyrredon*, and *Potrillo* arrived, so that the squadron was again complete.

It was mentioned in the last chapter that I had seized a considerable quantity of wheat at Mollendo, on account of a breach of the armistice. This was still on board, and the city being in a state of famine, General San Martin directed that the wheat, of which there were upwards of two thousand *fanegas*, should be landed at the Chorillos free of duty. As the *San Martin* was deeply laden, I objected to this from the dangerous nature of the anchorage, but more especially, that the only anchor on board was made from the remains of two broken anchors lashed together; this objection was nevertheless overruled, and, as I had anticipated, she went ashore at Chorillos, where, from the heavy swell which set in, she became a total wreck.

On the 17th I received an invitation from the *Cabildo* to visit the city, and on landing, found that preparations had been made to give the visit the character of a public entry, carriages being provided, with deputations from the various corporations. Finding this to be the case, I declined entering Lima in a manner so ostentatious, as General San Martin had entered the city privately by night. I was, however, compelled to hold a *levee* at the palace, where the compliments of the established authorities and principal inhabitants were tendered to me. General San Martin declined to attend this complimentary manifestation, remaining at La Legua, about halfway between Lima and Callao, where he had established his head quarters; probably considering such honours out of place towards one whom as Captain-General he might regard as a subordinate, and the more so, as no such compliment had been offered to himself.

On the following day, General San Martin directed a civic guard to be organized in place of the Spanish guard which had evacuated the city, the Marquis of Torre Tagle being appointed its commandant. At the same time the General retained the whole of the liberating army, though had even a portion of these followed the retreating Spaniards, the greater part would have joined the patriot standard—it being afterwards ascertained that Colonel Rodil who commanded them, had shot great numbers in the attempt to desert; even the patriot guerilla parties, unaided, had defeated those who were kept together; so that had a division of the liberating army been sent to co-operate with the guerillas, the entire Spanish force might have been annihilated, in place of forming the *nucleus*—as they afterwards did—of a force which, after my departure from Chili, threatened not only the independence of Peru, but even that of the Chilian Republic itself.

Being thus unopposed, and the towns which had given in their adhesion to the cause of independence being left defenceless—the retreating Spaniards committed great excesses amongst the inhabitants of the interior, who found themselves exposed to more than the rigours of martial law, without the least attempt for their protection; though a promise of this had formed one of the principal inducements for throwing off their allegiance to the Viceroy, at whose mercy—or rather want of it—they now found themselves exposed.

In place of protecting the Peruvians in the interior, a number of highly inflated proclamations were issued, in which it was left to be inferred that the city had been taken by hard fighting, though not a blow had been struck, except by the detachment of Colonel Arenales and the squadron, whose vigilance of blockade and previous actions had so dispirited the enemy and reduced them to such straits, that abandonment of the capital was inevitable. Nor was the large force present even required to maintain Lima, the inhabitants having for a long period been subjected to miseries which they had no disposition to re-encounter.

But General San Martin had other views in retaining the army than protecting those who had confided in his promises; the military force being required for very different purposes to that which had been set forth in his proclamations and in those entrusted to him by the Chilian government.

On the 24th I ordered Captain Crosbie to proceed to Callao in the boats, and cut out as many of the enemy's vessels as he could bring away. The service was gallantly performed, for on the following day he brought out two large merchantmen, the *San Fernando* and *Milagro*, and the sloop of war *Resolucion*, together with several launches; burning moreover two vessels within musket shot of the batteries.

On the 27th, the *Cabildo* sent me an invitation to be present at the public proclamation of the independence of Peru. As their letter fully recognises the obligations of the Limenos to the services of the squadron,—I shall transcribe it:—

"Lima is about to solemnize the most august act which has been performed for three centuries, or since her foundation; this is the proclamation of her independence, and absolute exclusion from the Spanish government, as well as from that of any other foreign potentate, and this *Cabildo*—wishing the ceremony to be conducted with all possible decorum and solemnity, *considers it necessary that your Excellency, who has so gloriously co-operated in bringing about this highly desired object*, will deign to assist at the act with your illustrious officers, on Saturday, the 28th instant."

Imagining that myself and officers had been mainly instrumental in establishing the independence of Peru—for I had in vain urged the Captain-General to action, as far as the army was concerned, the invitation was accepted, but judge of my surprise at the ceremony, when medals were distributed, ascribing to General San Martin and the army the whole credit of having accomplished that which the squadron had achieved! The inscription on the medals was as follows.—"Lima secured its inde-"pendence on the 28th of July, 1821, under the "protection of *General San Martin and the liberating* "*army*." The declaration of independence was however complete, according to the promises and intentions of the Chilian government. On hoisting the national flag, General San Martin pronounced the following words:—"Peru is from this moment "free and independent, by the general vote of the "people, and by the justice of her cause, which God "defend."

The inhabitants of Lima were in a state of great delight at this termination of centuries of Spanish misrule, and that their independence of action was fully recognized as had been stipulated by Chili. As a mark of gratitude, a deputation from the *Cabildo*, on the next day waited on General San Martin, offering him, in the name of the inhabitants of the capital, the first presidency of their now independent state. To the astonishment of the deputation they were curtly told that their offer was altogether unnecessary, as he had *already taken the command, and should keep it as long as he thought proper, whilst he would allow no assemblies for the discussion of public matters.* The first act of the freedom and independence so ostentatiously proclaimed on the previous day, being the establishment of a despotic government, in which the people had neither voice nor share; and this by the General of a Republic which existed only by the will of the people!

In this extraordinary assumption of power I had not been at all consulted, probably because it was known that I would not countenance anything but carrying out intact the intentions of the Supreme Director of Chili as declared in his proclamations. It now became evident to me that the army had been kept inert for the purpose of preserving it entire to further the ambitious views of the General, and that with the whole force now at Lima the inhabitants were completely at the mercy of their pretended liberator, but in reality their conqueror.

As the existence of this self-constituted authority was no less at variance with the institutions of the Chilian Republic than with its solemn promises to the Limeños, I again shifted my flag on board the *O'Higgins*, determined to adhere solely to the interests of Chili; but not interfering in any way with General San Martin's proceedings till they interfered with me in my capacity as Commander in Chief of the Chilian navy.

On the 3rd of August, General San Martin issued a proclamation to the same effect as his declaration to the now extinct *Cabildo*; setting forth that although it was abundantly notorious that he aspired only to retirement and tranquillity, nevertheless a moral responsibility required him to unite all government in his own person, and he therefore declared himself "Protector of Peru," with Don Juan Garcia del Rio, Don Bernardo Monteagudo, and Don Hipolito Unanue, as his three ministers of state.

Being at the time on board the flagship, I knew nothing of this proclamation; but as the squadron had not been paid their twelve months' wages, nor the 50,000 dollars promised by General San Martin, I went on shore on the 4th of August, to make the demand on behalf of the squadron, the seamen having served their time. Being ignorant of the self-imposed title which General San Martin had assumed, I frankly asked him to devise some means for defraying these payments.

I forbear personally to relate what passed at this interview; but as my secretary was present, and on his return to England published an account thereof, which is in every respect substantially true, I will give it in his words:—

"On the following morning, August 4th, Lord Cochrane, uninformed of the change which had taken place in the title of San Martin, visited the palace, and began to beg of the General in Chief to propose some means for the payment of the foreign seamen, who had served their time and fulfilled their contract. To this, San Martin answered, that 'he would never pay the Chilian squadron unless it was sold to Peru, and then the payment should be considered part of the purchase money!' To this Lord Cochrane replied, that 'by such a transaction the squadron of Chili would be transferred to Peru by merely paying what was due to the officers and crews for services done to that state.' San Martin knit his brows, and turning to his two ministers, Garcia and Monteagudo, ordered them to retire, to which his Lordship objected, stating that 'as he was not master of the Spanish language, he wished them to remain as interpreters, fearful that some expression, not rightly understood, might be considered offensive.' San Martin now turned round to the Admiral, and said—'Are you aware, my Lord, that I am Protector of Peru?'—'No,'—said his Lordship, 'I ordered my secretaries to inform you of it,' returned San Martin. 'That is now unnecessary, for you have personally informed me,' said his Lordship; 'I hope that the friendship which has existed between San Martin and myself will continue to exist between the Protector of Peru and myself.' San Martin then—rubbing his hands—said, 'I have only to say, that I am Protector of Peru!'

"The manner in which this last sentence was expressed, roused the Admiral, who, advancing, said—'Then it becomes me, as senior officer of Chili, and consequently the representative of the nation, to request the fulfilment of all the promises made to Chili and the squadron; but first—and principally—the squadron.' San Martin returned—" Chili! Chili! I will never pay a single *real* to Chili! As to the squadron, you may take it where you please, and go where you choose; a couple of schooners are quite enough for me;' '*Chili! Chili, yo nunca pagare 'un real a Chili! y en quanto a la esquadra, puede V llevarla donde quiere, e irse quando guste, con un par de golestas me basta a mi.*'

" On hearing this, Garcia left the room, and Monteagudo walked to the balcony. San Martin paced the room for a short time and turning to his Lordship, said,—' Forget, my Lord, what is past.' The admiral replied—' I will, when I can,' and immediately left the palace.

His Lordship was now undeceived by the man himself; the repeated reports he had heard of his past conduct crowded on his imagination, and knowing what might be attempted, from what had been already done, his Lordship agreed with me, that his life was not safe ashore. He therefore immediately took horse—rode to Boca Negra, and went on board his frigate*.

One thing has been omitted in the preceding narrative. General San Martin, following me to the staircase, had the temerity to propose to me to follow his example—viz. to break faith with Chilian Government to which we had both sworn—to abandon the squadron to his interests—and to accept the higher grade of " First Admiral of Peru." I need scarcely say that a proposition so dishonourable was declined; when in a tone of irritation he declared that " he would neither " give the seamen their arrears of pay, nor the gratuity " he had promised."

On arriving at the flagship, I found the following

* " *Twenty Years Residence in South America*," by W. B. STEVENSON, Secretary to Lord Cochrane, Vice-Admiral of Chili, &c. &c. 1825.

official communication, requesting me to fire a salute in honour of San Martin's self-elevation to the protectorship:—

Lima, 4th Aug 1821.

My Lord,

His Excellency the Protector of Peru commands me to transmit to you the annexed organic decree, announcing his exaltation to the Supreme Authority; in order that the squadron may be informed of this momentous event, and that the new Government may be acknowledged by the naval department under your command, belonging to the Republic of Chili.

I hope, that duly estimating this high act, you will cause it to be celebrated with all the dignity which is compatible with the martial usage of the naval service.

(Signed) MONTEAGUDO.

Attested by the *Rubrica* of the Protector.

Though this was a request to acknowledge General San Martin as invested with the attributes of a Sovereign Prince, I complied with it in the hope that quiet remonstrance might recal him to a sense of duty to the Chilian Government, no less than to his own true interests. On the 7th of August, I addressed to him the following letter.—

Callao Roads, 7th Aug. 1821.

My dear General,

I address you for the last time under your late designation, being aware that the liberty I may take as a friend might not be deemed decorous to you under the title of "Protector," for I shall not with a gentleman of your understanding take into account, as a motive for abstaining to speak truth, any chance of your resentment. Nay, were I certain that such would be the effect of this letter, I would nevertheless perform such an act of friendship, in repayment of the support you gave me at a time when the basest plots and plans were laid for my dismissal from the Chilian Service, for no other reason than that certain influential persons of shallow understanding and petty expedients hate those who despise mean acts accomplished by low cunning.

Permit me, my dear General, to give you the experience of eleven years during which I sat in the first senate in the world, and to say what I anticipate on the one hand, and what I fear on the other, nay, what I foresee; for that which is to come, in regard to the acts of Governments and Nations, may as certainly be predicted from history, as the revolutions of the solar system. You have it in your power to be the Napoleon of South America, as you have it in your power to be one of the greatest men now acting on the theatre of the world; but you have also the power to choose your course, and if the first steps are false, the eminence on which you stand will, as though from the brink of a precipice, make your fall the more heavy and the more certain.

The rocks on which the South American Government have split have hitherto been bad faith, and consequent temporary expedients. No man has yet arisen, save yourself, capable of soaring aloft, and with eagle eye embracing the expanse of the political horizon. But if in your flight, like Icarus, you trust to waxen wings, your descent may crush the rising liberties of Peru, and involve all South America in anarchy, civil war, and political despotism.

The real strength of Government is public opinion. What would the world say, were the Protector of Peru, as his first act, to cancel the bonds of San Martin, even though gratitude may be a private and not a public virtue? What would they say, were the Protector to refuse to pay the expense of that expedition which placed him in his present elevated situation? What would they say, were it promulgated to the world that he intended not even to remunerate those employed in the navy which contributed to his success.

What good can be arrived at by a crooked path that cannot be attained by a straight and open way? Who has advised a tortuous policy and the concealment of the real sentiments and intentions of Government? Has an intriguing spirit dictated the refusal of pay to the Chilian navy, whilst the army is doubly paid? Is it proposed thus to alienate the minds of the men from their present service, and by such policy to obtain them for the service of Peru? If so, the effect will, I predict, be the contrary, for they have looked, and do look, to Peru for their remuneration, and, if disappointed, they will feel accordingly.

See to what a state the Senate had brought the beautiful and fertile province of Chili. Nay, had not their notorious want of faith deprived them, notwithstanding their mines, their confiscated and public lands, of the means possessed even by the Spanish Government, and of the credit necessary to procure a dollar in any foreign country, or even in their own? I say, therefore, my dear General, that whoever has advised you to commence your Protectorship with devices unworthy of San Martin, is either a thoughtless or a wicked man, whom you should for ever banish from your counsels.

My dear General, look to the flattering addresses presented by the servile of all countries to the most base in power. Think not that it is to the person of San Martin that the public are attached. Believe not, that without a straight and dignified course you can obtain the admiration or love of mankind. So far yet you have succeeded, and, thank God, it is in your power to succeed yet farther. Flatterers are more dangerous than the most venomous serpents, and next to them are men of knowledge, if they have not the integrity or courage to oppose bad measures, when formally discussed, or even when casually spoken of.

What political necessity existed for any temporary concealment of the sentiments of Government in regard to the fate of the Spaniards in Peru? Were not the army and the people ready to support your measures, and did not the latter call aloud for their expulsion? Believe me, my dear General, that after your declaration, even the seizing on Spanish property belonging to those who remain, is an act which ought not to be resorted to without crime on their part subsequently committed.

In the feelings of my breast no man can deceive me. Of the sentiments of others, I judge by my own, and I tell you what they are as an honest man and a friend.

I could say much to you, my dear General, on other subjects of little inferior importance, but as the foregoing are the only acts immediately contemplated of which I have acquired a knowledge, and which are, in their consequences, ruinous, I shall, at present, only add, that had kings and princes but one man in their dominions who would, on all occasions, utter the naked truth, multifarious errors would be avoided, and the mischief to mankind would be infinitely less.

You will plainly perceive that I have no personal interests in these, or any other points, at variance with yours; but, on the contrary, if I were base and interested, I have now taken a decisive and irrevocable step to ruin my prospects; having no other security for such not being the consequence of my candour save my good opinion of your judgment and your heart.

Believe me, under all circumstances, your attached friend,

COCHRANE.

To this letter, on the 9th of August, General San Martin replied as follows:—

Lima, 9th August, 1821.

MY LORD,

The best proof of friendship that can be given by you is the sincere announcement of your opinions as to the course I should follow in my new political character.

Assuredly you have not erred, when, under the title of Protector, you do not anticipate any change in my personal character. Happily, the alteration is only in a name, which, in my opinion, was required for the benefit of the country; and if, in the character in which you have known me, you have met with *civility* and frankness, it would be an injustice to deny me confidence, having always listened to you as an enlightened person, experienced in the world; especially as you do me justice in enabling me to make observations on the spirit of your last communication.

I am aware that good faith in one who presides over a nation, is the vital spirit of its prosperity; and as, in this respect, a singular current of success has called me temporarily to the supreme magistracy of this country, I should renounce the advantages acquired and betray my principles, if vanity or servile acquiescence in bad advice were to induce me to deviate from the social interests of Peru, and so expose it to the evils which in such case you dread.

I know, my Lord, that one cannot fly with waxen wings. I perceive the course I ought to pursue, and that, however great the advantages already gained, there are rocks which, *without the aid of prudence and good faith*, must be encountered.

By good fortune, I have not forgotten the maxim of religiously adhering to the word of a gentleman, which, as General, has been the pivot on which my anticipations have rested.

It now behoves me to explain my engagements towards the Chilian squadron, to which, it is very gratifying to declare that Peru, in part, owes its liberty; an acknowledgment which would have been made on the medals coined, if, in the hurry of business, *I had been able to give my attention to the subject of the inscription that was presented to me as a model!* You yourself have heard me eulogise its merits and services.

I have offered to the crews of the squadron of Chili twelve months' pay, as an acknowledgment of its services, and am employed in providing the means, and also in endeavouring to collect the reward of 50,000 dollars which *you* offered to the seamen who should capture the *Esmeralda*, and I am not only disposed to pay these sums, but to recompense valour displayed in the cause of the country.

But you know, my Lord, that the wages of the crews do not come under these circumstances, and that I—*never having engaged to pay the amount—am not obliged to do so!* That debt is due from Chili, whose government engaged the seamen. Although it may be just, in the state of its finances, to indemnify Chili in some degree for the expeditionary expenses, that will be, for me, an agreeable consideration; but in no degree will I acknowledge a right to claim arrears of pay!

If I could forget the services of the squadron, and the sacrifices of Chili, I should manifest ingratitude, which, neither as a public or private virtue will I ever forego; but it is as imprudent to lavish rewards, as to withhold them from the meritorious. I am engaged in finding means to realize measures as regards the squadron, which I intend to propose to the Supreme Government of Chili, and thus conciliate all interests.

Your affectionate friend,
JOSE DE SAN MARTIN.

To Lord Cochrane, Vice-Admiral of Chili.

In this letter, San Martin attributes his usurpation to a "singular current of success;" omitting to state that he neither achieved one blow, nor devised one plan which led to it, whilst he had all along offered it every obstruction in his power. He declares that the arrogation of the fall of the Spaniards, attributed by the inscription on the medal to the army and himself, was a mistake, brought about by "his not being "able, in the hurry of business, to give attention to "the model presented to him;" whereas the inscription was his own writing, after days of deliberation and consultation with others, who advised him not to mention the squadron in the inscription.

In this letter he repudiates all connection with Chili, though he had sworn fidelity to the republic as its Captain General. He denies ever having engaged to pay the squadron their wages, though on no other condition had it put to sea from Valparaiso, and his own handwriting to this specific promise was accepted as the inducement. Though himself an officer of Chili, he treats Chili as a state with which he had nothing to do, whose debts he declares that he will not pay, as he had previously told me on the 4th of August; finally, he says that he will propose to Chili to pay its own seamen! As to his promises to give the men a twelvemonths' pay in acknowledgment of their services, this was neither intended nor given; whilst, as to the 50,000 dollars promised to the captors of the *Esmeralda*, which he is "endeavouring to "collect," he had long before "collected" many times the amount from the old Spaniards—who had offered a similar reward for the capture of any vessels of the Chilian squadron—and kept it. Fortunately, his own letters prove these matters, which otherwise I should have hesitated to mention, unsupported by testimony so irrefutable.

General San Martin afterwards denied to the Chilian Government that he refused, on the 4th of August, to pay the squadron. Here is the same assertion, in his own handwriting, on the 9th! During the whole of this time the squadron was in a state of literal destitution; even the provisions necessary for its subsistence being withheld from it, though the Protector had abundant means of supplying them; but his object was to starve both officers and men into desertion—so as to accelerate the dismemberment of the squadron which I would not give up to his ambitious views.

The sound advice contained in my letter General San Martin never forgave—and he afterwards fell exactly as I had predicted—there was no merit in the prophecy, for similar causes lead to like effects. Adhering to my own duty, I felt that I was free from his command, and determined to follow no other course than to carry out, as far as lay in my power, the pledge of the Chilian Government to the Peruvian people.

Concealing for the present his resentment, and reflecting that the forts of Callao were still in the hands of the Spaniards, the Protector endeavoured to explain away the disagreeable nature of our interview on the 4th of August, by asserting, " that he only " said, or meant to say, that it might be interesting " to Chili to *sell some of her vessels of war to Peru,* " because the latter wanted them for the protection " of her coasts;" adding, that " the Government of " Chili would at all times devote their squadron to " the furtherance of the cause of Peru." He repeated, that the arrears of pay to the squadron should be liquidated, as well as the rewards which had been promised.

As none of these were forthcoming, the squadron began to shew symptoms of mutiny at the conduct of the Protector. On the 11th of August I wrote to him, apprising him of the increasing discontent of the seamen, again requesting payment. On this a decree was issued, ordering one-fifth of the customs receipts to be set aside for the joint pay of the army and navy, but as the fortress and port of Callao were in the hands of the Spaniards, these receipts were most insignificant, and the measure was rightly regarded by the squadron as a subterfuge.

To this communication the Protector replied, on the 13th of August—at the same time hinting that I might *reconsider* my refusal to accept the command of the contemplated Peruvian navy.

The subjoined is his letter:—

Lima, 13th of August, 1821.

My Lord,

In my official letter addressed to you on the disagreeable business of paying the squadron, which causes us so much uneasiness, I have told you that it is impossible to do as we wish. I have nothing to add, unless my previous declaration, that I shall never view with indifference any thing that interests you. I told you in Valparaiso, that "*your lot should be equal to mine*," and I believe myself to have proved that my intentions have not varied—nor can vary, because every day renders my actions more important.

No, my Lord, I do not view with indifference anything which concerns you, and I shall be deeply grieved, if you do not wait till I can convince you of the truth, If, however, in despite of all this, you determine on the course, which, at our interview a few days ago, you proposed to take, it will be for me a difficulty from which I cannot extricate myself, but I hope that—*conforming yourself to my wishes*—you will conclude the work begun, on which our common lot depends.

Adieu, my Lord, I repeat that I am, with sincere esteem, your eternal friend,

JOSE DE SAN MARTIN.

The assertion, that he could not satisfy the seamen, was a subterfuge; he had abundance of money, derived from the wholesale spoliation of the Spaniards, to which indefensible course I had alluded in my letter of August 7th. He also hoped that "*conforming to* "*his wishes*," I would accept the appointment of "First Admiral;" the consequence of which—together with the decree transferring the Chilian officers —without their consent—to the service of Peru, would have been to turn over to his Government the Chilian squadron.

CHAPTER VII.

TAMPERING WITH CHILIAN OFFICERS—THE ARCHBISHOP OF LIMA—HIS EXPULSION—NEGOCIATION FOR SURRENDER OF THE FORTS—THIS COUNTERACTED—SAN MARTIN'S BOMBASTIC PROCLAMATIONS—HIS REFUSAL TO ENCOUNTER THE ENEMY—THE SPANIARDS RELIEVE CALLAO—DELUSIVE PROCLAMATION—THE UNBLUSHING FALSEHOOD—SPANIARDS CARRY OFF THE TREASURE—DISCONTENT OF THE SQUADRON.

Finding that I was indisposed to acknowledge his self-assumed authority, and still less to contribute to measures which would, in effect, have deprived Chili of the Navy, which by her patriotic sacrifices had been created, the Protector issued a proclamation, again *promising* the payment of arrears to the seamen, and a pension for life to the officers, *acknowledging them as officers of Peru*! No inference can be drawn from this other than a direct intimation to the officers to desert from the Chilian service.

The following are extracts from the proclamation, which was published in a Gazette Extraordinary of August 17th, 1821:—

"The Army and Squadron of Chili united, have, at last, completed the oath which they took, to liberate Peru, and have raised it to the rank which justice and the interests of the world demand. Their constancy and heroism will hand them down to posterity with gratitude. I should be deficient in my political duty, did I not manifest the appreciation due to their transcendent deeds, promoting the interests of both hemispheres.

" 1. The State of Peru acknowledges as a national debt the arrears of the Army and Squadron, as well as the promises made by me to both.

" 2. All the property of the State, and also twenty per cent. on the revenue, are pledged to the extinction of these debts.

" 3. All the officers of the Army and Squadron who sailed with the liberating expedition, and now remain in them, *are acknowledged as officers of Peru.*

" 4. Those comprehended in the preceding articles, and those employed in the said cause, shall receive, during the period of their lives, a pension of half their full pay, awarded on leaving Valparaiso, which pension shall be paid even in the case of their settling in a foreign country.

" 5. All shall receive a medal," &c., &c.

Not a penny of the arrears and the other emoluments promised, was, however, paid to the squadron; nor was any intended to be paid, the object being to get the officers quietly to transfer themselves from the Chilian squadron to the service of the Protector, on the strength of the promises made: and, in this, he was ably seconded by his instruments, Guise and Spry, who, in defiance of their desertion, and the sentence of court-martial on the latter, had been retained near his person for the accomplishment of this object.

One of the most fearless opponents of the Protector was the Archbishop of Lima, an excellent man, much beloved by the people—who made no secret of his indignation at the usurpation which had taken place, despite all the promises of Chili, declared "before God " and man"—as well as those of the Protector himself, to "leave the Peruvians free as regarded their own " choice of Government." As the honest prelate denounced, in no measured terms, the despotism which had been established in the place of the liberty guaranteed, it was determined to get rid of him.

The first step was an order to the Archbishop, dated August 22, 1821, to close all the houses of spiritual exercises. This was politely refused; but, at the same time, the prelate stated, that if any confessor disturbed public order, he would take the requisite measures for his punishment. On the 27th, the Archbishop was told in reply, that "the Protector's orders "were irrevocable, and he must at once decide on "the line of conduct he intended to adopt."

On the 1st of September, the prelate, in an admirable letter, told the Protector, that "the principal obligation "of a bishop was to defend the deposit of doctrine and "faith which had been confided to him, and, if "threatened by any great potentate, to remonstrate "with respect and submission, to the end that he "might not be a participator in crime by a cowardly "condescension. God had constituted bishops as "the pastors and guards of the flock, and he tells us, "that we are not to be cowards in the presence of the "greatest potentates on earth, but, if necessary, we "must shed our blood, and lay down our lives, in so "just a cause; anathematizing us, on the contrary, "as dumb dogs who do not bark when the spiritual "health of the flock is in danger."

The end of this was, that the Protector urged on the Archbishop to resign, promising him a vessel to convey him to Panama; relying on which promise, he sent in his resignation, and was ordered to quit

Lima in twenty-four hours! As the promise of a conveyance to Panama was broken, the Archbishop embarked in a merchant vessel for Rio de Janeiro, addressing to me the following letter previous to his departure.

Chancay, Nov. 2, 1821.

My dear Lord,

The time is arrived for my return to Spain, the Protector having granted me the necessary passport. The polite attention which I owe to your Excellency, and the peculiar qualifications which adorn and distinguish you, oblige me to manifest to you my sincere regard and esteem.

In Spain, if God grant that I arrive in safety, I request that you will deign to command me. On leaving this country, *I am convinced that its independence is for ever sealed.* This I will represent to the Spanish Government, and to the Papal See, and will do all in my power to preserve the tranquillity, and to further the views, of the inhabitants of America, who are dear to me.

Deign, my Lord, to receive these sentiments as emanating from the sincerity of my heart, and command

Your obliged servant and Chaplain,
BARTOLOMÉ MARIA DE LAS HERAS.

This forcible expulsion of the Archbishop was an act of political folly, as being tantamount to a declaration that he was too good a man to countenance the designs of those who had usurped an unjust dominion over his flock. Had the promises of Chili been carried out in their integrity, both the Archbishop and his clergy would have used all their influence to promote the cause of liberty—not more from interest than inclination. The expression of the Archbishop, that "the independence of Peru was *for ever* sealed," was, however, erroneous. Tyranny is not composed of enduring materials.

The Bishop of Guamanga, who resided at Lima, was also ordered to leave Peru within eight days, without reason assigned, and thus the opposition of the Church was got rid of, though not without deep feeling on the part of the Limeños, who were, however, powerless to help their clergy or themselves.

The affairs of the squadron becoming every day worse, and a mutinous spirit being excited from actual destitution, I endeavoured to obtain possession of the castles of Callao by negociation, offering to the Spanish Commandant permission to depart with two-thirds of the property contained in the fort, on condition of the remainder, together with the forts, being given up to the Chilian squadron. My object was to supply the crews with the absolute necessaries, of which they stood in need from the evasive conduct of the Protector, who continued to withhold, not only pay, but provisions, though the squadron had formed the ladder on which he had ascended to his present elevated position. There were large sums and a vast amount of plate in the possession of the Spanish garrison,—the wealthy citizens of Lima—fearing their liberators—having deposited both in the forts for security. A third of this would have relieved us from our embarrassments. The vessels were, in fact, in want of stores of every kind, their crews being without animal food, clothing, or spirits, indeed their only means of subsistence was upon money obtained from the Spanish fugitives, whom I permitted to ransom themselves by surrendering a third only of the property with which they were escaping.

As soon as my offer to the Spanish Commandant, La Mar, became known to the Protector—in order to counteract it, and ensure the success of his design to starve out the Chilian squadron, and so procure its transfer to himself—he offered La Mar unlimited and unconditional protection, both as to persons and property, on purchase of letters of citizenship! The Commandant, therefore, rejected my proposal, and the hope of obtaining a sufficient sum for the payment of the seamen, and for refitting the ships, was frustrated.

General San Martin afterwards accused me to the Chilian Government of aiming at the possession of the fortress of Callao, for the purpose of setting at defiance the Government of Peru! This was ridiculous; though, had it been my object, it would have been perfectly consistent with my duty to Chili, from which State the Protector of Peru had cast off his allegiance. My object was simply to obtain means to subsist the squadron; though, had I obtained possession of the forts, I would most certainly have dictated to General San Martin the fulfilment of his promises; and should as certainly have insisted on his performing his solemn engagement to the Peruvians, of giving them the free choice of their own government.

He also accused me of wishing to appropriate the sum proposed to be surrendered by the Spanish Commandant to my own use, though the seamen were in a state of mutiny from actual starvation! Instead of contributing to this useful end, as before the Protector's interference La Mar was not unwilling to do, the Spaniards were afterwards permitted to retire unmolested with the whole of their treasure; and to this, the most discreditable act which ever sullied the name of a military commander, we now come. As the whole transaction has been well described by another writer, who was present throughout, I prefer extracting his words, in order to prevent any suspicion of mental bias which I may be supposed to entertain on the subject:—

"The Spanish army at Janja, in the beginning of September, spread alarm in Lima, from advices received of their movements. It appeared that they were determined to attack the capital, and on the 5th of September the following proclamation was issued at head-quarters by the Protector:—

"INHABITANTS OF LIMA,

"It appears that the justice of heaven, tired of tolerating for so long a time the oppressors of Peru, now guides them to destruction. Three hundred of those troops who have desolated so many towns, burnt so many temples, and destroyed so many thousands of victims, are at San Mateo, and two hundred more at San Damian. If they advance on this capital, it will be with the design of immolating you to their vengeance (San Martin had 12,000 troops to oppose them), and to force you to purchase at a high price your decision, and enthusiasm for independence. Vain hope! The valiant who have liberated the illustrious Lima, those who protect her in the most difficult moments, know how to preserve her against the fury of the Spanish army. Yes, inhabitants of this capital, my troops will not abandon you; *they and myself are going to triumph over that army which—thirsty of our blood and property, is advancing*; *or we will perish with honour, for we will never witness your disgrace.* In return for this noble devotion, and that it may receive the favourable success of which it is worthy, all we require of you is, union, tranquillity, and efficacious co-operation. This alone is necessary to ensure the felicity and splendour of Peru.

"SAN MARTIN."

"On the morning of the 10th, Lord Cochrane received on board the *O'Higgins* an official communication, informing him that the enemy was approaching the walls of Lima, and repeating the request that his Lordship would send to the army every kind of portable arms then on board the squadron, as well as the marines and all volunteers; because the Protector was '*determined to bring* ' *the enemy to an action, and either conquer or remain buried in the* ' *ruins of what was Lima.*' This heroic note was, however, accompanied by a private one from Monteagudo, containing a request that the boats of the vessels of war might be kept in readiness, and a look out placed on the beach of Boca Negra.

" Lord Cochrane immediately pressed forward to San Martin's camp, where, being recognised by several officers, a murmur of congratulation was heard, and even Guise and Spry exclaimed, ' We shall have some fighting now the Admiral is come.' General Las Heras, acting as General-in-Chief, saluting the Admiral, begged of him to endeavour to persuade the Protector to bring the enemy to an action. His Lordship, on this, rode up to San Martin, and taking him by the hand, in the most earnest manner entreated him to attack the enemy without losing a single moment; his entreaties were, however, in vain, the only answer received being— ' My resolutions are taken'—' *mis medidas están tomadas.*'

" Notwithstanding this apathy, his Lordship remonstrated, stating the situation in which he had, not five minutes before, observed the enemy's infantry, and begged of the Protector to ascend an eminence at the back of the house, and convince himself how easily a victory might be obtained; but he only received the same cold reply— *mis medidas están tomadas.*' "

" The clamour of the officers in the *patio* of the house roused San Martin, who called for his horse and mounted. In a moment all was bustle, and the anticipated glow of victory shone in every countenance. The order to arms was given, and instantly obeyed by the whole army, amounting to about 12,000 men, including guerillas, all anxious to begin the fight. The Protector beckoned to the Admiral and General Las Heras, who immediately rode up to him, hoping that he was either about to consult them respecting the attack, or to inform them how it was to be conducted.

" At this moment a peasant approached San Martin on horseback, the General with most unparalleled composure lending an attentive ear to his communications as to where the enemy was the day before! The Admiral, exasperated at so unnecessary a waste of time, bade the peasant 'begone,' adding—'The General's 'time is too important to be employed in listening to your 'fooleries.' At this interruption, San Martin frowned on the Admiral, and turning his horse rode up to the door of the house, where he alighted and went in.

"Lord Cochrane then requested a private conference with San Martin—which was the last time he ever spoke to him—and assured him that it was not even then too late to attack the enemy, begging and entreating that the opportunity might not be lost, and offering himself to lead the cavalry. But to this he received the reply, 'I 'alone am responsible for the liberties of Peru.'—'*Yo solo soy res-'ponsable de la libertad del Peru.*' On this the Protector retired to an inner apartment of the house to enjoy his customary *siesta*, which was disturbed by General Las Heras, who came to receive orders, and recalled to the attention of the Protector that the force was still under arms, when San Martin ordered that the troops should receive their rations!

"Thus Gen. Cantarac, with 3,200 men, passed to the southward of Lima—within half-musket shot of the protecting army of Peru, composed of 12,000—entered the castles of Callao with a convoy of cattle and provisions, where he refreshed and rested his troops for six days, and then retired on the 15th, taking with him the *whole of the vast treasure deposited therein by the Limeños*, and leisurely retreating on the north side of Lima.

"After Cantarac had led his troops into the batteries of Callao, the success was announced by the firing of guns and other demonstrations which harrowed up the souls of the Chilian officers. The patriot army thereupon passively occupied their old camp at the Legua, between Callao and Lima.

"It would be an act of injustice not to mention that the second in command, General Las Heras, disgusted with the result, left the service of the Protector, and requested his passport to Chili, which was granted; his example being followed by several officers of the army, who, deeply wounded by what had taken place, preferred obscurity, and even poverty, to further serving under such circumstances.

"The British ship of war, *Superb*, was in the bay, and several of the officers, expecting to see the decisive blow struck in Peru, repaired to San Martin's head-quarters, and were astounded at the coolness of a general, who, commanding 12,000 men, could abandon a favourable position in which he might at least have intercepted the convoy of cattle, and so at once have compelled the surrender of Callao, instead of permitting them to pass without a single shot being fired *."

The preceding extract, published in London by one who was by my side during the whole affair, is perfectly correct. The Limeños were deeply humiliated by the occurrence, nor was their annoyance mitigated by the publication of the following proclamation in the ministerial Gazette of the 19th, in which General San Martin informed them that he had beaten the enemy and pursued the fugitives! though the said enemy had relieved and reinforced the fortress, and then coolly walked off unmolested with plate and money to the amount of many millions of dollars; in fact, the whole wealth of Lima, which, as has been said, was deposited by the inhabitants in the fortress for security.

Limeños,

It is now fifteen days since the liberating army left the capital, resolved not to permit that even the shadow of the Spanish flag should again darken the illustrious city of Lima. The enemy haughtily descended the mountains, filled with the calculations they had formed in their ignorant meditations. They fancied that to appear before our camp was enough to conquer us; but they found *valour armed with prudence!* They acknowledged their inferiority. *They trembled at the idea of the hour of battle, and profited by the hour of darkness!!* and they sought an asylum in Callao. My army

* "*Twenty years Residence in South America*," by W. B. STEVENSON. Vol. iii. London, 1825.

began its march, and at the end of eight days the enemy has had to fly precipitately—convinced of their impotency to try the fortune of war, or to remain in the position they held.

The desertion which they experience ensures us that, before they reach the mountains, there will only exist a handful of men, terrified and confounded with the remembrance of the colossal power which they had a year ago, and which has now disappeared like the fury of the waves of the sea at the dawn of a serene morning. *The liberating army pursues the fugitives. They shall be dissolved or beaten.* At all events, the capital of Peru shall never be profaned with the footsteps of the enemies of America—*this truth is peremptory.* The Spanish empire is at an end for ever. Peruvians! your destiny is irrevocable; consolidate it by the constant exercise of those virtues which you have shown in the epoch of conflicts. *You are independent,* and nothing can prevent your being happy, if you will it to be so.

SAN MARTIN.

To these monstrous assertions I only know one parallel, viz:—Falstaff's version of his victory over the robbers at Gadshill. The Protector asserts that "the shadow of the Spanish flag should never again "darken Lima." It nevertheless passed completely round the city within half-musket shot. "The enemy "thought that to view our camp was to conquer us." They were only 3,000 to 12,000. "They trembled at "the hour of battle, *and profited by the hour of darkness!*" The fact being that with droves of cattle and abundance of other provisions, they triumphantly marched into Callao *at mid-day!* viz from eleven A.M. to three P.M. "The liberating army pursues the fugitives." This is the only fact contained in the proclamation. The enemy *was* pursued by 1,100 men, who followed them at a distance for ten miles, when Cantarac suddenly facing about, let loose his cavalry at them, and nearly the whole were cut up! The Spaniards in fact came to relieve Callao, and fully effected their object.

Were not the preceding proclamation indelibly imprinted in the columns of the ministerial Gazette, it would be deemed a malicious fabrication. Yet the poor, *independent* Limeños dared not utter a voice against falsehood so palpable. Disarmed and betrayed, they were completely at the mercy of the Protector, who, if he can be said to have had a motive in not encountering the small force of Cantarac, no doubt founded it in keeping his own troops intact for the further oppression of the unhappy Limeños—with what effect we shall presently see.

This triumphant retreat of the Spanish force with its large amount of treasure was a disaster which, after the Limeños had risen against the tyranny of San Martin and forcibly expelled him from their city, entailed the shedding of torrents of blood in Peru, for the Spaniards were thus enabled to reorganize a force which would have subjected the country to its ancient oppressors, had not the army of Colombia stepped in to resist a common enemy. Even Chili trembled for her liberties, and, after I had left the Pacific, begged me to return and check disasters with which she was incompetent to grapple.

Had not the Protector prevented the Spanish Commandant, La Mar, from accepting my offer of permitting him to retire with two-thirds of the enormous treasure deposited in the fort, Chili would, at the lowest computation, have received ten millions of dollars, whilst the Spaniards would have retired with twenty millions. Surely this would have been better than to permit them—as General San Martin did—to retire unmolested with the whole.

Foiled in this attempt to relieve the necessities of the squadron, whilst the Protector's Government pertinaciously refused to supply them, it was impossible to keep the men from mutiny; even the officers—won over by Guise and Spry, who paid midnightly visits to the ships for the purpose—began to desert to the Protectoral Government.

The following letter, addressed to Monteagudo, will shew the state of the matter as regarded the squadron:—

MOST EXCELLENT SIR,

I have written you an official letter to-day, by which you will perceive that the consequences which I have long predicted will have so far come to pass, as to render the removal of the large ships of the squadron indispensable. If by a total neglect of all I tell the Protectoral Government through you, things happen prejudicial to the service, the Protector and yourself will at least do me the justice to feel that I have done my duty; the base, interested, and servile, for the promotion of their selfish views, may clamour, but I regard them not.

I would send you the *original* reports of the provisions and state of the ships issued by the captains, but I must hold these for my public justification, should such be necessary.

What is the meaning of all this, Monteagudo? Are these people so base as to be determined to force the squadron to mutiny? And are there others so blind as not to foresee the consequences? Ask Sir Thomas Hardy, and the British captains, or any other officers, what will be the result of such monstrous measures.

Believe me, with a heavy heart,

Yours, &c.

COCHRANE.

CHAPTER VIII.

PROLONGED DESTITUTION OF SQUADRON—THE MEN MUTINY IN A BODY—THE SEAMEN'S LETTERS—SAN MARTIN SENDS AWAY THE PUBLIC TREASURE—MY SEIZURE OF IT—PRIVATE PROPERTY RESTORED—SAN MARTIN'S ACCUSATIONS AGAINST ME—THE SQUADRON PAID WAGES—ATTEMPT ON THE OFFICERS' FIDELITY—I AM ASKED TO DESERT FROM CHILI—ORDERED TO QUIT ON REFUSAL—MONTEAGUDO'S LETTER—MY REPLY—JUSTIFICATION OF SEIZING THE TREASURE—NO OTHER COURSE POSSIBLE.

Previous to this time I had on board the flag-ship the unexpended portion of the money captured at Arica, but as the Chilian Government, trusting to Peru to supply the wants of the squadron, neither sent funds or provisions, I was compelled to spend for our subsistence the uncondemned portion of the prize money belonging to the seamen—a necessity which, no less than their want of pay or reward, irritated them beyond measure, as, in effect, compelling them to fight the battles of the Republic not only without pay but at their own expense. In addition to this, I was in possession of the uncondemned portion of other sums taken on the coast, and these also I was obliged to expend, at the same time transmitting accounts thereof to the Minister of Marine at Valparaiso, the appropriation being fully approved by the Chilian Government.

The destitute condition of the squadron, and the

consequent dissatisfaction of the crews, will be best shewn by a few extracts from the letters of the officers and the men themselves.

On the 2nd of September, Captain Delano, the Commander of the *Lantaro*, wrote to me as follows:—

"The officers as well as the men are dissatisfied, having been a long time on the cruise, and at present without any kind of meat or spirits, and without pay, so that they are not able to provide for themselves any longer, though, *until starved*, they have borne it without a murmur.

"The ship's company have now absolutely refused duty on account of short allowance. The last *charqui* (dried beef) they got was rotten and full of vermin. They are wholly destitute of clothing, and persist in their resolution not to do duty till beef and spirits are supplied, alleging that they have served their time, with nothing but promises so frequently broken that they will no longer be put off.

"In your Lordship's absence I took the liberty to write to the Government and make their complaints known, but the Minister of Marine did not even give me an answer.

"The greater portion have now left the ship and are all gone ashore, so that under existing circumstances, and with the dissatisfaction of the officers and the remainder of the ship's company I do not hold myself responsible for any accident that may happen to the ship until these difficulties are removed, as the cables are bad and not to be trusted to, and we have no anchor sufficient to hold her.

"PAUL DELANO, *Captain*."

On Captain Delano sending his first lieutenant on shore to persuade the men to return to the ship, he was arrested by order of the Government and put in prison, the Protector's object being to get all the men to desert, thus furthering his views towards the appropriation of the squadron.

The *Galvarino* was even in a worse condition, so that

I deemed it expedient to address a letter to the ship's company asking them to continue at their duty till I could devise means for their relief; with what result the following letter from Captain Esmond, commanding the *Galvarino* will shew.

Galvarino, Sept. 8th, 1821.

My Lord,

Pursuant to your Excellency's order, I have read your letter of the 6th instant to the ship's company, respecting your communication with His Excellency the Protector, concerning arrears of pay, prize-money, &c.

I am sorry to inform your Excellency that they still persist in their demands, *and are determined not to proceed to sea.*

I. ESMOND, *Captain.*

On the 19th, the foreign seamen of the flag-ship itself mutinied in a body, on which my flag-captain, Crosbie, wrote me the following letter:—

My Lord,

It is with the utmost regret I have to inform your Lordship that being ready for sea early this morning, the foreigners refused heaving up the anchor in consequence of arrears of pay and prize-money, and to my great surprise many of the natives also came aft.

I endeavoured by persuasive means to induce them to return quietly and willingly to their duty, which had no effect. Knowing well, had I commenced hostile measures to enforce those orders the consequence might be serious, I refrained therefrom, being aware of your Lordship's wish to conduct everything as peaceably as possible.

The names of the foreigners who refuse going to sea I have the honour to enclose to your Lordship, and also to enclose several letters sent me officially from Captain Cobbett, of the *Valdivia.*

I. S. CROSBIE, *Captain.*

Not to multiply these letters from other Commanders, I will adduce two written by the whole of the English and North-American seamen themselves.

Captin Crosby,

Sir, It his the request of us all in the Ship's Company to inform you that we would wish to acquaint his Lordship that we was promised by General San Martin to receive a bounty of 50.000 dollars and the Total Amount of the Spanish Frigate *Ismeralda*, it his the Sole thought of us all that if San Martin had any Honure he would not breck his promises wish out to have been fulfilled Long a go.

Ship's Company of *O'Higgins*.

Capt. Corbet

It is the request of us all On Bord the Chili States ship *Valdivia* To aquaint you that we are disatisfied on account of our pay and prize money, and likewise the promises made to us on leaving Valpariso, it is likewise our Determination not to weigh the anchor of the *Valdivia* untill we get the whole of our wages and prize money, likewise a number of us is a Bove twelvemonths aBove our time that we Shipt for And we should likewise wish our Discharge and let them that wish to Reenter Again May do as they think proppre as we consider this a patriot port.

The Ship's Company at large of the *Valdivia*.

Capt Crosby, Esq

We would wish to acquaint you of wot his bean read to us on board of the different C. States ship under his Lordship's Command Concerning the Capture of the *Ismeralda*.

Sir it was thus

the importance of the Service performed by your Lordship to the States by the Capture of the Spanish Frigat *Ismeralda*, and the brillant manner in which this noble enterprize was conducted under your Command on the memorable night of the fift of November, has aurgumented the claims which your previous services gave to the Consideration of the government and those that is Interested in thar cause as well as my present esteem.

All those who partook in the risk and glory of this Interprise deserves also the estermation of thar Companions in the Army, and I enjoy the pleasure of being the Organ of thar Sentiments of Admiration Wich so important an action as praduced in the officers and army, Permit me tharfore to express such thar sentiments to your Lordship that may be communicated to the Officers and Seamen and troops of the Sqwardon.

Regarding the premium for the Frigat It is to be regretted that the memorey of so herioic an Interprise should be mixed with the painful ideer that blood as been shed in Accomplishment, and we hope that your Lordship and the Gallant Officers and Seamen may be enabbled to give new days of Glorry to the cause of indispendence.

Ship s Company, *O'Higgins.*

N.B.—Warre One Single Sentiment his not been fulfilled.

This letter, though somewhat incomprehensible, was intended as a farewell complimentary address to myself, previous to the desertion of the flag-ship; and, had this taken place, there was no doubt that the ships' companies of the whole squadron would have followed the example, so that the Protector would have gained his ends, in spite of my endeavours to keep the men faithful to the flag under which they were engaged to serve.

Fortunately for Chili and myself, an occurrence took place which averted the evil, and was brought about by the very means which the Protector had devised to promote his individual views.

The occurrence alluded to, was the embarkation of large sums of money by the Protector in his yacht *Sacramento*, which had cast out her ballast to stow the silver, and in a merchant vessel in the harbour, to the exclusion of the *Lantaro* frigate, then at the anchorage. This money was sent to Ancon, on the pretence of placing it in safety from any attack by the Spanish forces, but possibly to secure it for the further purposes of the Protector. The squadron having thus ocular demonstration that its arrears could be paid, but were not, both officers and men refused longer to continue in a service which had brought them nothing but prolonged suffering.

My own views coincided with theirs, and I determined that the squadron should be no longer starved nor defrauded. I therefore sailed to Ancon, and personally seized the treasure, before witnesses; respecting all that professed to belong to private individuals, and also the whole of that contained in the Protector's schooner, *Sacramento*, considering it his private property, though it could not have been other than plunder wrested from the Limeños. Independently of this yacht-load of silver, there were also on board, seven *surrones* (sacks) of uncoined gold, brought down on his account by the Legate Parroisien; so that, after all the moveable wealth of Lima was supposed to have been previously deposited for safety in the castles of Callao, but carried off by Cantarac, the condition of the unhappy Limeños may be imagined, from the additional sums of which they were subsequently deprived.

I immediately made proclamation, that all private individuals, having the customary documents, might receive their property upon application, and considerable sums were thus given up to Dr. Unanue, Don Juan Aguero, Don Manuel Silva, Don Manuel Primo, Don Francisco Ramirez, and several others, though connected with the Government. Besides which, I gave up 40,000 dollars to the commissary of the army, who claimed it; so that, having returned all the money for which dockets were produced, there remained 285,000 dollars, which was subsequently applied to the payment of one year's arrears to every individual of the squadron; but relying on the justice of the Chilian Government, I took no part myself, reserving the small surplus that remained for the more pressing exigencies and re-equipment of the squadron.

Accounts of the whole money seized, were forwarded to the Minister of Marine at Valparaiso, as well as vouchers for its disbursement, and in due course, I received the approbation of the Chilian Government for what had been done.

General San Martin entreated, in the most earnest terms, the restoration of the treasure, promising the faithful fulfilment of all his former engagements. Letter after letter was sent, begging me to save the credit of the Government, and pretending that the money seized was all the Government possessed for indispensable daily expenses. To this I replied, that had I been aware that the treasure spared in the *Sacramento* was the property of Government, and not that of the Protector, I would have seized it also, and retained it till the debts due to the squadron were liquidated. Finding all arguments unavailing, and that no attention was paid to his threats, the Protector—to save the credit of his Government—addressed a proclamation to the squadron, confirming the distribution which was going on by my orders, at the same time writing to me, that I "might " employ the money as I thought proper."

San Martin afterwards accused me to the Chilian Government of seizing the whole of the treasure, that in his yacht included, which, at a low computation, must have been worth several millions of dollars, which were all left untouched. He also asserted, that I had retained the whole belonging to private individuals, though each *real* claimed was given up, as was well known to every individual concerned, and he also knew that I did not retain a penny on my own account. Nevertheless, he added, that I had kept the whole myself,—that, in consequence, the squadron was in a state of mutiny, and the seamen were abandoning their ships to offer their services to the Government of Peru! the fact being, that those who went on shore to spend their pay after the fashion of sailors, were prevented from returning on board, a lieutenant of my flag-ship being put in jail for attempting to bring them off again.

The first intimation of this outrage was conveyed by the officer himself, in the following letter, from his place of confinement.

MY LORD,

Whilst obeying your Lordship's orders in bringing off the men to the *O'Higgins*, Captain Guise sent his Lieutenant to tell me that I could not ship any more men. My answer was, that, till I received contrary orders from you I could not think of desisting. I then went to Captain Guise to tell him your orders, and he told me, that it was the Governor's order that I should not do it; he likewise told me, that several officers had spoken against the Government, instancing Captain Cobbett and others. He then asked me, whether I thought that your Lordship's *robbery*! of the money at Ancon was right? and, whether I believed that the

Government meant to keep its promise, and pay us, or not? My answer was, that I thought your Lordship had acted perfectly right, and that, in my opinion, the Government never intended to pay us; upon which, he ordered me to be seized.

My Lord, I am now a prisoner in the Case-mates, and am told that the Governor has written to you on the subject. The men, my Lord, will, I have no doubt, come off, as many have promised me to do so, to-morrow morning. Hoping that your Lordship will enquire into the circumstance, I remain, &c. &c.,

J. PAYNTOR.

On receipt of this, I immediately demanded his release, which was complied with.

Before distributing the money to the squadron, I took the precaution to request that a commissary of the Government might be sent on board to take part in the payment of the crews. As this was not complied with, I again urged it, but without effect—the object of not attending to the request being, as was afterwards learned, the expectation that I should place the money in his hands *ashore*, when it doubtless would have been seized, without payment to officers or men. This was, however, foreseen, the Government being informed by me that "the money was on board ready for "distribution, whilst the people were on board ready "to receive it, there was, therefore no necessity to "take it on shore;" it was then distributed by my own officers.

Annoyed beyond measure at my having taken such steps to restore order in the squadron by doing justice to the officers and men, the Protector, on the very day, September 26th, on which he told me by letter to "make what use I pleased of the money," sought to revenge himself by sending on board the ships of the squadron his two *aides-de-camp*, Colonel Paroissien and Captain Spry, with papers for distribution, stating that "the squadron of Chili was "under the command of the Protector of Peru, and "not under that of the Admiral, who was an inferior "officer in the service; and that it was consequently "the duty of the Captains and Commanders to obey "the orders of the Protector and not mine." One of these papers was immediately brought to me by that excellent and highly honourable officer, Captain Simpson, of the *Araucano* (now an Admiral in the Chilian service), to whose ship's company it had been delivered. These emissaries offered, in the name of the Protector, commissions, and the promise of honours, titles, and estates to all such officers as might accept service under the Government of Peru.

From the *Araucano*, the Protector's envoys went to the *Valdivia*, where similar papers were given to the men, and Captain Cobbett, nephew of the celebrated William Cobbett, was reminded of the preference which an officer, for his own interests, ought to give to the service of a rich state like Peru, in place of adhering to Chili, which must soon dwindle to comparative insignificance; besides which the authority of the Protector over the Chilian forces being unquestionable, it was the duty of the officers to obey the orders of the Protector as General-in-Chief. Captain Cobbett, who was a faithful and excellent officer, sarcastically inquired of Spry whether, if his disobedience to the Admiral brought him to a court-martial, the Protector's authority would ensure him an acquittal? This closed the argument; for Spry being at the time under sentence of court-martial, the question was much too pertinent to be pleasant, especially as he by no means felt confident that Cobbett might not seize him as a deserter.

Unfortunately for the emissaries, my flag-captain, Crosbie, was on a visit to Captain Cobbett, and on learning their errand he pushed off to the flag-ship with the intelligence. Observing this movement they immediately followed, judging it more prudent to visit me than to run the risk of being compelled so to do. At one o'clock in the morning their boat came alongside, when Paroissien solicited an interview, Spry remaining in the boat, having his own reasons for not wishing to attract my attention. Paroissien then addressed me with the most high-flown promises, assuring me of the Protector's wish, notwithstanding all that had occurred, to confer upon me the highest honours and rewards, amongst others the decoration of the newly-created order of "the Sun," and telling me how much better it would be for me to be First Admiral of a rich country like Peru, than Vice-Admiral of a poor province like Chili. He assured me, as one of the Commissioners of confiscated property, that it was the intention of the Protector to present me with a most valuable estate, and regretted that the present unlucky difference should form an obstacle to the Protector's intentions to confer upon me the command of the Peruvian navy.

Perceiving that he felt nervously uneasy in his

attempt at negociation, I reminded him that the Peruvian navy had no existence except in imagination; that I had no doubt whatever of his desire for my prosperity, but that it might be more agreeable to him to join me in a bottle of wine than to reiterate his regrets and lamentations. After taking a glass he went into his boat, and pulled off, glad no doubt to escape so easily, not that it occurred to me to resent the treachery of visiting the ships of the squadron in the dark, to unsettle the minds of the officers and men.

This, however, and other efforts proved but too successful, twenty-three officers abandoning the Chilian service, together with all the foreign seamen, who went on shore to spend their pay, and who were either forced, or allured by promises of a year's additional pay to remain, so that the squadron was half unmanned.

The fortress, notwithstanding the supplies so successfully introduced by General Cantarac, having again—by the vigilance of the squadron—been starved into surrender, I received an order immediately to quit Callao and proceed to Chili, although the Peruvian Government believed that from the abandonment of the squadron by the officers and foreign seamen, it would not be possible to comply with the order. The following is Monteagudo's letter conveying the commands of the Protector:—

Lima, Sept. 26th, 1821.

My Lord,

Your note of yesterday, in which you explain the motives

which induced you to decline complying with the positive orders of the Protector, *temporarily* to restore the money which you forcibly took at Ancon, has frustrated the hopes which the Government entertained of a happy termination to this most disagreeable of all affairs which have occurred during the expedition.

To answer your Excellency in detail, it will be necessary to enter into an investigation of acts which cannot be fully understood without referring to official communications and documents which prove the interest which has been taken in the necessities of the squadron.

(Here follows a reiteration of the *promises* and good intentions of the Protector, with which the reader is already well acquainted.)

This has been a mortal blow to the State, and worse could not have been received from the hand of an enemy, there only remaining to us a hope in the moderation and patient suffering of the valiant men who have sacrificed all!

You will *immediately* sail from this port to Chili, with the whole squadron under your command, and there deliver up the money which you have seized, and which you possess without any pretext to hold it. In communicating this order to your Excellency, the Government cannot avoid expressing its regret at being reduced to this extremity towards a chief with whom it has been connected by ties of friendship and high consideration since August 20th, 1820.

I have to complain of the style of your Excellency's Secretary, who, perhaps from his ignorance of the idiom of the Spanish language, cannot express himself with decency—his soul not having been formed to conceive correct ideas.

MONTEAGUDO.

The complaining tone of this letter about the "valiant sacrificing all," is worthy of the writer; when I had left untouched many times the amount seized, and the army, according to the admission of the Protectoral Government, had received two-thirds of its pay, whilst the squadron had even been suffered to starve. On the 28th I replied to the Minister as follows:—

SIR,

I should have felt uneasy, had the letter you addressed to me contained the commands of the Protector to quit the ports of Peru without reason assigned, and I should have been distressed had his motives been founded in reason, or on facts; but finding the order based on the groundless imputation that I had declined to do what I had no power to effect, I console myself that the Protector will ultimately be satisfied that no blame rests on me. At all events, I have the gratification of a mind unconscious of wrong, and gladdened by the cheering conviction that, however facts may be distorted by sycophancy, men who view things in their proper colours will do me the justice I deserve.

You address me as though I required to be convinced of your good intentions. No, Sir, it is the seamen who want convincing, for it is they who put no faith in professions so often broken. They are men of few words and decisive acts, and say that "for their "labour they have a right to pay and food, and will work no longer "than they are paid and fed"—though this may be uncourtly language, unfit for the ear of high authority. They urge, moreover, that they have had no pay whatever, whilst their fellow-labourers, the soldiers, have had two-thirds of their wages; they were starved, or living on stinking *charqui*, whilst the troops were wholly fed on beef and mutton; they had no grog, whilst the troops had money to obtain that favourite beverage, and anything else they desired. Such, Sir, are the rough grounds on which an English seaman founds his opinions. He expects an equivalent for the fulfilment of his contract, which, on his part, is performed with fidelity; but, if his rights are withheld, he is as boisterous as the element on which he lives. It is of no use, therefore, to convince me, but them.

In what communication, Sir, have I insisted on the payment of 200,000 dollars. I sent you an account of money due, but told you in my letter that it was the mutinous seamen who demanded the disbursements, and that I was doing all in my power, though without effect, to restrain their violence and allay their fears. You tell me in your letter that it was impossible to pay the clamorous crews. How, then, is it *that they are now paid out of the very money then lying at your disposal,* I having left untouched ten times as much? My warning to you, that they were no longer to be trifled with, was founded on a long acquaintance with their character and disposition; and facts have proved, and may more fully prove, the truth of what I told you.

Why, Sir, is the word "immediate" put into your order to go forth from this port? Would it not have been more decorous to have been less peremptory, knowing, as you do, that the delay of payment had unmanned the ships—that the total disregard of all my applications had left the squadron destitute—and that the men were enticed away by persons acting under the Peruvian Government? This being so, why are matters pushed to this extremity?

I thank you for the *approval of my services since the 20th of August,* 1820, and assure you that no abatement of my zeal for the Protector's interest took place till the 5th of August, when I became acquainted with his Excellency's installation, and when, in your presence, he uttered sentiments that struck a thrill through my frame, which no subsequent act, nor protestation of intentions, has been able to mitigate. Did he not say—aye, did you not hear him declare, that he would never pay the debt to Chili, nor that due to the navy, unless Chili would sell the squadron to Peru? What would you have thought of me as an officer, sworn to be faithful to the state of Chili, had I listened to such language in cold, calculating silence, weighing my decision in the scale of personal interest? No, Sir, the promise of San Martin, that "my fortune should be "equal to his own," will not warp from the path of honour

Your obedient, humble Servant,

COCHRANE.

After a lapse of nearly forty years' anxious consideration, I cannot reproach myself with having done any wrong in the seizure of the money of the Protectoral Government. General San Martin and myself had been, in our respective departments, deputed to liberate Peru from Spain, and to give to the Peruvians the same free institutions which

Chili herself enjoyed. The first part of our object had been fully effected by the achievements and vigilance of the squadron; the second part was frustrated by General San Martin arrogating to himself despotic power, which set at naught the wishes and voice of the people. As "my fortune in common with "his own" was only to be secured by acquiescence in the wrong he had done to Chili by casting off his allegiance to her, and by upholding him in the still greater wrong he was inflicting on Peru, I did not choose to sacrifice my self-esteem and professional character by lending myself as an instrument to purposes so unworthy. I did all in my power to warn General San Martin of the consequences of ambition so ill-directed, but the warning was neglected, if not despised. Chili trusted to him to defray the expenses of the squadron when its objects—as laid down by the Supreme Director—should be accomplished; but in place of fulfilling the obligation, he permitted the squadron to starve, its crews to go in rags, and the ships to be in perpetual danger for want of the proper equipment which Chili could not afford to give them when they sailed from Valparaiso. The pretence for this neglect was want of means, though at the same time money to a vast amount was sent away from the capital to Ancon. Seeing that no intention existed on the part of the Protector's Government to do justice to the Chilian squadron, whilst every effort was made to excite discontent among the officers and men with the purpose of procuring their transfer to Peru, I seized the public money, satisfied the men, and saved the navy to the Chilian Republic, which afterwards warmly thanked me for what I had done. Despite the obloquy cast upon me by the Protector's Government, there was nothing wrong in the course I pursued, if only for the reason that if the Chilian squadron was to be preserved, it was *impossible for me to have done otherwise.* Years of reflection have only produced the conviction, that, were I again placed in similar circumstances, I should adopt precisely the same course.

CHAPTER IX.

ARRIVAL AT GUAYAQUIL—ADDRESS TO GUAYAQUILENOS—INJURIOUS MONOPOLIES —MINISTERIAL FOLLY—DEPARTURE FROM GUAYAQUIL—ARRIVAL IN MEXICO—ANCHOR AT ACAPULCO—MOCK AMBASSADORS—PLOT AGAINST ME —RETURN TO GUAYAQUIL—VENGANZA TAKEN POSSESSION OF—AGREEMENT WITH JUNTA—GENERAL LA MAR—ORDERS TO WITHHOLD SUPPLIES— ABOMINABLE CRUELTY—COURTLY SPLENDOUR—DESTRUCTION OF A DIVISION OF THE ARMY—DISSATISFACTION OF OFFICERS—RENEWED OVERTURES FROM SAN MARTIN—THEIR REFUSAL BY ME—WARNING TO THE CHILIAN GOVERNMENT.

THE orders of the Protector to proceed to Chili were not complied with, 1st, because having thrown off his allegiance to Chili, he had no right to interfere with the squadron; and, 2ndly, as the Spanish frigates remained at large, my mission was incomplete till they were taken or destroyed.

Before going in quest of them, it was essential to repair, equip, and provision the ships, none of which purposes could be effected in Peru, the Protector not only having refused supplies, but having also issued orders on the coast to withhold necessaries of all kinds even to wood and water. From want of stores, none of the ships were fit for sea; even the *Valdivia*, so admirably found when captured, was now in as bad a condition as the rest, from the necessity which had arisen of distributing her equipment amongst the other ships; and to complete her inefficiency, the

Protector refused to restore the anchors which had been cut away from her bows at the time of her capture, thus adding to our embarrassment.

Many of the officers had gone over to the service of Peru, and the foreign seamen had been kept on shore in such numbers, that there were not sufficient left to perform the duties of reefing and steering. I therefore resolved on sending part of the squadron to Chili, and with the remainder to proceed to Guayaquil, in order to repair and refit for a cruise on the coast of Mexico in search of the Spanish frigates.

We reached Guayaquil on the 18th of October, and were extremely well received by the authorities, who saluted the Chilian flag, the like compliment being paid to their own. The work of repairing and refitting occupied six weeks, during which period the newly-constituted Government rendered us all the assistance in its power, entering into the most friendly intercourse with us. The expenses, which were heavy, were all defrayed out of the uncondemned prize-money remaining on board, this rightfully belonging to the officers and seamen, as never having had their previous claims satisfied by the Government, on which account it had been retained. To inspire the seamen with the reasonable expectation that the Chilian Government would reimburse them for their generosity, I added money of my own, on which they willingly consented to the appropriation of that due to the squadron.

Before quitting the anchorage, I was honoured with a public address, and thinking the opportunity good for striking a blow at those Spanish prejudices which, in spite of independence, still lingered from force of habit, the compliment was returned by the following address:—

GUAYAQUILENOS,

The reception which the Chilian squadron has met with from you not only shews the generosity of your sentiments, but proves that a people capable of asserting their independence in spite of arbitrary power must always possess noble and exalted feelings. Believe me, that the state of Chili will ever be grateful for your assistance, and more especially the Supreme Director, by whose exertions the squadron was created, and to whom, in fact, South America owes whatever benefit she may have derived from its services.

May you be as free as you are independent, and as independent as you deserve to be free! With the liberty of the press, now protected by your excellent Government, which discriminates enlightenment from that fount, Guayaquil can never again be enslaved.

See what difference a year of independence has produced in public opinion. In those whom you then looked upon as enemies, you have discovered your truest friends, whilst those formerly esteemed as friends have proved enemies. Remember your former ideas on commerce and manufactures, and compare them with those which you at present entertain. Accustomed to the blind habits of Spanish monopoly, you then believed that Guayaquil would be robbed, were not her commerce limited to her own merchants. All foreigners were forbidden by restrictive laws from attending even to their own business and interests: now you appreciate a true policy, and your enlightened Government is ready to further public opinion in the promotion of your riches, strength, and happiness, as well as to assist these, by disseminating through the press the political opinions of great and wise men—without fear of the Inquisition, the faggot, or the stake.

It is very gratifying to me to observe the change which has taken place in your ideas of political economy, and to see that you can appreciate and despise the clamour of the few who would still interrupt the public prosperity; though it is difficult to believe how any citizen of Guayaquil can be capable of opposing his private interest to the public good, as though his particular profit were superior to that of the community, or as if commerce, agriculture, and manufactures were to be paralysed for his especial behoof.

Guayaquilenos! Let your public press declare the consequences of monopoly, and affix your names to the defence of your enlightened system. Let it shew that, if your province contains 80,000 inhabitants, and that if 80 of these are privileged merchants according to the old system, 9,999 persons out of 10,000 must suffer because their cotton, coffee, tobacco, timber, and other productions must come into the hands of the monopolist, as the only purchaser of what they have to sell, and the only seller of what they must necessarily buy! the effect being that he will buy at the lowest possible rate, and sell at the dearest, so that not only are the 9,999 injured, but the lands will remain waste, the manufactories without workmen, and the people will be lazy and poor for want of a stimulus, it being a law of nature that no man will labour solely for the gain of another.

Tell the monopolist that the true method of acquiring general riches, political power, and even his own private advantage, is to sell his country's produce as high, and foreign goods as low as possible—and that public competition can alone accomplish this. Let foreign merchants who bring capital, and those who practise any art or handicraft, be permitted to settle freely; and thus a competition will be formed, from which all must reap advantage.

Then will land and fixed property increase in value; the magazines, instead of being the receptacles of filth and crime, will be full of the richest foreign and domestic productions, and all will be energy and activity, because the reward will be in proportion to the labour. Your river will be filled with ships, and the monopolist degraded and shamed. You will bless the day in which Omnipotence permitted the veil of obscurity to be rent asunder, under which the despotism of Spain, the abominable tyranny of the Inquisition, and the want of liberty of the press, so long hid the truth from your sight.

Let your customs' duties be moderate, in order to promote the greatest possible consumption of foreign and domestic goods; then smuggling will cease, and the returns to the treasury increase. Let every man do as he pleases as regards his own property, views, and interests; because every individual will watch over his own with more zeal than senates, ministers, or kings. By your enlarged views set an example to the New World; and thus, as Guayaquil is from its situation the *Central Republic*, it will become the centre of the agriculture, commerce, and riches of the Pacific.

Guayaquilenos! The liberality of your sentiments, and the justice of your acts and opinions, are a bulwark to your independence more secure than that of armies and squadrons. That you may pursue the path which will render you as free and happy as the territory is fertile, and may be rendered productive, is the sincere wish of your obliged friend and servant,

COCHRANE.

The English reader may consider a lecture of this nature superfluous to an emancipated people, but the adherence to injurious monoplies, in spite of independence, was one of the most marked features of the South American Republics, and one which I never lost an opportunity of combating. Even the Chilian Republic, which was amongst the first to assert its freedom, increased its monopolistic practices, instead of diminishing them. One or two examples will not be here out of place.

English malt liquor bore a very high price in Chili, from the heavy freight and customs' duties. An ingenious Scotchman, named Macfarlane, set up a brewery at considerable expense, and malt costing in Chili barely a shilling per *fanega* (about a bushel), soon produced beer of a fine quality, at a low price. The Government forthwith imposed a duty on his beer equal to the whole freight from England, customs' dues, and his profit, the consequence being, that the brewery was stopped and the capital employed lost. He had unwittingly interfered with the established duties on beer!

Some enterprising Americans formed a whale fishery on the Chilian coast near Coquimbo, where the sperm whale abounded, and so successful was the fishery, that the speculation promised a fortune to all concerned. A large plant had been provided, including abundance of casks to contain the oil. The Government directed the whole of the casks to be seized for the purpose of watering the squadron, that being easier than to provide them themselves, which being done, pursuant to orders, the Americans formed pits lined with clay, in which the oil was put till fresh casks could be procured. On this, the Governor of Coquimbo forbade the practice, as the wind might waft an unpleasant smell to Coquimbo, though the trade wind never blew in that direction. The Americans were therefore compelled to abandon the pursuit, and with it several sperm whales which were lying in the bay ready for boiling.

An enterprising English engineer, Mr. Miers, brought out complete machinery for smelting, rolling, and manufacturing copper, purchasing land whereon to erect his factory. As soon as his purpose became known, he was involved in a long and expensive lawsuit to prevent the use of the land which he had bought, the result being great pecuniary loss, complete prevention of his operations, and the final removal of such of his machinery as was not utterly spoiled, to Brazil.

It would be easy to multiply similar instances to a great extent, but these will show that my advice to the Guayaquilenos was not unnecessary; and to give counsel of this nature, wherever it could be applied, was my invariable practice, in place of engaging in petty intrigues, or bargaining for personal power or advantages, which, situated as I was, I could have commanded to any extent by a sacrifice of my own principles. Efforts of the above nature to enlighten the people, rendered me obnoxious to men in power, as interfering with their cherished monoplies, out of which they contrived to extract individual profit.

The necessity for a speedy pursuit of the enemy's frigates, precluded more than a temporary repair of the ships; nothing, indeed, had been done to remedy the leak in the hull of the flag-ship, as, from the rotten state of her masts, we durst not venture to heave her down, so that when we got in a sea-way she made six feet of water a day.

We quitted the Guayaquil river on the 3rd of December, coasting along the shore, and examining every bay for the objects of our search. On the 5th we reached Salango, where we again watered the ships, there being only twenty-three tons of water casks on board the flag-ship. On the 11th we reached Cocos Island, when we found and took possession of an English pirate, commanded by a man, named Blair. On the following day we captured a *felucca*, which turned out to be a deserter from Callao. From the men on board we learned that, after my departure, San Martin had refused to fulfil the promises by which they had been induced to remain, though he had thus allured nearly the whole of the foreign seamen, who comprised the only skilled portion of the Chilian squadron, into the service of Peru. The *felucca* thus manned, and sent as a *guarda costa* to Chorillas, the men took advantage of the absence of their captain on shore, and seized the vessel, which they named the *Retaliation*, having put to sea, no doubt with the intention of turning pirates. As they had committed no depredations, and I had no wish to be encumbered with them, they were suffered to escape.

On the 14th we made the coast of Mexico, the leak of the flag-ship daily increasing, and on the 19th we anchored in the bay of Fonseca, with five feet of water in the hold, the chain pumps being so worn as to be useless, there being no artificers on board to repair them, the ship was only kept afloat by the greatest possible exertions, in which my personal skill in smiths' work had to be called into requisition.

After three days' constant baling at the hatchways, we got two pumps from the *Valdivia*; but these proving too short, I ordered holes to be cut through the ships' sides, on a level with the berth deck, and thus managed to keep her clear till the old pumps could be refitted. Nearly all our ammunition was spoiled, and, in order to preserve the dry provisions, we were compelled to stow them in the hammock-nettings.

Having transferred forty men from the other ships to assist at the pumps, we quitted Fonseca bay on the

28th, and on the 6th of January, 1822, arrived at Tehuantepec, a volcano lighting us every night. This was one of the most imposing sights I ever beheld; large streams of molten lava pouring down the sides of the mountain, whilst at intervals, huge masses of solid burning matter were hurled into the air, and rebounding from their fall, ricocheted down the declivity till they found a resting place at its base.

On the 29th we anchored at Acapulco, where we met the *Araucano* and *Mercedes*, the latter having been sent on to gain intelligence of the Spanish frigates. We were civilly received by the Governor, though not without misgivings, on his part, that we might attempt to seize some Spanish merchantmen at anchor in the harbour; so that we found the fort manned by a strong garrison, and other preparations made to receive us in case of hostile demonstration.

We were not a little surprised at this, as nothing could be more friendly than our intentions towards the newly emancipated Republic. The mystery was, however, soon cleared up. When at Guayaquil, we met with two officers, General Wavell and Colonel O'Reilly, to whom the Chilian Government had given passports to quit the country, not estimating the value of their services as tantamount to their pay. As no secret was made of the object of the Chilian squadron, they had, owing to our delay on the coast, carried their own version of our mission to Mexico, and had reported to the Mexican Government, both personally and by letter, that Lord Cochrane had possessed himself of the Chilian Navy,—plundered the vessels belonging to Peru,—was now on a piratical cruise,—and was coming to ravage the coast of Mexico; hence the preparations which had been made.

The two worthies whom I have mentioned had represented to the authorities at Guayaquil that they were ambassadors from Chili to Mexico, deputed to congratulate the Mexican Government on their achievement of independence. Knowing this to be false, I requested them to shew their credentials, which of course they could not do. Their passports were then demanded, and evinced by their dates that the pretended ambassadors had quitted Chili prior to the intelligence of the establishment of independence in Mexico. This disclosure having become known to the lady of the Captain-General of Guatemala, who happened to be at Guayaquil, she forwarded the account to her husband, and he reported it to the Mexican authorities, who were thus informed of the true character of their visitors; who, in revenge, trumped up the story of our piratical intentions, to which the Governor of Acapulco attached sufficient importance to strengthen his forts as narrated.

The reserve, however, immediately wore off, and the most cordial relations were entered into; the President of Mexico, Iturbide, writing me a very polite letter, regretting that he could not visit me personally, but inviting me to repair to his court, assuring me of the most honourable reception. This, of course, I could not accept.

On the 2nd of February, a vessel arrived at

Acapulco, and reported the Spanish frigates to the southward, whither, notwithstanding the unseaworthy state of the ships, I determined to proceed in search of them.

During our stay an officer of marines, named Erescano—who by cruelty to his prisoners had made himself notorious at Valdivia—endeavoured to revenge my disapprobation of his conduct by representing to the men, that, notwithstanding the expenses we had been put to, there was still money on board the flagship, and that it ought to be divided amonst them. Failing in this, he had laid a plot to get possession of the chest, even at the cost of my assassination. All this was duly reported to me by the commander of the *Valdivia*, Captain Cobbett.

As I did not wish to produce a ferment by punishing this diabolical plot as it deserved, I contented myself with thwarting its execution, till we were under weigh, when I ordered Captain Cobbett to send Erescano on shore with a despatch to the Governor, detailing the whole plot; the result being, that the traitor was left on shore, the squadron sailing without him. What afterwards became of him I never heard.

After despatching the *Independencia* and *Araucano* to California for the purpose of purchasing provisions, with instructions to follow us to Guayaquil, we stood down the coast, and when off Tehuantepec, encountered a gale of wind, which, owing to the bad state of the frigate, threatened her destruction. To add to our distress, a sea struck the *Valdivia*—to which vessel we contemplated escaping—and forced in the timbers on her port side, so that she was only saved from sinking by passing a sail over the leak, till the damage could be repaired.

On the 5th of March we made the coast of Esmeraldas, and came to an anchor in the bay of Tacames, where we learned that the Spanish frigates had some time before left for Guayaquil. On receipt of this intelligence we immediately pursued our voyage, and on the 13th anchored off the forts of Guayaquil, where we found the *Venganza.*

Our reception was not of the same cordial nature as on the previous visit—two agents of San Martin having arrived, who by promises had gained over the Government to the Protector's interests, and had excited in their minds a jealousy of me which was as unexpected as ill-founded. Some attempts were even made to annoy me; but as, upon their manifestation, I laid the flagship alongside the *Venganza,* civility was enforced.

The *Prueba* and *Venganza,* being short of provisions, were compelled by our close pursuit, to put into Guayaquil, daily expecting us to follow. Previous to our arrival, the Peruvian envoy, Salasar, had so impressed upon the officers commanding the certainty of their being captured by the Chilian squadron, that he had induced them to give up the ships to Peru, on the promise that the Protectoral Government would pay the whole of the officers and crews all the arrears due to them, and that those who chose to remain in South America should be naturalized, with lands and pensions assigned to them; whilst such as were desirous of returning to Spain should have their passages defrayed by the Peruvian Government.

Many of the Spanish officers and most of the crews were adverse to the surrender of the ships, so that a mutiny was the consequence; when, at the instance of Salasar, the Government of Guayaquil was induced to sanction an assertion that the Chilian squadron was at anchor in the bay of La Manta, and that letters had been received from me announcing my intention to come to Guayaquil and seize the ships. This mendacity had the desired effect, and both officers and crews accepted the terms offered; so that San Martin's agents had thus tricked the Chilian squadron out of its prizes.

Under the before-mentioned impression the *Prueba* was hastily sent to Callao before our arrival, but the *Venganza*, being in a condition unfit for sea, remained at Guayaquil. On being positively assured of the dishonourable transaction which had taken place, on the morning of the 14th of March I sent Captain Crosbie on board the *Venganza* to take possession of her, for Chili and Peru jointly, being unwilling to embroil Chili in hostilities with Guayaquil by seizing her on our own account, as we were indisputably entitled to do, having chased her from port to port, until, destitute of provisions, she was compelled to take refuge in that port.

My orders to Captain Crosbie were to hoist at the peak of the *Venganza*, the flag of Chili conjointly with that of Peru. This act gave great offence to the Guayaquil Government, which manned its gun-boats, erected breast-works, and brought guns to the river side with the apparent intention of firing upon us; the Spanish sailors, who shortly before had sold their ships from the dread of having to fight, being extremely active in these hostile demonstrations.

Upon this, I ordered the *Valdivia* to drift with the flood tide in the direction of the gun-boats, now filled with Spanish officers and seamen. Imagining that the frigate was about to attack them—though there was no intention of the kind—these heroes ran the boats ashore, and took to their heels in most admired disorder, not stopping till they had gained the protection of the city.

The Junta, finding that we did not consider their warlike demonstration worthy of notice, remonstrated at my taking possession of the *Venganza*, but without effect, as I was not going to permit the Chilian squadron to be thus cheated out of its prize. I therefore proposed such terms as were best calculated to be accepted and ratified by the Junta of Government, composed of Olmedo, Kimena, and Roco, as follows:—

1st.—The frigate *Venganza* shall remain as belonging to the Government of Guayaquil, and shall hoist her flag, which shall be duly saluted.

2nd.—Guayaquil guarantees to the Chilian squadron, on responsibility of 40,000 dollars, that the frigate *Venganza* shall not be delivered to, nor negotiated for with any Government, till those of Chili and Peru shall have decided on what they may esteem most just. Moreover, the Government of Guayaquil is bound to destroy her rather than consent that the said vessel shall serve any other state till such decision be made.

3rd.—Any Government which may henceforward be established in Guayaquil shall be bound to the fulfilment of the articles here made.

4th.—These articles shall be understood literally, and in good faith, without mental reservations or restrictions.

(Signed) &c. &c.

After the ratification of this agreement, the Government of Guayaquil addressed to me a letter acknowledging the important services which had been conferred on the States of South America, and assuring me that "Guayaquil would always be the "first to honour my name, and the last to forget my "unparalleled achievements," &c., &c. Yet no sooner had I sailed from the port, than the *Venganza* was given up to the agent of Peru, but the 40,000 dollars have never been paid.

At Guayaquil, I met General La Mar, the late governor of the fortress of Callao; and a report having been circulated by the Peruvian Government that during the recent blockade I had made an offer to supply the fortress with provisions, in order to prevent its falling into the hands of the Protector, I requested the General to favour me with a statement whether I did or did not promise to succour his garrison, to which request the General obligingly returned the following answer:—

Guayaquil, March 13th, 1822.

Most Excellent Sir,

In consequence of the official note which I yesterday received from your Excellency through the hands of the Government, it is my duty to assert that I have neither said, nor written, nor ever heard that you proposed to supply with provisions the place of Callao during the whole of the time that it was under my charge.

God preserve your Excellency many years.

(Signed) JOSE DE LA MAR.

On the 27th we left the Guayaquil river, and on the 29th fell in with Captain Simpson, of the *Araucano*, whose crew had mutinied and carried off the ship. On the 12th of April we reached Guambucho, whither we had gone for the purpose of taking in water. To our surprise the Alcalde shewed a written order from San Martin, telling him that if any vessel of war belonging to Chili touched there he was to forbid their landing, and to deny assistance of every kind, not even permitting them to obtain wood and water.

To this order no attention was paid by us, and we took on board whatever was required, remaining further to repair the *Valdivia*. On the 16th we sailed, and on the 25th anchored at Callao, where we found the *Prueba* under Peruvian colours, and commanded by the senior Chilian captain, who had abandoned the squadron! On our arrival she was immediately hauled in close under the batteries, with guns housed, and ports closed, whilst she was so crammed with troops that three died on the following night from suffocation; these steps being taken to prevent her sharing the fate of the *Esmeralda*. To calm their fears, I wrote to the Government that there was no intention of taking her, otherwise I would have done so, and at midday too in spite of any such precautions.

Lima was at this time in an extraordinary condition, there being no less than five different Peruvian flags flying in the bay and on the batteries. The Protector had passed a decree ordering that all Spaniards who might quit the place should surrender half their property to the public treasury, or the whole should be confiscated, and the owners exiled. Another decree imposed the penalties of exile and confiscation of property upon all Spaniards who should appear in the streets wearing a cloak; also against any who should be found in private conversation! The punishment of death was awarded against all who should be out of their houses after sunset; and confiscation and death were pronounced on all who possessed any kind of weapons except table-knives! A wealthy lady in Lima was so annoyed at the rigour of these decrees, that her patriotism overcame her prudence, and having called the Protector ill names, she was compelled to give up her property. She was then habited in the garb of the Inquisition,—a garment painted with imaginary devils!—and taken to the great square, where an accusatory libel being fastened to her breast, a human bone was forced into her mouth—her tongue being condemned as the offending member—and then secured; in which state, with a halter round her neck, she was paraded through the streets by the common hangman, and afterwards exiled to Callao, where after two days she died from mental anguish arising from the treatment she had received. Such was the liberty conceded to Peru.

In the midst of this national degradation, the

Protector had assumed the style of a Sovereign Prince. An order of nobility was established, under the title of " The Institute of the Sun," the insignia being a golden sun suspended from a white ribbon, the Chilian officers who had abandoned the squadron coming in for a full share as the reward of their subserviency.

A quasi-royal guard was established, consisting of the leading youth of the city, who formed the Protector's escort in public; a precaution which, notwithstanding that the exasperated Limeños were weaponless, was not altogether unnecessary. The Solar nobility were permitted to place their armorial bearings in front of their houses, with the sun blazoned in the centre, which was certainly an addition to, if not an improvement on all previous orders of nobility. In short, the Limeños had a Republic swarming with marquises, counts, viscounts, and other titles of monarchy, to which consummation all expected the Protector to aspire; the more so, as the only unfettered portion of the press was that which saluted him under the title of Emperor. (*See Appendix, Ode of " The Dove," sung in celebration of our Protector and Emperor of Peru!*)

The strength of a State so constituted did not keep pace with the brilliancy of its court. On the 7th of April, General Cantarac had fallen upon a division of the liberating army, and cut up or made prisoners of the whole, capturing 5,000 muskets, the military chest, containing 100,000 dollars, and all their ammunition and baggage. It would have been thought that so serious a disaster occurring amongst a justly-exasperated people would have caused some embarrassment to the Government, but the *Gazette* of the 13th of April almost turned it into matter for congratulation.

LIMENOS,

The division of the south, *without having been beaten*, has been surprised and dispersed. In a long campaign all cannot be prosperity. You know *my* character, and you know that *I* have always spoken the truth! I do not mean to search for consolation in conflicts, notwithstanding, I dare to assure you, that the iniquitous and tyrannical empire of the Spaniards in Peru will cease in the year 1822. I will make an ingenuous confession to you. It was my intention to go in search of repose after so many years of agitation, but I believed your independence was not secured. Some trifling danger now presents itself, and so long as there remains the least appearance of it, till you are free you shall not be left by your faithful friend,

SAN MARTIN.

His proclamation to the army is still more extraordinary:—

COMPANIONS OF THE UNITED ARMY,

Your brothers in the division of the south have not been beaten—but they have been dispersed. To you it belongs to revenge this insult. You are valiant, and have known long ago the path to glory. Sharpen well your bayonets and your swords. The campaign of Peru shall finish in this year. Your old general assures it. Prepare to conquer!

SAN MARTIN.

To the inhabitants of the interior, proclamations of a still more bombastic nature were despatched, in which they were assured that a reverse of this kind "weighed nothing in the balance of destiny of Peru. "Providence protects us, and by this action will ac- "celerate the ruin of the enemies of Peru. Proud of "their first victory, *they will spare us part of our* " *march in search of them.* Fear not! the army that " *drove them from the capital* is ready to punish them " a third time, and to punish them for ever!"

The army, however, rightly dreaded another reverse, and what remained of the Chilian force was discontented, as no promise to them had been fulfilled. All gold and silver had disappeared, and paper money was issued by the Government in its stead. Contributions from the already drained inhabitants were increased, and had to be collected at the point of the bayonet. In short, on my arrival, Peru presented the extraordinary spectacle of a court whose minions indulged in every species of costly luxury, and a people impoverished to the dregs to administer to their rapacity.

Those who had condemned my conduct in taking possession of the money at Ancon, now admitted that I had adopted the only possible step to preserve the squadron of Chili. The officers of the liberating army sent me deplorable accounts of the state of affairs; and the regiment of Numantia, which had deserted from the Spaniards soon after the capture of the *Esmeralda*, sent an officer, Captain Doronso, with a message, asking me to receive them on board, and convey them to Colombia, to which province they belonged.

My appearance in the port of Callao caused serious, though, as far as I was concerned, unnecessary alarm to the Government, to which I transmitted a fresh demand for the sums due to the squadron, further alluding, in no measured language, to the events which had taken place at Guayaquil. Without replying to this by letter, Monteagudo came off to the *O'Higgins*, lamenting that I should have resorted to such intemperate expressions, as the Protector, before its receipt, had written me a private letter praying for an interview, but on the receipt of my note he became so indignant as to place his health in danger. Monteagudo further assured me that in that letter he had made me the offer of a large estate, and the decoration of the "Sun" set in diamonds, if I would consent to command the united navies of Chili and Peru, in a contemplated expedition to capture the Philippine Islands, by which I should make an immense fortune. My reply was, "Tell the Protector "from me, Mr. Monteagudo, that if, after the conduct "he has pursued he had sent me a private letter, "on any such subject, it would certainly have been "returned unanswered; and you may also tell him, "that it is not my wish to injure him; I neither fear "him nor hate him, but I disapprove of his conduct."

Monteagudo, in spite of his reception, begged of me to reconsider my determination, saying that the Marquis of Torre Tagle had got ready his house for my reception; asking me further to recal the letter I had written the day before, and accept the offers which had been made. I again told him that "I "would not accept either honours or rewards from a "Government constituted in defiance of solemn "pledges; nor would I set foot in a country governed "not only without law, but contrary to law. "Neither would I recal my letter, my habits were

" frugal, and my means sufficient without a fortune " from the Philippine Islands." Finding he could make no impression upon me, and not liking the scowl on the countenances of those on board, though he wore his blazing decoration of the first order of the " Sun," and was covered with ribbons and embroideries, the minister retired, accompanied by his military escort.

Consequent upon my refusal to comply with his wishes the Protector shortly afterwards, unknown to me, despatched Colonel Paroissien and Garcia del Rio to Chili with a long series of the most preposterous accusations, in which I was represented as having committed every species of crime, from piracy to petty robbery; calling on the Chilian Government to visit me with the severest punishment.

On the 8th of May, the schooner *Montezuma*, which had been lent to General San Martin by the Chilian Government, entered Callao *under Peruvian colours.* The insolence of thus appropriating a vessel of my squadron was too great for forbearance, so that I compelled her to come to an anchor, though not before we were obliged to fire upon her. I then turned all the officers ashore, and took possession of her; the Protectoral authorities, by way of reprisal, detaining a boat belonging to the flag-ship, and imprisoning the men; but, rightly calculating the consequences of such a step, they were soon set at liberty, and the boat was, on the same night, permitted to return to the ship.

On the 10th of May we quitted Callao, and arrived at Valparaiso on the 13th of June, after an absence of a year and nine months, during which the objects of the expedition had been completely accomplished.

Having satisfied myself, that, from the oppression practised, the Protectoral Government could not endure longer than the first favourable opportunity for a general revolt which might present itself to the Limeños, and judging that the fall of San Martin might involve serious consequences to Chili, I had addressed the following letter to the Supreme Director:—

Private and confidential.

Callao Roads, May 2, 1822.

MOST EXCELLENT SIR,

You will perceive by my public despatches the points of most interest as regards the proceedings of the squadron, and the result of our pursuit of the enemy's frigates, *Prueba* and *Venganza*, both of which I have embargoed, the one at Guayaquil and the other here, until your pleasure shall be known, whatever that may be, whether to give up the squadron of Chili, or to bring those vessels to you, shall be alike obeyed.

San Martin has now laid down the external pomp of Protector, and, like Cincinnatus, has withdrawn to retirement, but not with the same view. This modesty is to captivate the crowd, who are to call on him to convert the ploughshare *into an Imperial sceptre!* I have excellent information to this effect, having found means to obtain it from behind the scenes of this political actor.

Great hopes are entertained, from the mission to Chili, that the squadron will at least be withdrawn, and that when the sun of Peru shall rise on the ocean, the star (the national emblem of Chili) which has hitherto shone, will be for ever eclipsed! Some spots have, however, appeared on the sun's surface. Two thousand men have ceased to see its light at Pasco; and the Numantian regiment, once dazzled by its splendour, are about to grope their way to their native land.

As the attached and sincere friend of your Excellency, I hope you will take into your serious consideration the propriety of at once fixing the Chilian Government upon a base not to be shaken by the fall of the present tyranny in Peru, of which there are not only indications, but their result is inevitable; unless, indeed, the mischievous counsels of vain and mercenary men can suffice to prop up a fabric of the most barbarous political architecture, serving as a screen from whence to dart their weapons against the heart of liberty. Thank God, my hands are free from the stain of labouring in any such work, and, having finished all which you gave me to do, I may now rest till you shall command my further endeavours for the honour and security of my adopted land.

The enemy's forces, since the destruction of the division at Pasco, under Tristan, are superior to those of San Martin at Lima, and are said to be advancing on the capital.

Everything being fully explained in my despatches, I need not trouble your Excellency with a repetition. Trusting that you will judge of my conduct and intentions by my acts—not by the vile scandals of those who have deserted their flag, and set your proclamations at defiance,

I have the honor, &c.,

COCHRANE.

CHAPTER X.

RETURN TO VALPARAISO—THANKS OF THE GOVERNMENT—REASONS FOR SATISFACTION—ILLEGITIMATE TRADE—TURNED TO GOOD ACCOUNT—DENUNCIATION OF OFFICERS DESERTED—INVESTIGATION OF ACCOUNTS—SAN MARTIN'S CHARGES AGAINST ME—MY REFUTATION—GOVERNMENT REFUSES ITS PUBLICATION—CRUELTY TO SPANISH PRISONERS—RETIREMENT TO QUINTERO—POLITICAL FRUITS OF OUR SUCCESS—DESTITUTE CONDITION OF SQUADRON—INFAMOUS ATTEMPT TO PROMOTE DISSATISFACTION THEREIN—OBJECT OF THIS COURSE—STEPS TAKEN TO DEFEAT IT—DISAVOWED BY THE MINISTER—SYMPATHY OF OFFICERS—ATTEMPT TO GET RID OF GEN. FREIRE—ITS EVENTUAL RESULT—LETTER OF THE CAPTAINS.

On my arrival at Valparaiso, I found that San Martin's agents, Paroissien and Garcia del Rio, had produced his accusations against me to the Government at Santiago, though without effect, as I had taken care to keep it apprised of everything which had transpired, exercising the most scrupulous care in furnishing accounts of monies and stores taken from the Spaniards, but especially as regarded the public money of the Peruvian Government appropriated at Ancon.

The return of the squadron was announced by me to the Government in the following letter:—

The anxious desires of His Excellency the Supreme Director are now fulfilled, and the sacrifices of the Chilian people are rewarded. The naval power of Spain in the Pacific has succumbed and is extinguished, the following vessels having surrendered to the unceasing efforts of the squadron of this Free State:—

Prueba, 50 guns; *Esmeralda*, 44; *Venganza*, 44; *Resolution*, 34; *Sebastiana*, 34; *Pesuela*, 18; *Potrillo*, 16; *Prosperina*, 14; *Arausasu;* seventeen gun-boats; the armed ships *Aguila* and *Begonia;* the block ships at Callao; and many merchantmen.

It is highly gratifying to me, after labouring under such difficulties as were never before witnessed on board ships of war, to announce the arrival of the Chilian squadron in Valparaiso—its cradle; where, owing to its unceasing services in the cause of liberty and independence of Chili, Peru, Colombia, and Mexico, it forms an object of admiration and gratitude to the inhabitants of the New World.

(Signed) COCHRANE.

By the inhabitants of Valparaiso our return was hailed with every manifestation of delight, almost every house in the place being decorated with the patriot flag, whilst other demonstrations of national joy showed the importance which the Chilian people attached to our services, in spite of the obstacles which they well knew had been opposed to them.

On the 4th of June, the following letters of thanks were forwarded to me:—

Ministry of Marine,
Santiago de Chili, June 4th, 1822.

MOST EXCELLENT SIR,

The arrival of your Excellency at Valparaiso with the squadron under your command, has given the greatest pleasure to his Excellency the Supreme Director. In those feelings of gratitude which the glory acquired by your Excellency during the late campaign has excited, you will find the proof of that high consideration which your heroic services so justly deserve.

Among those who have a distinguished claim are the chiefs and officers, who, faithful to their duty, have remained on board the vessels of war of this State, a list of whom your Excellency has honoured me by enclosing. These gentlemen will most assuredly receive the recompense so justly due to their praiseworthy constancy.

Be pleased to accept the assurance of my highest esteem.

JOAQUIM DE ECHEVERRIA.

His Excellency the Vice-Admiral and
Commander-in-Chief of the Squadron,
the Right Honourable LORD COCHRANE.

From the preceding letter it will be observed that my old opponent, Zenteno, was no longer at the head of the Department of Marine, but was appointed Governor of Valparaiso, where he exercised the office of Port-Admiral, a position in which, with all his former enmity, he contrived, notwithstanding the complete satisfaction of the Government with my services, to give me great annoyance.

In addition to the above acknowledgment of our services, a decree was issued commanding a medal to be struck in commemoration thereof.

Ministry of Marine,
Santiago de Chili, 19th June, 1822.

MOST EXCELLENT SIR,

His Excellency the Supreme Director being desirous of making a public demonstration of the high services that the squadron has rendered to the nation, has resolved that a medal be struck for the officers and crews of the squadron, with an inscription expressive of the national gratitude towards the worthy supporters of its maritime power.

I have the honour to communicate this to your Excellency by supreme command, and to offer you my highest respects.

JOAQUIM DE ECHEVERRIA.

His Excellency the Rt. Hon. LORD COCHRANE,
Vice-Admiral and Commander-in-Chief, &c. &c.

It is here observable, that whereas San Martin, on the occupation of Lima, had caused a medal to be struck, arrogating the success of the expedition entirely to the army, which had done little or nothing towards it—leaving out all mention of the services of the squadron; the Chilian Government gave the credit, as was deserved, to the squadron—omitting all mention of the army, which remained under the standard of the Protector. Nothing can be more conclusive as to the opinions of the Chilian Government on the subject.

Chili had indeed reason to be grateful, no less for the management than the achievements of the squadron. I had now been in command something more than two years and a half, during which we either took, destroyed, or forced to surrender, every Spanish ship of war in the Pacific; the whole of the west coast was cleared of pirates, which before abounded; we had reduced unaided the most important fortresses of the enemy, either by storm or blockade; the commerce both of Chili and neutral powers had been protected; and the cause of independence placed on a basis so firm, that nothing but folly or corruption could shake it.

For these most important results, Chili had been at no cost whatever beyond the original ineffective equipment of the ships. With the exception of three or four cargoes of provisions sent to Callao, I had, by my own exertions, for the whole period, provided for the maintenance and subsistence of the squadron, its repairs, equipment, stores, provisions, and pay, as far as the men had been paid; not a dollar having been expended for these purposes by the Chilian Government, which trusted—but in vain—to Peru. To have been ungrateful—as far as the public expression of gratitude went, for other reward there was none—would have been a national crime.

As one of my modes of providing for the necessities of the squadron has not been mentioned, it must be here given.

Under the Spanish régime, no foreign vessel could trade at their ports in the Pacific. But, for the sake of revenue as well as to obtain supplies, it had become the practice of the Viceroy to sell licences, enabling British merchants to employ British vessels in the Spanish Colonial trade. These had to load in some port in Spain, and were there furnished with legalized Spanish papers.

Under the altered state of things in Chili, in order to secure such vessels from capture by the Chilian ships of war, as having Spanish property on board, the device of simulated papers was resorted to, representing the cargoes as British property, coming from the port of Gibraltar; one set of papers being used ashore, and the other afloat, or as occasion required. Several British vessels had been detained by the Chilian squadron, whereof the Spanish papers were found in the Peruvian custom-houses when taken possession of; they were accordingly liable to be libelled as Spanish property.

In order, however, to land their cargoes in safety, the commanders and supercargoes of such British vessels voluntarily offered terms which should confer upon their trade a legitimate character, viz. to pay a certain impost as an equivalent for customs' duties. I accepted these terms as furnishing me with means to supply the necessities and defray the expenses of the squadron, the wants of which were with great difficulty supplied, as the Protectoral Government refused to aid in any way, notwithstanding that it owed its very existence to our efforts.

The duties thus collected,—for the most part in contraband of war,—were duly accounted for by me to the Government of Chili, whilst such compromise was received as a boon by the British merchants, and highly approved of by the British naval authorities, Sir Thomas Hardy especially.

Yet General San Martin, and others interested in a line of policy which in its prosecution was inimical to the true interests of Chili, afterwards charged these proceedings upon me as "acts of piracy."

That the Chilian Government was, however, well satisfied with all the steps taken for provisioning and maintaining the squadron, as well as with the seizure and disposal of the public money at Ancon, is evident from the following acknowledgment:—

MOST EXCELLENT SIR,

I have informed the Supreme Director of the note which you addressed to me on the 7th of October, accompanying the accounts of the monies supplied to the payment of the officers and seamen of the squadron, and to the other objects of the naval service; as well as the accounts of money and bars of silver returned at Ancon to their respective owners.

His Excellency approves of all that you have done in these matters and orders me in reply to convey his approbation, which I have the honour now to do.

Accept the assurance of my high consideration,

(Signed) JOAQUIM DE ECHEVERRIA,
Ministry of Marine, Santiago de Chili.

To LORD COCHRANE,
Vice-Adm. & Comm -in-Chief. Nov. 13, 1821.

On the same date, the following was received relative to the officers who had deserted from the squadron, for the purpose of entering the service of the Protector:—

Santiago de Chili, Nov. 13, 1821.

MOST EXCELLENT SIR,

His Excellency the Supreme Director has received with the greatest dissatisfaction a list of the naval officers who have deserted from the squadron. These will not fail to be noted in order to be tried by a court-martial, in case they should again tread the soil of Chili. It is fortunate that your Excellency has altered the private signals, lest Capt. Esmonde should divulge those which were in use.

(Signed) JOAQUIM DE ECHEVERRIA.

Vice-Adm. LORD COCHRANE.

Immediately after my arrival, an intimation was forwarded to me by the Supreme Director of his wish to confer with me privately on the subject of my letter of May 2nd, in which had been pointed out the danger arising in Peru, from the tyranny exercised by the Protectoral Government.

Santiago, June 4th, 1822.

MY DISTINGUISHED FRIEND LORD COCHRANE,

I do not wish to delay a moment in expressing my satisfaction at your arrival, of which you have informed me in your letter of the 2nd inst. As in that letter you acquaint me that you will speedily be in this Capital, with a view to communicate matters which would be better conveyed in a verbal conference, I shall anxiously await the day to express to you all the consideration with which I am

Your sincere friend,

BERNARDO O'HIGGINS.

Having as yet received no official acknowledgment of the accounts of the squadron, beyond the previously mentioned general expression of entire satisfaction on the part of the Government, I applied to the Minister of Marine for a more minute investigation into their contents, as from the charges made against me by San Martin, I was desirous that the most rigid inquiry should be instituted forthwith, and indeed expressed my surprise—from the time which had elapsed since they were forwarded—that this had not been done. On the 14th of June, the Minister replied as follows:—

MOST EXCELLENT SIR,

The accounts of monies applied by your Excellency in the necessary requirements of the vessels of war under your command, which you conveyed to me in your two notes of the 25th of May last, have been passed to the office of the Accountant-General, for the purpose indicated by your Excellency.

JOAQUIM DE ECHEVERRIA.

Knowing the dilatory habits of the departments of State, I did not deem this satisfactory, and being engaged in preparing a refutation of San Martin's charges, I again urged on the Minister to investigate the accounts without further delay, when, on the 19th of June, he acknowledged—in a letter too long for insertion—the specific items; at the same time declaring his "high consideration for the manner in "which I had made the flag of Chili respected in "the Pacific."

This was satisfactory, but it is perhaps necessary to assign a reason why so much importance is attached to a mere matter of routine, especially after the Government had declared its satisfaction with all my proceedings. The reason is this—that for all the services so warmly acknowledged, the Government of Chili restrained from conferring either upon myself or the squadron the slightest pecuniary recompense, even the prize-money due to the officers and seamen, part of which the ministry had appropriated. On pressing these claims year after year subsequent to my departure from Chili, I was informed *sixteen years afterwards!* that my accounts required explanation! the reason for this unworthy proceeding being, that, as the claim could not be disputed, it might thus be evaded.

My refutation of San Martin's accusations was drawn up in the most minute manner, replying to every charge *seriatim*, and bringing to light a multitude of nefarious practices on the part of his Government, which had been previously kept back. Lest I might appear in the invidious light of an accuser, I was strongly dissuaded from its publication, as being unnecessary, the Chilian Government paying no attention whatever to his charges, but being afraid of embroiling themselves with Peru, the weakness of which they failed rightly to estimate.

Having, however, my own character to defend, I

did not think proper to comply, and therefore forwarded my refutation to the Government, the Minister of Marine acknowledging its receipt, with an intimation that it had been deposited in the archives of the Republic.

As, from the Minister of Marine's reply, the document was evidently intended to remain there without further notice, I addressed the following letter to the Supreme Director:—

MOST EXCELLENT SIR,

As the game attempted to be played by the Government of Peru for the annihilation of the marine of Chili is now being put in practice in another form, conjointly with further attacks on my character, I have to request permission from the supreme authority to publish my correspondence with San Martin and his agents on these subjects; together with a copy of his accusation against me, with my reply thereto, in order that the public may no longer be deceived, and falsehood pass for truth.

I have the honour, &c.

COCHRANE.

To this the following reply was returned:—

Santiago, Oct. 1, 1822.

MOST EXCELLENT SIR,

Your Excellency is too well acquainted with political affairs not to understand the reasons which oppose the publication of the disagreeable occurrences which have taken place with the Protector at the termination of the Peruvian campaign. Were they made public, it would be opening a vast field of censure to the enemies of our cause, and also weakening the credit of the independent Governments, by shewing dissensions amongst themselves.

Already have we felt the inconveniences of the injurious impressions *made on the British Cabinet* by the dissensions between your Excellency and Gen. San Martin; for they had no sooner been informed thereof, than the diplomatic negociations which had been established with our Envoy at that Court were paralysed; and had he not laboured to counteract the rumours, which had been exaggerated by distance, there is no doubt but that his influence in advocating the cause of South America would have most prejudicially failed.

His Excellency the Supreme Director feels confident that these reflections will have in your mind all the weight they merit; but if you still insist on the publication of your reply to Gen. San Martin, you may nevertheless avail yourself of the liberty of the press which prevails in Chili.

(Signed) JOAQUIM DE ECHEVERRIA.

It was "*the injurious impressions made on the* "*British Cabinet*," which made me chiefly desirous of replying to the Protector's charges; but being thus adjured not to sacrifice the interests of South America, and being, moreover, strenuously requested to let the matter drop, as being of no consequence to me in Chili, I reluctantly yielded, contenting myself with sending a copy of my reply to the Peruvian Government. Further to assure me of the disbelief of the Chilian Government in the charges made, an additional vote of thanks was given me by the Senate, and inserted in the Gazette.

On my return to Valparaiso, I found a lamentable instance of the cruelty practised by the military tyrants of Peru. It has been mentioned that the old Spaniards were ostensibly permitted to quit Lima on surrender of half their property—a regulation of which many availed themselves rather than submit to the caprices of the Protectoral Government. In place of the security which they thus purchased for the remainder of their property, they were seized and stripped on their way to Callao of the whole that remained, thrust on board the prison ship, and finally sent, in a state of complete destitution of the necessaries of life, to be added to the Spanish prisoners in Chili. The *Milagro* had arrived in Valparaiso full of these miserable people, many of whom were shortly before amongst the most respectable inhabitants of Lima; and, to add to the bitterness of their treatment, they were accompanied to Chili by the agents of the Protector, Paroissien and Garcia del Rio, with his charges against me, no doubt for the further purpose of again tampering with the officers of the squadron. I did all in my power to interfere on the part of the unhappy prisoners, but in vain; they were at length transferred to the hospital of San Juan de Dios, where they were confined with the common felons, and would have been starved but for the English inhabitants of Valparaiso, who raised a subscription on their behalf, and appointed one of their body to see their daily food distributed. They were afterwards transferred to Santiago. The cruelty practised towards these prisoners in Peru, is of itself a reason why their tyrants did not venture to encounter the Spanish General Cantarac. Cruel people are invariably cowards.

On my arrival at Santiago, I found the Supreme Director on the point of resigning his high office, from the opposition he had to encounter by adhering to a ministry which in one way or other was constantly bringing his Government into discredit, and from being supposed to favour the designs of

General San Martin, though to this I attached no credit, believing that his high sense of principle led him to take upon himself the obnoxious acts of his Ministers, who were partisans of the Protector. The dissatisfaction increasing, the Supreme Director at length tendered his resignation to the Convention, who, being unprepared for this step, insisted on reinstating him in the supreme executive authority.

Being indisposed to mingle in the conflicting state of parties which distracted Chili after my return, and being in need of relaxation after the two years and a-half of harassing anxiety which I had encountered, I requested permission of the Government to retire to my estate at Quintero, intending also to visit the estate which had been conferred upon me at Rio Clara as an acknowledgment of services rendered at Valdivia; my object being to bring it into a state of cultivation, which might give an impetus to the low condition of agriculture in Chili.

At this juncture, the *Rising Star*, the steamer which was spoken of as having been left behind in England, arrived in Valparaiso, too late, however, to take any part in the operations which were now brought to a close by the surrender of the Spanish navy. This delay had been caused by want of funds to complete her equipment, which could not even now have been accomplished, had not large means been furnished to the Chilian agent in London, by my brother, the Hon. Major Cochrane, who, to this day, has not been reimbursed a shilling of the outlay advanced on the faith of the accredited Chilian

Envoy! Though the *Rising Star* was now of little use as regarded naval operations, she was the first steamer which had entered the Pacific, and might, had she not been repudiated by the Government, have formed the nucleus of a force which would have prevented an infinity of disasters which shortly after my departure from Chili befel the cause of independence, as will presently be seen.

The political fruits of our successes in Chili and Peru now began to manifest themselves in the recognition of the South American Republics by the United States, so that Chili had assumed the rank of a recognised member of the family of nations.

I took with me as a guest to Quintero, my former prisoner, Colonel Fausto del Hoyo, the Commandant at Valdivia on our reduction of that fortress. Previous to my departure for Peru, I had obtained from the Government a promise for his generous treatment, but no sooner had the squadron sailed, than he was thrust into prison, without fire, light, or books, and in this miserable condition he had remained till our return. As he received the promise of generous treatment from me, I insisted on and obtained his liberation, and he was now on parole. By paying him every attention, I hoped to inculcate that national greatness does not include cruelty to prisoners of war.

No sooner had I arrived at Quintero, than I zealously entered on my improvements, having now received from England a variety of agricultural implements, such as ploughs, harrows, spades, &c., all of which were new to Chili; also European agricultural seeds, such as carrots, turnips, &c., which, previous to their introduction by me were unknown in the country.

But I was not long permitted to enjoy the "*otium*" marked out for myself. Letter after letter came from the squadron, complaining that, like the Spanish prisoners, they too were in a state of destitution, without pay, clothes, or provisions. Starting again for Valparaiso, I found their complaints to be more than realized, upon which I addressed to the Minister of Marine the following letter :—

MOST EXCELLENT SIR,

Three months having passed since the squadron anchored in this port, and the same period since my representations on its condition were made to the Supreme Government, relative to the nakedness and destitute condition of the crews; who still continue in the same state as that in which they passed the winter, without beds or clothes, the sentinel at my cabin door being in rags, no portion of which formed his original uniform. As it is impossible that such a state of things can continue, without exciting dangerous discontent and mutiny, I beg that you will order such clothing as may be found in Valparaiso to be supplied through the Commissary of the squadron, in order that it may immediately be distributed to the naked crews.

(Signed) COCHRANE.

The determination with which I had entered upon the relief of the seamen, was so offensive to those who, in popular estimation, were deserving of blame, that a report was circulated of my having surreptitiously shipped on board the English frigate *Doris*, then lying in the harbour of Valparaiso, 9000 ounces of coined gold, and also a quantity of gold and silver bars to the like amount! the object no doubt being to induce a belief in the popular mind, that money had been applicable for the use of the squadron, but that it had been dishonestly appropriated by myself.

As I had returned to Quintero, this rumour did not reach me till it had become widely disseminated amongst the Chilian people. The first intimation I had of it, was contained in the following letter from Captain Cobbett, of the *Valdivia*:—

MY DEAR LORD,

When I informed you, on my arrival at Quintero, that something unpleasant would take place, I was not altogether ignorant of a report which has now become prevalent. It was said on the day of your departure, that your Lordship had placed a large sum of money on board one of the British men of war in the harbour, 9,000 ounces in gold in a package directed to Lady Cochrane, and an equal amount in gold and silver bars to wait further orders from your Lordship. Every exertion was made by one interested in injuring your Lordship, to convince me of the fact, my reply being, that I had too long been accustomed to rely in your Lordship's integrity to believe any such report without proof.

Yesterday the same person came again to my house to inform me that the matter was cleared beyond doubt, for that the master of the *Doris* frigate had told him that the two boxes of gold and silver were on board, directed as above-mentioned. This report has created great sensation here, and the greatest pains are being taken to spread it far and wide. On making inquiry on board the *Doris*, Captain Wilkinson and myself found that no packages of the kind were on board, and on telling the parties engaged in spreading the report the result of our inquiry, they seemed much chopfallen, but would not retract their charge, which I am certain they intend to carry to the Supreme Director, the consequence of which would be, that were the report true or false, the Government would blame your Lordship, and accuse us of being your abettors; whilst, as the want of pay and prize-money renders the officers irritable, they are ready for anything and everything which might promise to relieve their necessities.

I have told your Lordship all I know, and have conceived the rumour to be of so much importance, as to send one of my own horses with the little doctor to inform you immediately of what is going on, as such reports ought not to be treated lightly. I beg to subscribe myself, with the greatest respect,

Your Lordship's grateful Servant,

HENRY COBBETT.

Another letter, from Captain Wilkinson, was to the same effect:—

My dear Lord,

A report is in circulation that your Lordship has put on board the British frigate *Doris* nine thousand ounces in gold. I feel it my duty to acquaint you of this, as no person can have your Lordship's reputation more at heart than myself. I have been told this by two or three persons after your Lordship left for Quintero, and in the evening by Moyell, who must have known it to be false, and I declared it so to him. I trust your Lordship will be able to trace the shameless offender.

I am, my Lord, &c. &c.

W. WILKINSON.

As soon as these letters were received, I lost no time in repairing to Valparaiso, not doubting that Zenteno and the Peruvian agents were again at work to disorganize the squadron, and in case of the overthrow of the Supreme Director, which was still impending, to place it in the hands of San Martin. The object of the party was to cause dissension amongst the seamen, by making them believe that, amidst their poverty and sufferings, I had been taking care of myself, and hence they hoped to destroy that confidence in me which officers and men had all along exhibited, notwithstanding their privations. As they had never before been so wretchedly destitute, this circumstance was considered favourable to the impression, that having secured all I could for myself, I was about to abandon them.

Though there was not a word of truth in the report which had been thus sedulously disseminated, it was too serious to be trifled with; accordingly, on the receipt of Captain Cobbett's letter, I hastened to Valparaiso, and to the chagrin of Zenteno, again hoisted my flag on board the *O'Higgins.*

My first step was to demand from the Government the appointment of a commission to go on board the *Doris*, and there ascertain whether I had placed any packages on board that frigate for transmission to England or elsewhere. The reply was, that no such commission was requisite, as no one gave credit to the assertion that I had done so, or suppose me capable of acting in the way which had been falsely reported!

The re-hoisting my flag was a step which had not been anticipated, and as it was unbidden, a remonstrance was addressed to me upon having taken such a step unauthorised by the Government. My reply was, that I had taken the step upon my own responsibility, and that as such an infamous accusation had been promulgated against me, for the purpose of promoting mutiny amongst the men, I intended to keep my flag flying till they were paid. At the same time I addressed the following letter to the Minister of Marine:—

MOST EXCELLENT SIR,

Aroused from the tranquillity in which I had vainly hoped to spend at least the short period of my leave of absence by imputations against my character, propagated with a view to excite dissatisfaction and mutiny in the squadron, by taking advantage of the irritation occasioned by the necessities of the officers, and the destitute and naked condition of the men, which I have so often implored you to remedy; I have reluctantly proceeded to this port to refute the calumny and prevent the evil anticipated, for which purpose I have re-hoisted my flag, to haul it down when the discontent shall cease, by the people being clothed and paid, or when I shall be ordered to haul it down for ever.

I enclose a copy of a letter which I have sent to the Governor of Valparaiso.

(Signed) COCHRANE.

It is unnecessary to give the letter to Zenteno, as being to the same effect with the preceding, with some additional guesses at the infamous author of the report, these proving sufficient for his discreet silence on the subject. The following reply from the Minister of Marine was immediately forwarded to me:—

Santiago, Oct. 1, 1822.

MOST EXCELLENT SIR,

His Excellency the Supreme Director is impressed with deep disgust at the calumny to which you allude in your note, a copy of which I have forwarded to the Governor of Valparaiso. Your Excellency may rest satisfied that the authors thereof will not remain unpunished if discovered.

Accept the assurance of my high consideration.

The Minister of Marine,

JOAQUIM DE ECHEVERRIA.

To the Vice-Admiral Com.-in-Chief of the Squadron.

As a matter of course the libeller was neither discovered nor punished, otherwise the Governor of Valparaiso, and the agents of San Martin would have been placed in an unpleasant position. But they had nothing to fear, as, from the daily increasing perplexities of the Chilian Government, it was in no condition to defend itself, much less to assert the majesty of the law.

From the promptitude displayed in meeting a charge as utterly groundless as it was infamous, and from the conviction of the squadron that I was incapable of acting in the manner imputed to me, the calumny produced the opposite effect to that which was intended, viz. by inspiring in the minds of the officers and men the most intense disgust towards its originators. On my re-hoisting my flag, I was received with every demonstration of enthusiasm and affection, the officers unanimously uniting in the following address ;—

MAY IT PLEASE YOUR EXCELLENCY,

We, the undersigned officers of the Chilian squadron, have heard with surprise and indignation the vile and scandalous reports tending to bring your Excellency's high character in question, and to destroy that confidence and admiration with which it has always inspired us.

We have seen with pleasure the measures your Excellency has adopted to suppress so malicious and absurd a conspiracy, and trust that no means will be spared to bring its authors to public shame.

At a time like the present, when the best interests of the squadron and our dearest rights as individuals are at stake, we feel especially indignant at an attempt to destroy that union and confidence which at present exists, and which we are assured ever will exist, while we have the honour to serve under your Excellency's command.

With these sentiments we subscribe ourselves,

Your Excellency's most obedient humble Servant,

(Signed) J. P. GRENFELL, Lieut.-Com. *Mercedes*,

And all the Officers of the Squadron.

The excellent officer whose name is prominently attached to this address, is now Admiral Grenfell, Consul-General in England of the Brazilian Empire. He was my flag-lieutenant at the capture of the *Esmeralda*, under the batteries of Callao, and it is no more than justice to mention, that his distinguished gallantry in that affair in an eminent degree contributed to the success of the enterprise.

But I was not the only person of whom the envoys of San Martin and their creatures in the Chilian Government desired to get rid. General Santa Cruz was openly appointed to supersede General Freire as Governor of Conception and Chief of the Army of the South; the keen discrimination of Freire having estimated San Martin and his proceedings in Peru as they deserved, and hence he had become obnoxious to those whose design it was to lay Chili at the feet of the Protector. On Santa Cruz proceeding to Conception to take up the command, the troops unanimously refused to obey his authority, or to permit General Freire to leave them. The people of Conception, who had suffered more from their patriotism than any other in Chili, were equally resolute, not only from attachment to Freire, but because they knew that if the ministry gained their ends, Conception would be destroyed as a port; it being their object to shut up every port but Valparaiso, in order that by the corrupt practices prevalent there, they might monopolize the whole advantage to be personally gained from the commerce of the country.

The Supreme Director was, as usual, made the scapegoat for the unsuccessful attempt of his ministers to depose General Freire, and the consequence was that in three months after the attempt was made, General O'Higgins was deposed from his authority, and General Freire elevated to the Supreme Directorate!

As I had been falsely accused of stealing money which ought to have been divided amongst the seamen, I was determined that no ground for future accusation of the kind should arise in consequence of their not being paid; and with this view, pertinaciously insisted on the payment of the arrears due to the squadron. These efforts were seconded by the commanding officers of ships, who, in a temperate address to the Government, set forth the nature of their claims. From this address, the following extracts are given, as forming an excellent epitome of the whole events of the war:—

"Ever since the capture of the *Isabel*, the dominion of the Pacific has been maintained by the Chilian navy, and such have been the exertions of our Commander and ourselves that with Chileno crews unaccustomed to navigation, and a few foreign seamen whom we alone could control, not only have the shores of this State been effectually protected from injury and insult, but the maritime forces of the enemy have been closely blockaded in the face of a superior force. By means of the navy the important province, fortifications, and port of Valdivia have been added to the Republic. By the same means the Spanish power in Peru was brought into contempt, and the way opened for the invasion of that country. The enemy's ships of war have all fallen into our hands or by our means have been compelled to surrender. Their merchant vessels have been seized under their very batteries, whilst the Chilian transports and trading vessels have been in such perfect security that not even the smallest has been compelled to haul down its flag. Amongst these achievements, the capture of the *Esmeralda* has reflected lustre on the Chilian marine equal to anything recorded in the chronicles of ancient States, greatly adding to Chilian importance in the eyes of Europe; whilst, from the vigilance of the naval blockade, the fortifications of Callao were finally compelled to surrender.

"This happy event, so long hoped for, was by all considered to complete our labours in Peru, and to entitle us if not to a remuneration from that State, *as in the case of those officers who abandoned the Chilian service!* yet, at least, to a share of the valuable property taken by our means, as awarded under similar circumstances by other States, which, by experience, are aware of the benefit of stimulating individuals by such rewards for great enterprises undertaken for the public good. But, alas! so far from either of these modes of remuneration being adopted, *even the pay so often promised was withheld, and food itself was denied, so that we were reduced to a state of the greatest privation and suffering; so great, indeed, that the crew of the Lautaro abandoned their ship for want of food, and the seamen of the squadron, natives as well as foreigners, were in a state of open mutiny, threatening the safety of all the vessels of the State.*

"We do not claim merit for not relieving ourselves from this painful situation by an act of a doubtful nature, viz. by an acquiescence in the intentions of the General Commanding-in-Chief the expeditionary forces; *who, having declared us officers of Peru,* offered, through his *aides-de camps,* Colonel Paroissien and Captain Spry, honours and estates to those who would further his views. *Nor do we envy those who received those estates and honours;* but having rejected these inducements to swerve from our allegiance, we may fairly claim the approbation of Government for providing the squadron of Chili with provisions and stores at Callao, *out of monies in our hands justly due for the capture of the Esmeralda, when such supplies had been refused by General San Martin.* We may also claim similar approbation for having repaired the squadron at Guayaquil, and for equipping and provisioning it for the pursuit of the enemy's frigates, *Prueba* and *Venganza*, which we drove from the shores of Mexico in a state of destitution to the shores of Peru; and if they were not actually brought to Chili, it was because they were seized by our late General and Commander-in-Chief, and appropriated in the same manner as he had previously intended with respect to the Chilian squadron itself. We may add, that every endeavour short of actual hostilities with the said General, was made on our part to obtain the restitution of those valuable frigates to the Government of Chili. In no other instance through the whole course of our proceedings, has any dispute arisen but what has terminated favourably to the interests of Chili, and the honour of her flag. Private friendships have been preserved with the naval officers of foreign powers; no point has been conceded that could be maintained consistently with the maritime laws of civilized nations, by which our conduct has been scrupulously guided; and such has been the caution observed, that no act of violence contrary to the laws of nations, nor any improper exercise of power, can be laid to our charge. The Chilian flag has waved in triumph, and with universal respect, from the southern extremity of the Republic to the shores of California; population and the value of property have by our exertions increased threefold; whilst commerce and its consequent revenue have been augmented in a far greater proportion; which commerce, so productive to the State, might, without the protecting aid of its navy, be annihilated by a few of those miserable privateers which the terror of its name alone deters from approaching.

"The period has now arrived at which it is essential for the well-being of the service in general, and especially for our private affairs, that our arrears, so long due, should be liquidated; and far as it is from our desire to press our claims on the Government, yet we cannot abstain from so doing, in justice to the State, as well as to ourselves; because want of regularity in the internal affairs of a naval service is productive of relaxation of discipline, as just complaints cannot be redressed, nor complainants chastised—discontent spreading like a contagious disease, and paralysing the system.

"Permit us, therefore, to call to the notice of the Government that since our return to Valparaiso *with our naked crews, even clothes have been withheld for four months*, during which no payment has been made, the destitute seamen being *without blankets, ponchos, or any covering to protect them from the cold of winter*, the more severely felt from the hot climates in which they have for nearly three years been employed.

"The two months' pay offered the other day could not now effect its purpose, as the whole—and more is due to the Pulperia keepers, to whose benefit, and not that of the seamen, it must have immediately accrued. Judge, then, of the irritation produced by such privations, and the impossibility of relieving them by such inadequate payment; also whether it is possible to maintain order and discipline amongst men worse circumstanced than the convicts of Algiers! Under such circumstances, it is no exaggeration to affirm that confidence will be for ever gone, and the squadron entirely ruined, if measures of preservation are not immediately resorted to.

"With respect to the offer of *one month's pay to ourselves!* after our faithful and persevering services, undergoing privations such as were never endured in the navy of any other State, we are afraid to trust ourselves to make any observations; but it is quite impossible that it could have been accepted under any circumstances, as it would have placed us in no better situation than if, on our arrival here four months ago, we had actually paid the Government three months' salary for the satisfaction of having served it, during a period of two years, with unremitting exertions and fidelity.

"In conclusion, we respectfully hope, that the Supreme Government will be pleased to take what we have stated into its serious consideration, and more especially that it will be pleased to comply with its existing engagements to us, with the same alacrity and fidelity with which we have acted towards the Government; the duties of each being reciprocal, and equally binding on both parties."

Signed by all the Captains.

The preceding statement of the captains is a faithful statement of the case as regarded the injustice done to the squadron, which had throughout supported itself, even to the repairs and equipment of the ships. As to the ruin which the captains predict, it was no doubt intended by the envoys of San Martin and their creatures in the Chilian Ministry, as the effect would have been to have driven the men to desertion, when the ships would have been turned over to Peru, and manned with fresh crews. Fortunately for Chili, this consummation was prevented by an occurrence as strange as unexpected by her short-sighted rulers, though long before predicted by myself.

CHAPTER XI.

NEGOCIATIONS WITH BOLIVAR—EXILE OF MONTEAGUDO—COMPLAINTS OF THE LIMENOS—EXTRAVAGANCE OF THE GOVERNMENT—EXCULPATION OF SAN MARTIN—EFFECTS OF POPULAR DISSENSION—DISAGREEMENT OF BOLIVAR AND SAN MARTIN—VOTE OF PERUVIAN CONGRESS—EXTRAORDINARY NEGLECT OF THE CHILIAN SQUADRON—SAN MARTIN'S ARRIVAL AT VALPARAISO—I DEMAND HIS TRIAL—COUNTENANCE OF THE SUPREME DIRECTOR—SQUADRON AT LENGTH PAID WAGES—REVOLT OF CONCEPTION—GENERAL FREIRE APPRISES ME OF IT—FREIRE ASKS FOR MY SUPPORT—HIS LETTER NOT REPLIED TO—SAN MARTIN'S INFLUENCE.

MENTION has been made in a previous chapter of the all but total destruction of a division of the liberating army by General Canterac, and of the bombastic proclamations issued on that occasion by San Martin, to the effect that they were "only "dispersed, not beaten," &c. The Protector was however ill at ease, and entered into a correspondence with Bolivar, with a view to procure the assistance of Columbian troops against the Spaniards, who, following up their success, were making demonstrations of attacking the patriot forces in Lima. To this request was added another soliciting an interview with Bolivar at Guayaquil. A similar despatch was sent to Santiago, asking, in the most urgent terms, for aid from the Chilian Government.

The whole affair—as narrated at the time, for personally I had nothing to do with it—was somewhat curious. San Martin's designs on Guayaquil having got wind, Bolivar marched the Columbian troops across the Cordillera, successfully invaded Quito, and was hastening towards Guayaquil, with a view of being beforehand with San Martin, of whose intentions upon that province he was aware. After the above-mentioned defeat of the Peruvian army by Canterac, San Martin had been compelled to withdraw his forces from Truxillo, on which Sucre, the next in command to Bolivar, advanced to Guayaquil and took possession of it. At this time, as was afterwards well known, the Limeños were privately soliciting Bolivar to give them his assistance in liberating Peru, *both from the Protector* and the Spaniards!

Ignorant of this, the Protector, having delegated the supreme authority to the Marquis of Torre Tagle, and appointed General Alvarado Commander-in-Chief in his absence, departed for Guayaquil, for the purpose of the proposed interview.

No sooner had San Martin turned his back, than a public meeting of the Limeños took place in the Plaza, and insisted on the reconstitution of the *Cabildo*, which assembly had been put down by the Protector immediately after the declaration of independence. The members having complied, it was decided that "the Minister Monteagudo should be deposed, tried, "and subjected to the severity of the law," a note being despatched to this effect to the Supreme Delegate, Torre Tagle. The Council of State met, and informed Monteagudo of what had taken place, when he was induced to resign; the Supreme

Delegate politely informing the *Cabildo* that the ex-Minister should be made to answer to the Council of State for the acts of his administration.

This note not satisfying the municipality, the *Cabildo* requested that Monteagudo should at once be placed in arrest till called upon for his defence, which was immediately complied with; but the step was disapproved by the Limeños, who feared that some crafty subterfuge might again place him in authority. The *Cabildo*, therefore, in order to satisfy the people and get rid of the ex-Minister, requested of the Government that he might be put on board ship, and exiled for ever from Peru. This was also acceded to; and, on the anniversary of his arrival in Lima, Monteagudo was sent under escort to Callao, and forthwith taken to sea.

Torre Tagle was unable to cope with the returning spirit of the Limeños, nor did he attempt it, as the army was as much disgusted as were the inhabitants, and would not have raised a hand against them. The liberty of the press returned, and the first use of it was the following picture of the exiled Minister, taken from the Lima newspapers; this would not have been inserted here, except to shew the class of men with whom I had so long to contend.

"Every honourable citizen found in Don Bernardo Monteagudo, (this is the name of the man of whom we speak,) an enemy who at any price would have sacrificed him. How many victims has he not immolated in his one year's ministry! More than eight hundred honourable families have been reduced by him to extreme indigence, and the whole city to misery! Amongst the patriots of Lima, nothing was thought of but where they might find an asylum in a foreign land. Without agriculture, commerce, industry, personal security, property, and laws, what is society here but a scene of the most afflicting torments?

"The religion of our forefathers suffered an equal persecution in its ministers and its temples; these were deprived of their riches, not for the service of our country, but for the reward of *espionage*, and to deceive us with useless trickeries. The satellites of this bandit were equally despotic with himself, and committed under his protection the most horrid crimes. This is not a proper place in which to insert the baseness with which he abused the delicacy and weakness of females. Fathers of families * * * *. Every man was intimidated. Every feeling man wept, because all were the victims of the caprice of this insolent upstart, who made an ostentation of atheism and ferocity.

"It is impossible to recapitulate his actions. Volumes would be necessary to shew the world the arbitrary crimes of this atrocious individual. It would appear that for the commission of so many offences he must have had some cause that impelled him, for they could not possibly be the effect of ignorance. It was impossible to believe that by insulting and ruining every one, plundering our property, despising the ingenuity and talents of the Peruvians, and endeavouring to introduce anarchy, he could be longer tolerated in this capital. Was the reduction of Peru to the most degrading slavery, the means to make us or even himself happy?" &c. &c. &c.

The reader can—from what has been narrated in these pages,—form pretty correct opinions upon the majority of the enormities which drove Monteagudo into exile. Of his private character I have always foreborn to speak, as considering it a thing apart from official acts—but as the Limeños themselves have forcibly alluded to it, I can say that in no respect can their allegations be called in question.

The opinion of the roused Limeños, that for Monteagudo's plunders, insults, and cruelties, there "must have been an impelling cause," is correct, though it is rather surprising that they should not have more justly estimated that cause. The vast amount of silver and gold which I spared in the *Sacramento* at Ancon, as being the property of the Protector, shews the gulf which swallowed up his plunder of the inhabitants. The costly extravagance of the Government—amidst which the degraded Minister's ostentation was even more conspicuous than that of the Protector himself—could have had no other source but plunder, for of legitimate revenue there was scarcely enough to carry on the expenses of the Government—certainly none for luxurious ostentation; which, nevertheless, emulated that of the Roman Empire in its worst period—but without the "*panem et circenses.*"

The "impelling cause" was the Protector himself. Ambitious beyond all bounds, but with a capacity singularly incommensurate with his ambition, he believed that money could accomplish everything. Monteagudo supplied this literally by plunder and cruelty, whilst San Martin recklessly flung it away in ostentation and bribes. In return for the means of prodigality, the Minister was permitted to carry on the Government just as he chose, the Protector meanwhile indulging in the "*otium cum dignitate*" at his country palace near La Legua—his physical powers prostrated by opium and brandy, to which he was a slave, whilst his mental faculties day by day became more torpid from the same debilitating influence. This was well known to me, and alluded to in my letter to him of August 7th, 1821, in which I adjured him to banish his advisers and act as became his position. I now mention these things, not to cast a slur on San Martin, but for the opposite purpose of averting undue reproach, though my bitter enemy. The enormities committed in his name were for the most part not his, but Monteagudo's; for, to paraphrase the saying of a French wit, "San Martin reigned, but his Minister "governed." Duplicity and cunning were San Martin's great instruments when he was not too indolent to wield them; and while he was wrapped in ease, his Minister superadded to these qualities all the cruelty and ferocity which sometimes converts a ruler into a monster, as the Limeños very appropriately designate him. San Martin was not innately cruel, though, as in the execution of the Carreras, he did not hesitate to sacrifice men of far greater patriotism and ability than himself, regarding them as rivals; but he would not, as Monteagudo did, have endeavoured to tempt me ashore to the house of Torre Tagle, for the purpose of assassinating me; nor, failing in this, would he as Monteagudo also did, have liberated a convict for the express purpose of murdering me on board my own ship. At this distance of time these things may be mentioned, as there can be no delicacy in thus alluding to Monteagudo, who, having lived the life of a tyrant, died the death of a dog; for having sometime afterwards imprudently returned to the Peruvian capital, he was set upon and killed in the streets by the enraged Limeños.

This bad commencement of the Peruvian Government subsequently entailed on the country years of misery and civil war, from intestine feuds and party strife—the natural results of the early abuse which unhappily inaugurated its liberation. No such features have been exhibited in Chili, where the maritime force under my command at once and for ever annihilated the power of Spain, leaving to the mother country neither adherents nor defenders, so that all men agreed to consolidate the liberty which had been achieved. The same good results followed my expulsion of the Portuguese fleets and army from Brazil, where, whatever may have been the contentions of the parties into which the country was divided, the empire has ever since been preserved from those revolutions which invariably characterise states based at the outset upon virulent contentions. In Peru, the liberty which had been promised was trodden under foot by the myrmidons of San Martin, so that a portion of the people, and that the most influential, would gladly have exchanged the degradation of their country for a return to Spanish rule, and this was afterwards very nearly achieved. Another portion, dreading the Spaniards, invited Bolivar to free them from the despotism to which, in the name of liberty, they had been subjected. A third party sighed for independence, as they originally hoped it would have been established. The community became thus divided in object, and, as a consequence, in strength; being in constant danger of the oppressor, and in even more danger from its own intestine dissensions; which have continued to this day, not in Peru only, but in the majority of the South American States, which, having commenced their career in the midst of private feud and public dissension, have never been able to shake off either the one or the other monuments of their own incipient weakness.

The intelligence of Monteagudo's forced exile was received at Valparaiso on the 21st of September; and if this excited the surprise of the Chilians, still greater must have been their astonishment when, on the 12th of October, General San Martin himself arrived at Valparaiso, a fugitive from his short-lived splendour, amidst the desolation of despotism.

The story of this event is brief, but instructive. Having met Bolivar, as previously agreed upon, the Liberator, in place of entering upon any mutual arrangement, bitterly taunted San Martin with the folly and cruelty of his conduct towards the Limeños; to such an extent, indeed, that the latter, fearing designs upon his person, precipitately left Guayaquil, and returned to Callao shortly after the expulsion of Monteagudo. Finding what had taken place, he remained on board his vessel, issuing vain threats against all who had been concerned in exiling his minister, and insisting on his immediate recal and reinstatement. A congress had however, by this time been appointed, with Xavier de Luna Pizarro as its head, so the remonstrances of the Protector were unheeded. After some time spent in useless recrimination, he made a virtue of necessity, and sent in his abdication of the Protectorate, returning, as has been said, to Chili.

One of the first acts of the Peruvian Congress, after his abdication, was to address to me the following vote of thanks, not only marking my services in the liberation of their country, but denouncing San Martin as a military despot:—

Resolution of thanks to Lord Cochrane by the Sovereign Congress of Peru.

The Sovereign Constituent Congress of Peru, in consideration of the services rendered to Peruvian liberty by Lord Cochrane, by whose talent, worth, and bravery, the Pacific Ocean has been liberated from the insults of enemies, and the standard of liberty has been planted on the shores of the South,

HAS RESOLVED,—

That the Supreme Junta, on behalf of the Nation, shall offer to Lord Cochrane, Admiral of the Chilian squadron, its most expressive sentiments of gratitude for his hazardous exploits on behalf of Peru, hitherto under the tyranny of military despotism, but now the arbiter of its own fate.

This resolution being communicated to the Supreme Junta, they will do that which is necessary for its fulfilment, by ordering it to be printed, published, and circulated.

Given in the Hall of Congress, at Lima, September 27th, 1822.

XAVIER DE LUNA PIZARRO, President.
JOSE SANCHEZ CARRION, Deputy and Secretary.
FRANCISCO XAVIER MARIATIQUE, Deputy and Secretary.

In fulfilment of the preceding Resolution, we direct the same to be executed.

JOSE DE LA MAR,
FELIPE ANTO. ALVARADO,
EL CONDE DE VISTA FLORIDA.

By order of His Excellency,
FRANCISCO VALDIVIESO.

San Martin had, however, played his cards so cunningly, that, in order to be well rid of him, the

Peruvian congress had been induced to give him a pension of 20,000 dollars per annum, whilst nothing but thanks were awarded to me, both for liberating their country and for freeing them from military despotism! notwithstanding that the new Peruvian Government was in possession of our prizes, the *Prueba* and *Venganza*, the latter only to be given up by paying 40,000 dollars to the Chilian squadron, which at its own cost had run it down in Guayaquil—these sums, no less than the value of the other frigate, being, in common honesty, due from Peru to the Chilian squadron to this day. To have thanked me so warmly as the exclusive instrument of their independence and deliverance from military tyranny—yet to have rewarded the tyrant and not myself in any form beyond the acknowledgment of my services, is a circumstance to which the Peruvian Government of the present day cannot look back with satisfaction; the less so as Chili has, after the lapse of thirty years, partially atoned for the ingratitude of a former Government in availing itself of my aid, without a shilling in the way of recompense, though I had supported its squadron by my own exertions, with comparatively no expense to the Government, during the whole period that I held the command.

To add to this palpable injustice, the Peruvian Congress distributed 500,000 dollars amongst twenty general and field officers of the army; but the officers of the squadron, whose prowess had freed the Pacific of the enemy, and by the admission of the Congress itself Peru also—were not only excluded from the Peruvian bounty, but were denied the prize-money which they had won and generously given up to the temporary exigencies of Chili. Such a monstrous perversion of justice and even common honesty, never before reflected discredit on a state. But more of this hereafter.

It having been circulated in Lima that San Martin had secreted a quantity of gold in the *Puyrredon*, steps were taken to verify the rumour, on which, at midnight on the 20th of September, he ordered the Captain to get under weigh, though the vessel was not half manned, and had scarcely any water on board. He then went to Ancon, and despatched a messenger to Lima, on whose return, he ordered the Captain instantly to weigh anchor and proceed to Valparaiso, where on his arrival, it was given out that an attack of rheumatism compelled him to have resource to the baths of Cauquenes.

On the arrival of the Ex-protector, two *aides-de-camp* were sent by Zenteno to compliment him, and his flag was regularly saluted, the Governor of Valparaiso's carriage being sent to convey him to the Government house. Yet shortly before, this very Governor of Valparaiso had rightly branded those who abandoned the Chilian flag for that of Peru, as "deserters;" but now he received the man who had not only first set the example, but had also induced others to desert—with the honours of a Sovereign Prince! The patriots were eager that I should arrest General San Martin, and there were those in power who would not have complained had I done so, but

I preferred to leave the Government to its own course.

On the following day, General San Martin was forwarded in one of the Director's carriages to Santiago with an escort, the pretence for this mark of honour being fears for his personal safety, in which there might be something of truth, for the Chilian people rightly estimated his past conduct. Without troubling myself about such matters, I immediately forwarded to the Supreme Director the annexed demand, that he should be tried for his desertion and subsequent conduct:—

MOST EXCELLENT SIR,

Don Jose de San Martin, late Commander-in-Chief of the Expeditionary forces from Chili for the liberation of Peru, having this day arrived at Valparaiso, and being now within the jurisdiction of the laws of Chili, I lose no time in acquainting you that, if it be the pleasure of Government to institute an inquiry into the conduct of the said Don Jose de San Martin, I am ready to prove his forcible usurpation of the Supreme Authority of Peru, in violation of the solemn pledge given by his Excellency the Supreme Director of Chili; his attempts to seduce the navy of Chili; his receiving and rewarding deserters from the Chilian service; his unjustifiably placing the frigates, *Prueba* and *Venganza*, under the flag of Peru; with other demonstrations and acts of hostility towards the Republic of Chili.

Given under my hand this 12th day of October, 1822, on board the Chilian ship *O'Higgins*, in the harbour of Valparaiso.

(Signed) COCHRANE.

In place of my demand being complied with, San Martin was honoured by having the palace appointed as his residence, whilst every mark of public attention was paid him by the Ministry, the object being no other than to insult me, both as regarded the countenance given to him in the face of my demand for his trial, and the infamous accusations which he had made against me, but which he did not dare to sustain.

The passive acquiescence of the Supreme Director in the treachery of his advisers caused an amount of popular discontent which ended in his exile also; both Chilenos and Spaniards revolting at the idea of San Martin being thus publicly honoured. To see the Supreme Director parade himself as the friend and ally of such a man, was more than the patriot spirit could bear, and the voice of dissatisfaction was loud in every direction. By the partisans of San Martin this was attributed to the squadron; and at his instigation, as was generally believed, troops were sent to Valparaiso for the purpose of overawing it. I was cautioned to be on my guard against personal seizure or assault, as had been attempted in Peru, but did not place sufficient reliance on the courage of my opponents to adopt any steps evincing doubt of the Chilian people, who were well disposed to me.

On the 21st of November there occurred an earthquake, which completely destroyed the town of Valparaiso, so that scarcely a house remained habitable; the people rushing to the hills or to the ships in the harbour. On the first shocks, knowing that terrible disasters would ensue, I went on shore to restore what order could be maintained amongst the terrified people, and met with the Supreme Director, who had narrowly escaped with his life when hurrying out of his house. It being impossible to render the unhappy townspeople any service, I paid His Excellency every possible attention, even though I had reason to believe that his visit was unfriendly to me, he being falsely persuaded that my incessant demands for the payment of the squadron was an act of hostility to himself, instead of a measure of justice to the officers and men.

Finding me determined, after what had occurred, to procure the payment of the squadron, the now tottering Government gave in, and thus far decided on doing justice; but even in this—as I had reason to believe—the counsels of San Martin induced them to adopt a plan of making the payments ashore, and paying the men and petty officers first—after which, they were to be allowed a furlough of four months. As this plan was palpably meant to unman the squadron, and thus place the officers and myself at the mercy of the intriguers, I would not suffer it to be carried into effect, the men were therefore paid on board their respective ships.

A new system of annoyance was hereupon practised towards me by Zenteno, who had again assumed the office of Minister of Marine. From the neglect to repair the ships—which were left in the same wretched condition as when they returned from Peru and Mexico—the *Independencia* was alone seaworthy; and was sent to sea by Zenteno without even the formality of transmitting the requisite orders through me.

But a crisis was now at hand. The insult offered to General Freire, by sending Santa Cruz to supersede him, will be fresh in the reader's recollection. Soon after this the Provincial Convention of Conception met, and passed a vote of censure upon the Council of Government at Santiago, for re-electing General O'Higgins as Supreme Director after his resignation—an act which it considered illegal, as no such power was vested in the Ministry—and it became known that General Freire was about to march with the troops under his command to enforce these views. On the 17th, General Freire had advanced his troops as far as Talca, and a division of the army at Santiago was ordered to be in readiness to meet him. The marines belonging to the squadron, under the command of Major Hind, were also ordered to reinforce the Director's troops.

I was at this time at my country residence at Quintero, but learning what was going on, I immediately went to Valparaiso and resumed the command of the squadron, to which I found that orders had been issued at variance with the arrangements which had been entered into in regard to the prize-money due to the officers and men—the *Galvarino*, which was pledged to be sold for that purpose, being under orders for sea, to convey San Martin to some place of safety, for, not anticipating the disorganisation which he found in Chili, he was afraid of falling into the hands of General Freire, from whom he would doubtless have experienced the full amount of justice which his conduct deserved. The squadron in my absence had, however, taken the matter into its own hands, by placing the *Lautaro*, with her guns loaded, in a position to sink the *Galvarino* if she attempted to move. The forts on shore had also loaded their guns for retaliation, though of these the squadron would have made short work.

No sooner had I restored order, by resuming the command, than I received from General Freire the subjoined letter, which no longer left me in doubt of his intentions:—

Conception, Dec. 18th, 1822.

MY LORD,

The province under my command being tired of suffering the effects of a corrupted administration, which has reduced the Republic to a state of greater degradation than that under which it was labouring when it made the first struggle to obtain its liberty; and when, by means of an illegitimately-created convention, without the will of the people, they have traced the plans of enslaving them, by constituting them as the patrimony of an ambitious despot, whilst, in order to ensure him the command, they have trodden under foot the imprescriptible right of the citizens, exiling them in the most arbitrary manner from their native country.

Nothing now remains for us but heroically to resolve that we will place the fruit of eleven years of painful sacrifices in the way of saving it; to which effect I have deposited in the hands of its legal representatives who are united in this city the authority that I have hitherto exercised; but notwithstanding my want of merit, and sincere renouncement, the constituent power has deigned to place upon my weak shoulders this enormous weight, by again depositing the civil and military command in my person, which the adjoining resolution I have the honour of remitting will explain to your Lordship.

God preserve your Lordship many years.

(Signed) RAMON FREIRE.

In short, a revolution to depose the Supreme Director had commenced, and General Freire, supported by the inhabitants of Conception and Coquimbo, was in arms to effect it. With this revolution I was determined to have nothing to do, because, as a foreigner, it was not desirable for me to become a party to any faction, though it was evident that the authority of General O'Higgins would shortly be at an end.

Regarding General Freire's letter as an indirect request to me to aid him in deposing General O'Higgins, I did not even reply to it. On the 20th of September he made the following direct overture to me to join in the revolution:—

Conception, Nov. 20th, 1852.

MY BEST AND MOST DISTINGUISHED FRIEND,

The time has arrived when circumstances and the country require the protection of those who generously and judiciously know how to maintain its sacred rights. Let us withdraw the curtain from the scene which trifles with the interests of the Republic, leading it to inevitable ruin. Its deplorable state is public and notorious. There is not a man who is unacquainted with it, and who does not bewail the prospective loss of its independence, with a thraldom also in view more grievous than the Spanish yoke.

The self-assumed powers of the Government, the restrictions on commerce, and, above all, the constitution recently promulgated, place the ambitious views of the Chief Magistrate and the corruption of his Ministers in a clear light. Every act proves that the intentions of the Supreme Director have undergone a change. Fortune, which has hitherto favoured him, has given a new turn to his ambition, as if the proposal of a crown could no longer be resisted—all the measures pursued throughout the state leading to that end. It is grievous to see laurels thus stained in the grasp of one who so gloriously obtained them. It is, however, needless to trespass on you with further reflections on these occurrences, as your judgment cannot fail to be formed both on the facts and their consequences. Let us therefore touch on other subjects.

Permit me, without offence to your delicacy, to make some reflections on subjects equally public and notorious.

You enjoyed honours, rank, and fortune, amidst a people the most distinguished in Europe. You generously abandoned ease and comfort in order to aid in the attainment of our liberty, and you have been the chief instrument which has enabled us to achieve it. The whole world is acquainted with your gallant efforts to abolish tyranny and give liberty to South America. The people of this Republic are full of the most lively gratitude, and are grieved that it is not in their power to give you an effectual proof of their deep attachment. This Province, holding valour and merit in estimation, idolizes you, whilst it holds in abhorrence and detestation the tyrant "Liberator of Peru!" who has stained our soil with tears of blood shed for his pretended services. Chacabuco would have terminated the war throughout the Republic, had it not been deemed necessary to foster its continuance for the interests of this individual.

This Province (Conception) having been completely sacrificed, has arrived at the point of exasperation. Its inhabitants are unanimously determined on a change and a reform of Government, and declare that in Arauco they will breathe the air of liberty, and that they will perish in the field of battle to obtain it. This is the decision universally adopted without exception. This is the determination of the gallant troops which I have the honour to command, and of their valiant officers, and is moreover sanctioned by the holy orders of the clergy.

Compromised by these declarations, what am I to reply to them? Must I profess my sympathy and accordance of opinion with them, and admit to you, that, though yesterday a private citizen, with a heart burning to be freed from fetters, *I must to-day gird on the sword*. May Heaven favour my lot in the absence of personal merit! To my country I owe my life and the position I hold—from having contributed to its welfare—can I then neglect the duty that I owe to it? No, my dear friend, far be that course from me.

Freire has sworn to live or perish for the liberty of his native country, and he now repeats that solemn oath, grieved at the cause which compels him to renew it, but trusting in the hope that God will avert the effusion of blood in the accomplishment of the object.

I know that you are deeply interested in securing the liberty of Chili, for which you have so gloriously contended. I know you will deeply feel the privation of hope--for neither in your generous heart, nor in mine, can such events be received with indifference. Let us then pursue a course in uniformity with the glory of Chili, and the opinion of the world. Let us listen to the voice of the country, which calls us to avert evils when repose might have been anticipated. I count, together with the whole Province, on your co-operation to avert mischief and advance the good of the country.

Act as you judge best, but for the promotion of that object, the moment has arrived for action. Answer me with promptitude and frankness. Let us have the satisfaction of applying effective remedies to the evils which afflict the country, zealously and disinterestedly for the good of the Republic, and without personal views.

I hold the residence of San Martin in any part of Chili as suspicious and dangerous. Let him be off to make some other quarter happy, where he can sell his protection to the ill-fated inhabitants.

I hope my intentions meet your approbation, and will be seconded by the officers of the squadron.

I trust you will receive this as the sincerest proof that I can give of the high consideration with which I am

Your most faithful and unchangeable Friend,

RAMON FREIRE.

To Vice-Adm. LORD COCHRANE,
Commanding the squadron of Chili.

I did not reply with promptitude, for I felt that it was no part of my mission to mingle in civil warfare. This letter, however, corroborated my opinion as to the fact of San Martin's influence over the Supreme Director, and the recent coolness in his conduct towards me. If General Freire's information was correct, there was evidently a desire to restore San Martin to the Empire of Peru! when possession could be got of the squadron, and he in return had deluded General O'Higgins into the plot by promise of support. Whether this was so in reality is problematical, but there is General Freire's letter, for the first time published, and the Chilian people can thence draw their own conclusions.

Fortunately an occurrence took place, which relieved me from the dilemma in which I was placed, as will be narrated in the succeeding chapter.

CHAPTER XII.

THE SQUADRON TAKEN FROM ME—I ACCEPT INVITATION FROM BRAZIL—LETTER TO THE SUPREME DIRECTOR—SAN MARTIN QUITS CHILI—HIS PRUDENCE—OPINION OF HIS AIDE-DE-CAMP—MINISTERIAL NEGLECT—PERMISSION TO QUIT CHILI—LETTER TO GENERAL FREIRE—FOR THE FIRST TIME MADE PUBLIC—LETTER TO THE CAPTAINS AND OFFICERS—TO THE CHILIAN PEOPLE—TO THE FOREIGN MERCHANTS—TO THE PRESIDENT OF PERU—SAN MARTIN ACTUATED BY REVENGE—THIS SHEWN FROM HIS LETTERS.

THE event alluded to in the last chapter was the arrival of an express from the Brazilian *Charge d'Affaires* at Buenos Ayres, with a request from the Imperial Court at Rio de Janeiro, to the effect that, as by my exertions the Spaniards had now been driven from the Pacific, I would accept the command of the Brazilian navy, for the purpose of expelling the Portuguese, who still maintained their hold upon the greater portion of that side of the South American Continent. As acquiescence in this offer would relieve me from the embarrassing situation in which I was placed in Chili, I began seriously to consider the expediency of accepting it.

At this juncture Freire commenced his march towards the capital, at the same time sending Captain Casey to Valparaiso with an armed merchantman, to ascertain the effect of his last letter to me. Without coming to an anchor, Captain Casey sent a boat on board the *O'Higgins* to ascertain my sentiments, but meeting with a refusal to acquiesce in the revolution, he again sailed. The ministers, however, judging me by themselves, and suspecting that I was about to become a party to General Freire's designs, began to withdraw the ships from my command, on the pretence of repairs or converting them into store-ships, several being thus taken from the squadron. I was also ordered to place the *O'Higgins* and *Valdivia* under the charge of the Commandant of Marine, to be repaired, and to make a store-ship of the *Lautaro*, and being thus deprived of the slightest authority over them, I was now considered as a sort of state prisoner; but in pursuing this course, the little schooner *Montezuma*, which I had rescued from Peru, had been overlooked, and on board of her I hoisted my flag.

The *Galvarino* was now sent to sea without my permission, and without an Englishman in her. The *Lautaro*, the pretended store-ship, was also being got ready for sea, when I addressed the following note to Captain Worcester, who commanded her:—

MEMO,

Having received directions from the Supreme Government to cause the *Lautaro* to be placed as a store-ship, under the command of the Governor, and observing that the said order is in process of violation by the preparations making for sea; you are hereby required and directed to hoist my flag, and obey all such orders as you shall receive from me on the service of the State.

Given under my hand this 8th day of January, 1823, on board the *Montezuma*.

COCHRANE.

Tired of this heartless ingratitude, and disgusted with the suspicion that I was about to join General

Freire with the squadron—an idea which could only have arisen from the expectation that I should thus resent the injuries inflicted on me—I resolved to accept the invitation from His Majesty the Emperor of Brazil, leaving all which the Chilian Government owed me to the honour of a juster and more enlightened administration. Accordingly I addressed to the Supreme Director the following letter:—

Valparaiso, Jan. 8, 1822.

MOST EXCELLENT SIR,

The difficulties which I have experienced in accomplishing the naval enterprizes successfully achieved during the period of my command as Admiral of Chili, have not been effected without responsibility such as I would scarcely again undertake, not because I would hesitate to make any personal sacrifice in a cause of so much interest, but because even these favourable results have led to the total alienation of the sympathies of meritorious officers, —whose co-operation was indispensable,—in consequence of the conduct of the Government.

That which has made most impression on their minds has been, not the privations they have suffered, nor the withholding of their pay and other dues, but the absence of any public acknowledgment by the Government of the honours and distinctions promised for their fidelity and constancy to Chili; especially at a time when no temptation was withheld that could induce them to abandon the cause of Chili for the service of the Protector of Peru; even since that time, though there was no want of means or knowledge of facts on the part of the Chilian Government, it has submitted itself to the influence of the agents of an individual whose power having ceased in Peru, has been again resumed in Chili.

The effect of this on me is so keenly sensible that I cannot trust myself in words to express my personal feelings. Desiring, as I do, to extenuate rather than accuse, nothing shall enter into a narrative of these circumstances which is not capable of undeniable proof.

Whatever I have recommended or asked for the good of the naval service has been scouted or denied, though acquiescence would have placed Chili in the first rank of maritime States in this quarter of the globe. My requisitions and suggestions were founded on the practice of the first naval service in the world—that of England; they have, however, met with no consideration, as though their object had been directed to my own personal benefit.

Until now I have never eaten the bread of idleness. I cannot reconcile to my mind a state of inactivity which might even now impose upon the Chilian Republic an annual pension for past services; especially as an Admiral of Peru is actually in command of a portion of the Chilian squadron, whilst other vessels are sent to sea without the orders under which they act being communicated to me, and are despatched by the Supreme Government through the instrumentality of the Governor of Valparaiso (Zenteno.) I mention these circumstances incidentally as having confirmed me in the resolution to withdraw myself from Chili for a time; asking nothing for myself during my absence; whilst as regards the sums owing to me, I forbear to press for their payment till the Government shall be more freed from its difficulties. I have complied with all that my public duty demanded, and if I have not been able to accomplish more, the deficiency has arisen from circumstances beyond my control—at any rate, having the world still before me, I hope to prove that it is not owing to me.

I have received proposals from Mexico, from Brazil, and from an European state, but have not as yet accepted any of these offers. Nevertheless, the active habits of my life do not permit me to refuse my services to those labouring under oppression, as Chili was before the annihilation of the Spanish naval force in the Pacific. In this I am prepared to justify whatever course I may pursue. In thus taking leave of Chili, I do so with sentiments of deep regret that I have not been suffered to be more useful to the cause of liberty, and that I am compelled to separate myself from individuals with whom I hoped to have lived for a long period, without violating such sentiments of honour as, were they broken, would render me odious to myself and despicable in their eyes.

Until this day I have abstained from pressing upon your Excellency's attention my reply to the infamous accusations presented against me by the agents of San Martin—knowing that your Excellency had more urgent objects to attend to. Nevertheless, I now beg your Excellency's consideration of this matter, in order that—as has been the case in Peru—these falsehoods may be rendered manifest—as well as the despicable character of that man who falsely arrogated to himself the attributes of a General and a Legislator, though destitute of courage or legislative knowledge—the substitution for which was duplicity and cunning.

(Signed) COCHRANE.

Foiled in getting one of the ships of the squadron, wherein to escape from the impending storm, San Martin remained in Santiago till the beginning of January, 1823, when finding matters in Chili becoming dangerous to his safety, he crossed the Cordillera to Mendoza, and from thence went to Europe to avoid reprobation in retirement.

Throughout this narrative I have been careful that San Martin's proceedings should be shown from his own acts and letters, there not being in this volume one which has not been published in the gazettes of Chili and Peru, or of which the originals are not now in my possession. Of the latter, I could communicate San Martin's letters to me by dozens, and had I so far trespassed on the patience of the reader, his acts would have appeared in a yet more invidious light. What have been given are strictly relative to public transactions, and belong to the people of Chili as part of their national history, which, rather than any defence of my own conduct—which was never brought in question by the Chilian Government—is my chief reason for now making them public.

There may be, however, some who think that I have mistaken General San Martin's *prudence* in not approaching Lima when every advantage was before him—for a worse quality, which until my letter to the Supreme Director O'Higgins, just quoted, I had never publicly attributed to him, though, in the estimation of every officer of the army and squadron, richly deserving it. It will be in the recollection of the reader, that instead of marching on Lima, he wasted nearly two months at Haura, and that from the pestilential character of the climate, a fearful amount of sickness amongst the troops was the consequence. I will here give a letter to me from his *Aide-de-camp* Paroissien, who was subsequently employed by San Martin to promulgate his infamous accusations against me, when he had no longer any hope of securing my co-operation; premising that in my ardour to get the army at once to Lima, and unsuspicious at that time of San Martin's secret designs, I had laid Paroissien a wager that by a given day we should be in the Peruvian capital; the *Aide-de-camp* being a better judge of his chief than I was, accepted the wager, and as a matter of course, won it.

Haura, 10 April, 1821.

My dear Lord,

With what pleasure would I lose twenty bets like that which I have unfortunately won of you, if you could but tell me that I should be *the loser*. Nay more, I will lay you the same wager now, that in another three weeks we shall not get to the little room over the great entrance of the Palaccio. I have received this afternoon a fine fat turtle; and egad, if I thought I *should lose*, I would fatten him up all the more—but, alas! I fear we shall have to calipee and calipash it in Haura; however, the bustle that has lately prevailed seems to indicate some movement; and those of us who are well, are ready to march at an hour's notice—but of course you are infinitely better acquainted with these things than I am. Still, I think that *were we more active and enterprising, a great deal might be done, particularly with our cavalry—whose swords for want of use are getting rusty. If we do not make a push now, God knows when we shall do so.*

* * * * * * *

The General appears desirous of striking a blow against Baldez. It may be right—and I dare say it is; *but I should rather we had a touch against the Capital.* Thank God we are about to do something.

Yours very truly,

PAROISSIEN.

The reader will have gathered from the narrative, that San Martin struck no blow anywhere, even hesitating to enter Lima when no blow was required to be struck. His *Aide-de-camp's* view of the matter can hardly be mistaken.

It is not a little remarkable, that in a letter addressed to the Supreme Director, before sailing on the liberating expedition to Peru, I should have, from the first, correctly estimated San Martin's character in persisting not to make any military movement without an unnecessary force to ensure his personal safety, though our recent victory at Valdivia with a force of 350 men only, could not have given him any very great idea of the difficulties to be encountered. As this letter was omitted in its place, I will here transcribe it.

May 4, 1820.

MOST EXCELLENT SIR,

Finding that all the measures proposed in the expedition to Peru are made public—that all that is decided on to-day is contradicted to-morrow—that no system is followed, either in regard to naval or state matters, which can promote your interest—that mischievous delays of all kinds are opposed to the success of an enterprise, which your Excellency is desirous of promoting—that the expedition of 2,000 men (abundantly sufficient) was not to be delayed on any pretence, but that it has been delayed in order to increase it to 4,000—and that even now it is kept back, in order to ascertain the position and force of the enemy at Callao, of which we know just as much now as we should when the *Montezuma* may return, some forty days hence, after an investigation to no purpose—in short, finding that everthing stipulated and agreed upon has been deviated from. I am desirous to give up the command of the squadron to whoever may enjoy the confidence of your Excellency; which act will, I hope, add to your tranquillity, by relieving you from my opinions in regard to what ought to be done, but has not been done—and to that which could be effected, but has not even been attempted.

I have abstained from sending the *Montezuma* on a meaningless voyage of forty days to Callao, till I receive your Excellency's definitive commands—considering that the despatch of that vessel is not only useless, but a pretext for delay, and is calculated to frustrate all that your Excellency has in contemplation. Would that you could yourself note the palpable treachery which prevents anything of importance being collected for the expedition—I say palpable treason—as not a single article necessary has yet been procured.

Can your Excellency believe, that only one vessel is in the hands of the contractor; and even she is not prepared for sea? Will you believe that the only provisions that the contractor's agent has in hand is twenty-one days' rations of bread, and six days' of salt meat, whilst to my query whether he had any *charqui* ready, his reply was, "There is plenty in the country." Will your Excellence believe that there are only 120 water casks ready for 4,000 troops and the crews of the squadron?

Your Excellency may be assured that only your interest and that of the State could induce me to utter these opinions; but, in order to convince you that I have no wish to abandon the service, if my continuance in it can be of any use—my only wish being to avoid becoming the butt of disasters after their occurrence—I now offer to give up the command of the squadron, and to accept in lieu thereof, the command of the four armed prizes taken by the O'Higgins in the last cruise, and with 1,000 troops selected by myself, to accomplish all that is expected from the 4,000 troops and the squadron; the former being a manageable force, capable of defeating all the defensive measures of the enemy—whilst the latter, solely under military command, will not only be unmanageable for desultory operations, but, from its unhandiness, will paralyse naval movements.

Lastly, I must repeat to your Excellency that the inviolable secresy of determinations and the rapidity of operations under present circumstances, are the only security for the prosperity of the Chilian Government and the hoped-for liberty of Peru. If those are to be set at nought, I hereby again place at your Excellency's disposal the commission with which I have been honoured, in order that you may be convinced of my having no other object than to serve your Excellency in every way compatible with honour.

I have the honour, &c.

To his Excellency the Supreme Director, COCHRANE.
&c. &c.

To return to my, now in reality, approaching departure from Chili. The request to be permitted to retire for a time from the service, was promptly complied with, and no doubt gladly so, from the belief of the Government that I might otherwise ally myself with General Freire, though, that I had no such intention, the annexed reply to his communications—made shortly after I had left Chili, and when he had succeeded in overthrowing the Government of General O'Higgins—will shew.

Bahia, June 21, 1823.

My respected Friend,

It would give me great pleasure to learn that the change which has been effected in the Government of Chili proves alike conducive to your happiness and to the interests of the State. For my own part—like yourself—I suffered so long and so much, that I could not bear the neglect and double dealing of those in power any longer, but adopted other means of freeing myself from an unpleasant situation.

Not being under those imperious obligations which, as a native Chileno, rendered it incumbent on you to rescue your country from the mischiefs with which it was assailed by the scandalous measures of some of those who were unhappily in the confidence of the late Supreme Director, I could not accept your offers. My heart was with you in the measures you adopted for their removal; and my hand was only restrained by a conviction that my interference, as a foreigner, in the internal affairs of the State, would not only have been improper in itself, but would have tended to shake that confidence in my undeviating rectitude which it was my ambition that the people of Chili should ever justly entertain. Indeed, before I was favoured with your communications, I had resolved to leave the country, at least for a time, and return to England, but accident so ordered it that at the very moment I was preparing to execute this intention, I received an offer from the Emperor of Brazil to command his navy, and conditionally accepted it.

Brazil has one great advantage over other South American States, it is free from all question as to the authority of its Chief, who has nothing to fear from the rivalry to which those elevated to power are so frequently subject. I pray God that this may not be your case. The command of the army will enable you to accomplish great things without jealousy, but the possession of the Supreme power of the State will hardly fail to excite the envy of the selfish and ambitious to a degree that may operate to the destruction of your expectations of doing good, and to the injury of the cause in which you have embarked.

Permit me to add my opinion, that whoever may possess the Supreme authority in Chili—*until after the present generation, educated as it has been under the Spanish colonial yoke, shall have passed away*, will have to contend with so much error, and so many prejudices, as to be disappointed in his utmost endeavours to pursue steadily the course best calculated to promote the freedom and happiness of the people. I admire the middle and lower classes of Chili, but I have ever found the Senate, the Ministers, and the Convention, actuated by the narrowest policy, which led them to adopt the worst measures. It is my earnest wish that you may find better men to co-operate with you; if so, you may be fortunate, and may succeed in what you have most at heart—the promotion of your country's good.

Believe me that I am—with gratitude for the disinterested and generous manner in which you have always acted towards me—your unshaken and faithful friend,

COCHRANE.

To His Excellency Don Ramon Freire,
Supreme Director of Chili, &c.

This letter has never before seen the light, and I here make it public, in order to show that the Government of General O'Higgins had nothing to fear, even from its ingratitude to me; my only desire being to escape from it, even at the cost of leaving behind the whole amount due to my services, none of which was conceded.

Previous to my departure, I addressed the following letter to the squadron:—

To the Captains and Officers generally of the Chilian Navy,

Gentlemen,

As I am now about to take my leave of you, at least for a time, I cannot refrain from expressing my satisfaction at the cheerful manner in which the service has been carried on, the unanimity which has prevailed, and the zeal which, on all trying occasions, you have shown. These have compensated me for the difficulties with which I have had to contend, and which I am confident have been such as never before presented themselves in any service. Your patience and perseverance under privations of all kinds were such as Chili had no right to expect, and such as no other country would have demanded, even from its own native subjects. In all maritime states the strictest attention is paid to the necessities of officers and men—regularity of pay and adequate reward for services are deemed necessary as excitements to per severance, and the achievement of effective and heroic exploits—but your exertions and achievements have been made independently of any such inducements.

Gentlemen, by our united exertions, the naval power of the enemy of these seas, though superior to our own, has been annihilated, and the commerce of the Pacific is everywhere carried on in security under the protection of the independent flag of Chili. To me it is highly gratifying to reflect, that these services have not been sullied by any act of illegality or impropriety on your part; and that, while you have asserted the rights of Chili, and maintained and confirmed her independence, you have so conducted yourselves, as uniformly to preserve the strictest harmony and good fellowship with the officers of the ships of war of all neutral states. The services you have rendered to Chili will, however, be better appreciated at a future period, when the passions which now actuate individuals shall have ceased to influence those in power, and when your honourable motives shall no longer be felt as a reproach by those whose selfishness has withheld the reward of your fidelity, and whose jealousy has denied you even the official expression of public approbation.

Gentlemen, the best approbation is that of your own hearts—of that, none can deprive you. However, if it be any satisfaction to you to receive my assurance that your conduct has, on all occasions, merited my warmest applause, I can say with perfect truth that I have great pleasure in rendering you that assurance, and in conveying to you my heartfelt thanks for your uniform cordial and efficient co-operation in the cause in which we have been engaged.

Towards the brave seamen under my command I entertain similar sentiments, which you will oblige me by communicating to them in terms most gratifying to their feelings.

In taking my leave of you and them, I have only to add, that if I have not been able to evince my gratitude so fully as I ought, it has not been owing to any deficiency of zeal, but to circumstances over which I had no control.

I remain, Gentlemen,
Your grateful and faithful friend and servant,

Jan. 18th, 1823. COCHRANE.

On my acceptance of the Brazilian command becoming known, several highly meritorious officers begged to accompany me—giving up, like myself, all present hope of adequate payment for their services. Knowing that in Brazil—as had been the case in Chili—it would be necessary to organize a navy, I gladly complied with the requisition; so that neither then, nor afterwards, did they receive from Chili any recompense for their unparalleled bravery and perseverance in the cause of independence.

To the people of Chili—amongst whom, disgusted with the treatment I had received at home, I had once hoped to spend the remainder of my days in the bosom of my family—I issued the following address:—

Chilenos—My fellow Countrymen!

The common enemy of America has fallen in Chili. Your tricoloured flag waves on the Pacific, secured by your sacrifices. Some internal commotions agitate Chili. It is not my business to investigate their causes, to accelerate or retard their effects; I can only wish that the result may be favourable to the national interest.

Chilenos. You have expelled from your country the enemies of your independence, do not sully the glorious act by encouraging discord and promoting anarchy—that greatest of all evils. Consult the dignity to which your heroism has raised you, and if you must take any step to secure your national liberty—judge for yourselves—act with prudence—and be guided by reason and justice.

It is now four years since the sacred cause of your independence called me to Chili. I assisted you to gain it. I have seen it accomplished. It only remains to preserve it. I leave you for a time, in order not to involve myself in matters foreign to my duties, and for other reasons, concerning which I now remain silent, that I may not encourage party spirit.

CHILENOS. You know that independence is purchased at the point of the bayonet. Know also, that liberty is founded on good faith, and on the laws of honour, and that those who infringe upon these, are your only enemies, amongst whom you will never find

COCHRANE.

Quintero, Jan. 4th, 1823.

On the same day I issued another address to the English and other merchants at Valparaiso, who at the outset had given me every confidence and assistance, but—notwithstanding the protection imparted by the squadron to their legitimate commerce, the minds of some had become alienated because I would not permit illegitimate trading at which the corrupt ministers not only connived, but for their own individual profit, encouraged,—by granting licences to supply the enemy, even to contraband of war. In the subjoined, allusion is made to this matter—

To the Merchants of Valparaiso.

GENTLEMEN,

I cannot quit this country without expressing to you the heartfelt satisfaction which I experience on account of the extension which has been given to your commerce, by laying open to all the trade of these vast provinces, to which Spain formerly asserted an exclusive right. The squadron which maintained the monopoly has disappeared from the face of the ocean, and the flag of Independent South America waves everywhere triumphant, protecting that intercourse between nations which is the source of riches, power, and happiness.

If, for the furtherance of this great object, some restraints were imposed, they were no other than those sanctioned by the practice of all civilized states; and though they may have affected the immediate interests of a few *who were desirous to avail themselves of accidental circumstances presented during the contest*, it is a gratification to know that such interests were only postponed for the general good. Should there, however, be any who conceive themselves aggrieved by my conduct, I have to request them to make known their complaints, in order that I may have an opportunity of particular reply.

I trust that you will do me the justice to believe that I have not determined to withdraw myself from these seas, whilst anything remained within my means to accomplish for your benefit and security.

I have the honour to be, gentlemen,
Your faithful humble servant,

COCHRANE.

Quintero, Chili, Jan. 4, 1823.

Though I remained in Chili a fortnight after the date of this letter, not a complaint of any kind was forwarded from the merchants; indeed, considering the protection which the squadron had afforded to their existing commerce, and the facilities which it had given for extending it, I had no reason to suppose that any complaint would be made.

The above addresses were printed by a lithographic press in my house at Quintero, this being the first introduced into the Pacific States. I had sent for this press from England, together with other social improvements, and a number of agricultural implements, hoping thereby, though at my own expense, to give an impetus to industry in Chili. All this was, however, frustrated, and the mortification was not a little enhanced by the circumstance that, whilst turning printer for the nonce, there lay opposite my house at Quintero one of our best prizes, the *Aguila*, a wreck, tenanted only by shell-fish—she having gone ashore whilst waiting the decision of the Chilian Government, previous to being sold for the benefit of her captors!

As the Chilian Government refused to permit my refutation of San Martin's charges against me in a way as public as they had been promulgated, I addressed the following note to the Peruvian congress, together with a copy of the refutation:—

To His Excellency the President of the Congress of Peru.

Sir,

I have the honour to transmit through you to the Sovereign Congress a copy of a letter addressed by me to Don Jose de San Martin, translations of which I have forwarded to Europe and to North America, to be issued to the world through the press. Mankind will then cease to accuse the Peruvians of ingratitude, and will no longer wonder that an Imperial Crown was withheld from the Protector as the reward of labours in the cause of liberty, but will applaud your resolution to select from amongst yourselves the most enlightened of your citizens—men capable of securing the independence and promoting the prosperity of the State on principles of national freedom under the rule of law.

Be pleased to solicit in my name that the Sovereign Congress may deign to deposit in their archives that letter and the charges against me thereto annexed, which were preferred by Don Jose de San Martin to the Chilian Government relative to my conduct in Peru, in order that a record may remain whereby to judge of facts when the actors shall have passed from this scene. Then the even hand of time shall poise the scale of justice, apportioning to all the due measure of approbation or reproach.

That the acts of the Sovereign Congress and of the Executive Government of Peru may be such as shall call forth the admiration and secure the affections of its people, is the prayer of

Your Excellency's obedient humble Servant,

COCHRANE.

Valparaiso, Dec. 12, 1822.

One word more with regard to these accusations of San Martin. It was not till all his offers to me to abandon my allegiance to Chili, and to join him in his defection had proved unavailing, that he sought to revenge himself by such charges, well knowing that Zenteno and his party in the Chilian ministry would second any chance of injuring me in public estimation from their unabating personal enmity to me, arising from my constant opposition to their selfish measures for private advantage. Into these matters I have no inclination to enter, though possessing abundant materials for disclosing a career of state dishonesty without parallel in the history of Governments.

Up to the time of my last refusal of San Martin's offers, made through Monteagudo, everything was "*couleur de rose*"—with all kinds of declarations that "*my lot should be equal to his own*"—though, thank God, my lot has been of a far different nature. It was within a week of my last refusal that his charges against me were trumped up. I will select one more from his numerous letters now in my possession, to show that nothing but revenge at being disappointed in my co-operation to ensure his personal aggrandisement, could have influenced him to perpetrate such an act of meanness.

Lima, 20 Aug., 1821.

MY ESTEEMED FRIEND,

Your appreciated letter, received yesterday, has convinced me that the frankness of your sentiments is only equalled by the regard you entertain for the public cause—especially as to matters under my charge. I cannot view the counsel and opinions you offer, otherwise than as proof of the zeal you entertain for my interests. Aware of the estimation in which you hold glorious acts, I cannot do otherwise than sympathize with you, as you desire that I shall augment those I have acquired. Without entertaining a doubt that I shall contribute effectually in the field still open to us—*more particularly to you,* I wish that the enterprises in which you evince so much zeal, *did not require so great temerity to carry them out, and such enthusiasm to bring them to a successful result.* Believe me, my Lord, that nothing will make me swerve from the determination that the *lot of Lord Cochrane shall be that of Gen. San Martin.*

I hope that in your correspondence with Sir Thos. Hardy, all difficulties will be smoothed in a manner satisfactory to both. I understand that he is desirous to accord to *our* flag all that justice demands and the policy of England will permit. On these points I confide in your prudence.

Never doubt, my Lord, of the sincere friendship with which I am your affectionate

JOSE DE SAN MARTIN.

It is so utterly incredible that a man entertaining such opinions of me should believe in the charges he afterwards made against me, *with regard to acts occurring long previous to this period*, even to accusing me of " endangering the safety of the squadron from " the first moment of our quitting Valparaiso," that I will not weary the reader's patience in commenting further upon them.

CHAPTER XIII.

FREIRE MARCHES ON VALPARAISO—ELECTED SUPREME DIRECTOR—HE BEGS OF ME TO RETURN—MY REPLY—SUBSEQUENT LETTER TO GENERAL FREIRE.

On the 18th of January, 1823, I hauled down my flag, hoisted in the *Montezuma* schooner—the only vessel which the suspicious jealousy of the Chilian ministers had left me—and sailed for Rio de Janiero in the chartered brig, Colonel Allen, though my brother's steamer, the *Rising Star*—or rather the Chilian Government's steamer, upon which he had a lien for money advanced for its completion and equipment—was lying idle at Valparaiso. Could I have taken this vessel with me to Brazil, on the refusal of Chili to repay the sums which my brother had advanced on the guarantee of its London envoy Alvarez—the Brazilian Government would have eagerly availed itself of an advantage to which the Chilian ministry was insensible: though recently by the exertions of Admiral Simpson, and the more enlightened views of the present Government, Chili is now beginning to appreciate the advantage of a steam marine, which, at the period of her liberation, she so perversely rejected by refusing to honour the comparatively trifling pecuniary engagements of her minister in London. The probable reason why the Chilian Government refused to acknowledge these obligations was—that the war being now ended by the annihilation of the Spanish naval power in the Pacific through the instrumentality of sailing ships alone, there was no necessity for a steam ship of war—the narrow-minded policy of the ministers who have figured in these pages never conceiving that to maintain maritime preponderance is scarcely less difficult than to achieve it. Hence, to get rid of the paltry sum of £.13,000 due—and still due—to my brother for his advances on the ship, she was rejected; the consequence was, that after my departure, the independence of Chili was again placed in jeopardy, whilst Peru was only saved from a Spanish reconquest by the intervention of the Colombian liberator, Bolivar.

Shortly after my departure, the partisans of General Freire, and the enemies of General O'Higgins, having entered into a combination—the former marched on Valparaiso, where the people ardently espoused his cause; so that abandoned by his evil genius, San Martin, and equally so by others who had caused his downfall, the Supreme Director found himself a prisoner in the hands of the very man who had most conduced to his overthrow, viz., Zenteno, in whose charge he was placed on pretence of being made accountable for the expenditure of those who now held him in durance!

The end of this was, a five months' examination of O'Higgins, which resulted in his being permitted to leave the country; General Freire having, meanwhile, been elected to the Supreme Directorate, in the midst of internal dissensions in Chili, and disasters in Peru, where the Spaniards, under Cantarac—emboldened by the pusillanimity of the Protector in permitting them to relieve Callao unmolested, and elated with their decisive victory over a division of his army, as narrated in a previous chapter—had availed themselves of the treasure carried away from Callao in reorganising their forces, which now threatened Lima, and would no doubt have recovered Peru, had not Bolivar, foreseeing the result, sent a division of his army, under General Sucre, to the assistance of the beleaguered city.

In the midst of these embarrassments, the New Government of Chili despatched the following letter to Rio de Janeiro, for the purpose of inducing me to return, and reorganise the navy, the officers and men of which had, as I learned, shortly subsequent to my departure been turned adrift, without any reward whatever for their extraordinary privations and exertions in the cause of independence.

Ministry of Foreign Affairs.

Santiago de Chili, April 11, 1823.

MOST EXCELLENT SIR,

The Representatives of the people of Chili, legally assembled, having elected Don Ramon Freire as Supreme Director of the State, this event has happily terminated the internal movements which agitated the country. The new Government, on entering on its delicate functions, has been impressed with the want of your Excellency to give preponderance to this maritime state, by the imposing aptitude of your Excellency's measures and extraordinary renown, so highly prized by the Chilenos, and dreaded by their enemies.

The loss of the Allied army in Moquegua, where it has been beaten by General Cantarac, has occasioned such an effect on the result of the war, that possibly the capital of Peru may fall into the hands of the enemy in consequence of the ascendancy thus acquired.

In consequence of this event, Chili must give a new impulse to her maritime affairs, especially as an expedition is about to sail from Cadiz, composed of two ships of the line, to restore the Spanish authority in Peru.

Your Excellency, on leaving Chili, promised not to abandon the cause of independence; and Chili—which has ever admired in your Excellency one of its most illustrious protectors—must not therefore be deprived of your services in a time of danger, and your great work thus be left incomplete. These considerations his Excellency desires me to lay before you in the name of the nation, and in his own name, to request that you will return to this State, at least during the period of danger. His Excellency trusts in your generosity and zeal for the cause of humanity, that you will return as speedily as circumstances require, without taking into account fatigue or sacrifices in supporting the cause which you have advocated since its commencement.

Be pleased to accept the expression of my high consideration.

(Signed) MARIANO DE EGANA.

It is almost unnecessary to state that my engagements with Brazil, and the fact that when the invitation to resume the command of the Chilian navy was received, I was blockading the Portuguese fleet in Bahia—rendered it impossible to comply with the request. That a state whose ministers had, by the greatest injustice, compelled me to quit it—should, in so short a period, have thus earnestly entreated me to return and free it from impending disaster, is not more a proof of the peril in which the Government was placed, than of its thorough satisfaction with my conduct as its admiral, and of its anxiety for my renewed assistance.

In reply to the request, I addressed the following letter to the minister:—

MOST EXCELLENT SIR,

I have just been honoured with your letter of April 11th, announcing the elevation of Mareschal Don Ramon Freire to the high dignity of Director of the State of Chili, by acclamation of the people—a choice at which I cordially rejoice, as it has placed in power a patriot and a friend. My sentiments with respect to His Excellency have long been well known to the late Supreme Director, as well as to his Ministers, and I would to God that they had availed themselves of Gen. Freire's able and disinterested services in the expedition to Peru—in which case the affairs of South America would have now worn a different aspect; but the Buenos Ayrean faction, being actuated by ambitious motives and more sordid views, interfered, and rendered abortive those plans which, under Gen. Freire's management, would have brought the war to a speedy and successful termination.

On my quitting Chili, there was no looking to the past without regret, nor to the future without despair, for I had learned by experience what were the views and motives which guided the councils of the State. Believe me, that nothing but a thorough conviction that it was impracticable to render the good people of Chili any further service under existing circumstances, or to live in tranquillity under such a system, could have induced me to remove myself from a country which I had vainly hoped would have afforded me that tranquil asylum which, after the anxieties I had suffered, I felt needful to my repose. My inclinations, too, were decidedly in favor of a residence in Chili, from a feeling of the congeniality which subsisted between my own habits and the manners and customs of the people, those few only excepted who were corrupted by contiguity with the Court, or debased in their minds and practices by that species of Spanish Colonial education which inculcates duplicity as the chief qualification of statesmen in all their dealings, both with individuals and the public.

I now speak more particularly of the persons late in power—excepting, however, the late Supreme Director—who I believe to have been the dupe of their deceit; and I do assure you that nothing would afford me greater pleasure, for the sake of the ingenuous Chilian people, than to find that with a change of Ministers, a change of measures has also taken place, and that the errors of your predecessors, and their consequent fate, shall operate as an effectual caution against a course so destructive.

Point out to me one engagement that has been honourably fulfilled—one military enterprise of which the professed object has not been perverted—or one solemn pledge that has not been forfeited; but my opinions on this want of faith, at various periods of the contest, when everything was fresh in my recollection, are recorded in my correspondence with the Minister of Marine, and more particularly in my private letters to His Excellency, the late Supreme Director, whom I unavailingly warned of all that has happened. My letter also to San Martin, in answer to his accusations—a copy of which was officially transmitted to your predecessor in office—contains a brief abstract of the errors and follies committed in Peru; as my public letters and those documents are, of course, in your possession, I shall abstain from trespassing on your attention with a repetition of facts with which you are acquainted.

Look to my representations on the necessities of the navy, and see how they were relieved! Look to my memorial, proposing to establish a nursery for seamen by encouraging the coasting trade, and compare its principles with the code of Rodriguez, which annihilated both. You will see in this, as in all other cases, that whatever I recommended in regard to the promotion of the good of the marine, was set at naught, or opposed by measures directly the reverse. Look to the orders which I received, and see whether I had more liberty of action than a schoolboy in the execution of his task. Look back into the records of the Minister of Marine's office, and you will find that, while the squadron was nearly reduced to a state of starvation, provisions were actually shipped at Valparaiso, *apparently for the navy, but were consigned to Don Luiz de Cruz, and disposed of in such a way as to reflect eternal reproach and disgrace.* You may probably find also, the copy of an order, the original of which is in my possession, (not rubricated by the Supreme Director) *to permit a vessel laden with corn to enter the blockaded port of Callao at the period of its greatest distress*, and which did enter in my absence, and was sold for an enormous amount; whilst funds could not be found to send even 500 troops on an eight days' voyage from Chili to secure Upper Peru, when the greater part of the country was actually in our possession, and when the minds of the people, afterwards alienated by the base conduct of San Martin, were universally in our favour.

Sir, that which I suffered from anxiety of mind whilst in the Chilian service, I will never again endure for any consideration. To organise new crews—to navigate ships destitute of sails, cordage, provisions, and stores—to secure them in port without anchors and cables, except so far as I could supply these essentials by accidental means, were difficulties sufficiently harassing; but to live amongst officers and men—discontented and mutinous on account of arrears of pay and other numerous privations—to be compelled to incur the responsibility of seizing by force from Peru, funds for their payment, in order to prevent worse consequences to Chili—and then to be exposed to the reproach of one party for such seizure, and the suspicions of another that the sums were not duly applied, though the paybooks and vouchers for every material item were delivered to the Accountant-General—are all circumstances so disagreeable and so disgusting that until I have certain proof that the present Ministers are disposed to act in another manner, I cannot possibly consent to renew my services, where, under such circumstances, they would be wholly unavailing to the true interests of the people. Intrigue and faction might again place me in the predicament in which I found myself previous to my departure from Valparaiso, viz., a cypher and a public burthen; for the ships of war might again be placed in the hands of a Governor Zenteno, for the purpose of exposing me to popular odium, as a person receiving a large salary from the state, for which—without a vessel under my command—no adequate services could be rendered. That this was the intention of the late ministers in withdrawing the ships from my command, on the false pretence of repairing them, there can be no doubt; for whilst every honorary reward was withheld from me, they refused to accept the remission which I offered of 4,000 dollars from my annual pay—treating me at the same time with every neglect and indignity.

Such proceedings, I am aware, are far distant from the contemplation of the excellent person who now presides over the affairs of Chili, as in my conscience I believe that they were no less distant from the mind and heart of the late Supreme Director, who, being placed in that elevated situation, was unfortunately exposed to the errors that arise from listening to the reports of interested individuals who ever surround the powerful, making a gain by concealing the truth and propagating falsehood.

It is a fact—as is well known to all my friends—that I had determined to quit Chili, previous to my receiving any proposition from the Government of Brazil. By that Government I have been hitherto treated with the utmost confidence and candour, and the orders they have given me are in everything the reverse of those narrow and restricted instructions with which I was hampered by the Senate, the Ministers of Chili, and San Martin, under whose orders they had placed me. The Government of Brazil, having in view the termination of the war, gave orders to that effect, without any of those miserable restrictions which are calculated to retard, if not finally to defeat, their object. The consequence is, that the war in Brazil is already successfully terminated—though we have had to contend with a much superior force—by the evacuation of Bahia—the flight of the Portuguese fleet—the capture of great part of their transports and troops—and the surrender of Maranham—all in fewer months than the Chilian Government have employed years without having even yet accomplished their object, nay, with no other result than that of removing the independence of Peru, and their own peace and security to a greater distance.

I must now call your attention, although I have already addressed a letter on the subject to the Minister of Finance, to a breach of faith on the part of the late Government of Chili in respect to the contract between Senor Alvarez, their Envoy in England, and my brother, the Honourable William Erskine Cochrane, for the completion, outfit, and navigation to Chili of the steamer *Rising Star*, by which my brother has been involved in expenses to a very great amount. Whether the inconvenience he is sustaining from the perfidy of the late Ministers is in the course of removal by the good faith of their successors I have yet to learn, but if not, I must respectfully state to you on behalf of my brother that I demand payment of the amount due to him under the contract above-mentioned.

I also respectfully suggest, that it is your duty to examine the accounts of Mr. Price, and cause him to pay over the bonus of 40,000 dollars which was granted by the Government on account of the *Rising Star*, which bonus Mr. Price prematurely obtained in advance nearly three years ago, although it did not become due till the arrival of the ship. This sum, which is part of the remuneration due to my brother on account of the said ship, Mr. Price, or the house of which he is a member, refuses to deliver up, under the pretence that its detention is necessary to their own security, in the event of the Chilian Government requiring it to be restored. This is a most extraordinary way of justifying the detention of another's property, and I trust, Sir, that you will immediately take the necessary steps to cause both that sum, and all other sums due to my brother for the *Rising Star*—the particulars of which you may receive from Mr. Barnard—to be paid without further delay. To that end, and in order to prevent the risk and serious expense attending the remittance of money to so great a distance, I beg to suggest that the best mode of payment will be by an order on your agents in London.

I am much less solicitous on the subject of the debt due to myself, but after repeatedly requesting the Accountant-General, Correa de Saa, during the last six months of my residence in Chili, to investigate and determine on my accounts, without his proceeding therein in any effectual way, I was astonished to receive from him a communication calling upon me to appoint an agent to explain certain particulars, which I had considered as explicitly set forth in the documents delivered. This delay and these obstacles, I cannot consider in any other light than *as mere pretexts to avoid the payment of the balance due to me for my services*, and for the expenditure of monies that were my own, inasmuch as I might, with perfect justice—instead of employing them for the maintenance of the Chilian navy—have applied them to the liquidation of the debt due to myself, and have left the service, as the Government did, to shift for itself. Besides, Sir, let me call to your recollection that not a *real* of these monies came out of the pocket of any Chileno, but that the whole were captured or collected by me from sources never before rendered available to supply the necessities of a destitute squadron.

I call upon you, Sir, as the Minister of Marine, to see justice done on the above subjects, and if in my accounts or demands you find anything false or fraudulent, let it be printed in the *Gazette*, and give me the privilege of reply.

I trust you will excuse my entering into the present detail, and do me the justice to feel that no part of it is irrelevant to the subject of your letter. Indeed, if I were not desirous of troubling you as briefly as possible, I could assign numerous other reasons for desiring to have demonstration of a change of ministerial conduct in the management of affairs in Chili, before again exposing myself to difficulties of so painful a nature, and re-occupying a situation which I have found to be harassing, thankless, and unprofitable.

When the *puertos non habilitados* (unlicensed ports) shall be thrown open to the national commerce—when those obstacles shall be removed which now render the transport by sea more expensive than carriage by land—when the coasting trade, that nursery for native seamen, shall be encouraged instead of prohibited, it will be time enough to think of re-establishing the marine, for, with regard to foreign seamen, such is the disgust they entertain for a service in which they have been so neglected and deceived, that I am confident that the ships of Chili will never again be effectively supplied with men of that description. Indeed, there was not an individual amongst the foreign seamen under my command during the latter period of my services in Chili whose fidelity was not shaken to such a degree as to be undeserving of confidence on any occasion of danger or emergency. Could the late Ministers even expect the natives to serve them faithfully without pay and without food?—but His Excellency the present Director can solve this question in a similar case with regard to the army.

It will be well if the foreign seamen have sufficient forbearance to refrain from revenging—by acts of hostility to the state—the deception and breach of promise which they experienced from San Martin, and that destitute condition to which they were reduced, especially during the last six months of my stay at Valparaiso, by similar frauds on the part of Rodriguez, who, I believe, as Minister of Finance, has been actuated by the hope of compelling the men to abandon their country without remuneration for their services, when they appeared to him and to other short-sighted individuals to be no longer useful.

The Chilian expedition to the Intermedios, and the mean methods by which it was proposed to obtain Chiloe without my intervention, excited in my mind at the time no other feeling than pity and contempt, mixed with regret that the sacrifices of so good a people should be rendered unavailing by the imbecility of their rulers. The failure of both these wretched attempts I predicted. From the men now in power I hope better things, and it will gratify me extremely to observe that you succeed in establishing just laws—a free constitution—and a representative body to direct civil affairs. In fine, that you succeed in all you undertake for the public good; and when I see you entered on the right path, my most zealous co-operation—if required—shall not be withheld.

I cannot conclude without expressing my high sense of the honour which His Excellency the present Director conferred upon me, by desiring my continuance in the command of the navy. To him I return my heartfelt thanks, and to you also for the polite manner in which you communicated his obliging wishes.

(Signed) COCHRANE.

To His Excellency Don Mariano Egana,
Minister of Foreign Affairs, &c.

I will quote one more letter, subsequently addressed by me to the Supreme Director, General Freire, in whose administration I felt a sincere interest, knowing him to be a truly honest man, having only at heart the good of his country; but from his rough training in the camp, without the administrative ability to contend with the intrigues by which he was surrounded.

Rio de Janeiro, Dec. 14, 1823.

MY RESPECTED AND ESTEEMED FRIEND,

It would afford me great satisfaction to learn that everything you contemplated for the advancement and happiness of your country, has succeeded to the extent of your wishes and endeavours, but here we live at so great a distance, and the communication by letter is so scanty, that we have no certain knowledge with respect to your proceedings. I dare not venture to offer you my congratulations, being well aware that the re-union of the Congress would present difficulties which might possibly be insuperable, fearing also that you may have been subjected to much uneasiness by the diversity of views entertained by the members, and their deficiency in those habits, and that general information in affairs of Government, so necessary in the deliberations of a Legislative Assembly.

Here we have had our Cortes, but their meeting has produced nothing beneficial to the State. There existed indeed amongst them so great a discordance of opinion, and the temper of those who found their crude notions opposed was so violent, that the Emperor—finding it impracticable to act with them—determined to dissolve them, which he did on the 12th of last month, and issued his commands for the meeting of a new Cortes, but I much doubt whether the people in the various provinces can find others competent to the task. Everything here is quiet, and I have no doubt will remain so in the neighbourhood of the capital, but I have some fear as to the disposition of the northern provinces. I shall regret much should anything occur which will disturb the public tranquillity, now that all the provinces are entirely free and independent of European authority.

With regard to myself, the friendship you have always expressed and entertained towards me, justifies my belief that you will be gratified to learn that everything has succeeded here to the full extent of my expectations, the foreign war being entirely brought to a close within the short space of six months; during which period about seventy vessels have fallen into our hands, including several ships of war, amongst which is a beautiful new frigate of the largest dimensions.

We have gone on here in the happy manner that I fondly anticipated we should have done in Peru, and which would have been the case if the expedition which was intended to be sent to the Puertos Intermedios three years ago under your command, had not been prevented by the intrigues of San Martin, who was jealous of anything being done in which he was not personally engaged, though he had neither the courage nor talent to avail himself of circumstances when appointed to the command of the Peruvian expedition.

I have heard that my reply to San Martin's accusations has been published in Peru, but as it is chiefly a personal defence, it cannot be very interesting to the public, to whom I feel a great inclination to address a letter on the causes of the miscarriage of their *military enterprises*, and the origin and progress of those intrigues which led to the mismanagement of public affairs, and disappointed the hopes and expectations of the worthy people of Chili, who conducted themselves so long with patient submission to rulers who governed without law, and often without justice.

In my letter to you of the 21st of June last, I mentioned at some length my reasons for leaving Chili, but as that letter may possibly have miscarried, I think it well to repeat here—which I do with great truth—that it would have given me great pleasure to have been at liberty to co-operate with you; but having, long previous to your communications, determined from the ill-treatment I received to quit the country, I considered that it was better in every point of view to conform to that resolution, without mixing myself in its internal affairs, it being my province, as a foreigner, to leave all parties uncontrolled, aud in the free exercise of their civil rights. In adhering to this resolution, I sacrificed both my inclination to have acted with you in overthrowing the ministers, and my own personal interests—abandoning nearly all that I had individually hoped to attain; but I had predetermined to do this, rather than endure any longer the base intrigues of those men, and their packed Convention; whose injustice became the more conspicuous after their receiving the stars and distinctions bestowed by San Martin, with the promise of estates and further bounties. Indeed, the reception which even the late Supreme Director influenced by these persons gave to San Martin after his apostacy to Chili, his cowardice, ambition, and tyranny in Peru, formed a sufficient contrast with the conduct pursued towards me, to convince me that my presence in Chili was no longer desired by the Government, and could not, under existing circumstances, be useful to the people.

I hear that O'Higgins has proceeded to Peru. Personally I wish him well, and hope that the lesson he has received will enlighten him, and enable him in future to distinguish between sincere friends and insidious enemies. I fear, however, that his asylum in Peru will not meet his expectations, because his passive acquiescence in the barbarities inflicted by San Martin on the Spaniards to whom he had tendered protection cannot be forgotten; and the Peruvian people are not ignorant that the miseries which they have suffered might have been averted by a little firmness on the part of O'Higgins.

I have no reason to believe that the old intrigue on the part of Puyrredon and San Martin, is again revived by the latter, and that a French frigate which lately sailed hence for Buenos Ayres, has a commission on that subject. Whether these intrigues extend from Mendoza over the Cordilleras, or not, I have no means to ascertain, but I know that the French *Charge d'Affaires* here has been endeavouring underhand to induce this Government to give up the fortifications of Monte Video to the State of Buenos Ayres, which can only be with the view of extending the influence of France in that quarter.

I fear that I have already trespassed too long on the time of your Excellency, otherwise I might take the liberty to throw out some suggestions which it appears to me ought to be useful, though you may probably have anticipated them. The principal one is the benefit which might be derived from having some accredited agent here; and from the reciprocal and formal acknowledgment of the independence of the respective States. Treatises of commerce and, if possible, alliance and mutual protection against any hostile attempts on the independence of South America should be entered into. This country possesses a squadron of considerable force, in addition to which six new frigates and eight large steam gallies have been ordered to be built in North America, England, and the northern ports of the Empire.

I shall be gratified if you will do me the favour to honour me with the continuance of your friendly correspondence, and believe me to be,

Your respectful and attached friend,

(Signed) COCHRANE and Marenhaõ.

His Excellency Don Ramon Freire,
Supreme Director of Chili.

P.S. I did not intend to have trespassed on you with anything of a private nature, having written at length to the Accountant-General on the subject of my brother's claim for the steamer "*Rising Star*," and my own claims for monies disbursed *for the maintenance of the Chilian squadron, whilst in pursuit of the Prueba and Venganza;* but, on consideration, I think it well to request you to do me the favour to cause justice to be done.

CHAPTER XIV.

INJUSTICE TO THE SQUADRON—INCONSISTENCY OF THIS—ESTATE TAKEN FROM ME—MY LOSSES BY LITIGATION—ENDEAVOURS TO ENFORCE MY CLAIMS—PETTY EXCUSES FOR EVADING THEM—I AM CHARGED WITH EXPENSES OF THE ARMY—AND WITH COSTS FOR MAKING LEGAL CAPTURES—MY CONDUCT APPROVED AT THE TIME—MINISTERIAL APPROBATION—PALTRY COMPENSATION AT LENGTH GIVEN—MINISTERIAL CORRUPTION—PROVED BY SAN MARTIN—CAUSE OF OFFICIAL ANIMOSITY TO ME—CONCLUSION.

MY services to Chili and Peru have been so fully narrated in these pages, that recapitulation is unnecessary. I will, therefore, briefly notice their reward.

I was compelled to quit Chili by the political dissensions previously related—without any of the emoluments due to my position as Commander-in-Chief of the Navy, or any share of the sums belonging to myself, officers, and seamen; which sums, on the faith of repayment had, at my solicitation, been appropriated to the repairs and maintenance of the squadron generally, but more especially at Guayaquil and Acapulco, when in pursuit of the *Prueba* and *Venganza*. Neither was any compensation made for the value of stores captured and collected by the squadron, whereby its efficiency was chiefly maintained during the whole period of the Peruvian blockade.

The revolutionary movements already detailed, also

compelled me to quit the Pacific without any compensation from Peru, either to myself or the officers who remained faithful to Chili—though my absence ought not to have operated as a bar to such compensation as the Sovereign Congress awarded to the generals and field officers of the army, who, though restrained by General San Martin from effecting anything of importance towards the liberation of the country, nevertheless received 500,000 dollars as a reward, whilst nothing was bestowed on myself or the squadron, except thanks for "hazardous exploits on "behalf of Peru, hitherto," as the Congress expressed it, "under the *tyranny of military despotism*, but now "the arbiter of its own fate." To the "military "despot" himself, a pension of 20,000 dollars was granted, no doubt, as has been said, in order to be rid of him; but it was I who gave the death-blow to his usurped power, by seizing the treasure at Ancon to pay the squadron, and by my constant refusal of his insidious overtures to aid him in further treading under foot the liberties of Peru. It is scarcely possible that the Government of Peru, even at this day, can contrast with any degree of satisfaction, the empty thanks which were alone given to one—to use the words of the Sovereign Congress in its laudatory vote to myself—"by whose talent, worth, and bravery, the "Pacific Ocean has been liberated from the insults of "enemies, and the standard of liberty has been "planted on the shores of the South"—and its lavish reward to the enemy of that liberty, and even to those officers who deserted from Chili to aid the specious views of the Protector, of which rewards all who remained faithful to their duty were wholly deprived.

Still more inconsistent has been the neglect of succeeding Peruvian Governments in not fulfilling existing obligations. The Supreme Director of Chili, recognising—as must also the Peruvians—the justice of their paying, at least, the value of the *Esmeralda*, the capture of which inflicted the death-blow on Spanish power, sent me a bill on the Peruvian Government for 120,000 dollars, which was dishonoured, and never since paid by any succeeding Government. Even the 40,000 dollars stipulated by the authorities at Guayaquil as the penalty of giving up the *Venganza* was never liquidated, though the frigate was delivered to Peru contrary to written stipulations previously adduced—and was thus added to the Peruvian navy without cost to the State, but in reality at the expense of the Chilian squadron, which ran it down into Guayaquil. How the successive Governments of Peru can have reconciled this appropriation to the injury of one whom their first independent Government so warmly eulogised, it is difficult to conceive.

To return, however, to my relations with Chili. Shortly after my departure for Brazil, the Government forcibly and indefensibly resumed the estate at Rio Clara, which had been awarded to me and my family in perpetuity, as a remuneration for the capture of Valdivia, and my bailiff, Mr. Edwards, who had been left upon it for its management and direction, was summarily ejected. Situated as this estate was, upon the borders of the Indian frontier, it was, indeed, a trifling remuneration for overthrowing the last remnant of Spanish power in the continental territory of Chili. To have resumed it then, without pretext of any kind, was an act reflecting infinite discredit upon those who perpetrated that act, whether from revengeful feelings or baser motives.

The sum of 67,000 dollars, the speedy payment of which was promised to me by the Supreme Director after our return from Valdivia, was never paid, though the conquest of that fortress proved the immediate cause of success in negociating a loan in England, which, before that event, had been found impracticable. By a remarkable coincidence, the first instalment of the loan arrived at Valparaiso at the period of my departure; but the English merchants to whose care it was consigned, refused to permit the money to be landed, in consequence of the disorganization in which the corrupt conduct of the ministry had involved the State.

No compensation for the severe wounds received during the capture of the *Esmeralda* was either offered or received—though for these all States make separate provision. Even the Grand Cross of the Legion of Merit, conferred for the capture of the *Esmeralda*, was suspended; whilst, in its place, I was exposed to the greatest imaginable insults, even to the withdrawal of every ship of war from under my command.

Unhappily, this ingratitude for services rendered

was the least misfortune which my devotedness to Chili brought upon me. On my return to England, in 1825, after the termination of my services in Brazil, I found myself involved in litigation on account of the seizure of neutral vessels by authority of the then unacknowledged Government of Chili. These litigations cost me, directly, upwards of £.14,000, and indirectly, more than double that amount; for, in order to meet the expenses, I was compelled to dispose of property at a great sacrifice, amongst which the loss arising from the sale of my residence and grounds in the Regent's Park alone was upwards of £.6,000—whilst that on other property also sacrificed was as much more; thus, in place of receiving anything for my efforts in the cause of Chilian and Peruvian independence, I was a loser of upwards of £.25,000, this being more than double the whole amount I had received as pay whilst in command of the Chilian squadron: in other words, not only did I obtain no compensation for my services in Chili—but was, in addition, compelled to sacrifice all I afterwards earned in Brazil to satisfy claims arising from seizures made under the authority of the Chilian Government! No consideration whatever for these losses has been shewn by those whom I so zealously and faithfully served in their hour of need; not even by Peru, in behalf of which country nearly all these litigations arose, though the services of the squadron cost nothing to that country or Chili, beyond the expense to the latter of its original ineffective equipment, the provisioning and maintenance of the ships having been provided for at the cost of the enemy, even to the payment of the crews with their own prize-money, none of which was ever refunded!

For sixteen years I made unceasing efforts to induce the succeeding Governments of Chili to liquidate my claims, but without effect. At the expiration of that period, I was no less surprised than annoyed by receiving from the Accountant-General a demand for explanation of my accounts, though, whilst I remained in Chili, I had urged incessantly their official investigation, for, notwithstanding that the Government had pronounced its approbation upon all I had done, I foresaw that quibbles might arise as the pretext for continued injustice.

That the accounts were not adjusted previous to my departure from Chili, was no fault of mine, as I was, in self-defence, compelled to quit the country, unless I chose to take part with the late Supreme Director, in supporting a ministry which, unknown to him, were guilty of the most avaricious and injurious acts—or aid Gen. Freire in overthrowing one to whom I was attached, as having always believed him to be a sincere and honourable man.

To call upon me, therefore, in the year 1838, for an explanation of complicated accounts delivered to the Chilian Government and unquestioned in 1821–2, was an unworthy course, the more so as most of the explanations required were of a paltry description, even to the expenditure of a single dollar in the purser's accounts—as though amidst operations of such magnitude as had successfully resulted in the accomplishment of every object proposed, my time could be occupied in minor details, yet even to these I was compelled to attend, the Government not furnishing me with a competent person to register the expenditure of the squadron.

The explanations thus demanded, after a lapse of nearly twenty years, were one hundred in number—no great amount in a series of accounts extending over more than three years' prosecution of an arduous service, during which I had to find the means of supporting the squadron, the expenditure of which was now, for the first time, called into question. The paltry character of many of the matters in dispute will be best judged of from the following items:—

No. 4. Vouchers demanded for ten dollars' worth of mutton.

23 to 32. Certificates for cases of gin lost in the San Martin.

40. Deficiency of nine dollars in the pay-books of the Lautaro.

42. Do. of three dollars in the pay-books of the Independencia.

69. Error of three dollars in the valuation of goods captured at Arica.

73. Forty dollars for repairing pumps at a time when the ships could hardly be kept afloat.

75. Imputed error of *one dollar!* in the purchase of 756 gals. of gin, &c. &c.

In addition to many such petty items, I was accused of giving bounty to seamen unauthorised—though the seamen had captured the very monies with which they were rewarded—and was expected to refund some which had been stolen. My having supplied rudders and rigging to the vessels cut out from before the batteries at Callao, was called into question, though the ships could not be sent from the port without re-equipment, the Spaniards having dismantled them before their capture. I was expected, after the lapse of sixteen years, to produce the pursers' books of the division of stores captured, the books having been sent in due course to the Minister of Marine's office; yet the Government had not furnished the squadron with the necessary articles for the safety of the ships, whether under sail or at anchor, whilst the stores which were taken from the enemy and applied to the use of the expedition, were so much clear gain to the State.

A still more unjust act of the Chilian Government was that of calling upon me for vouchers for the expenditure of 50,000 dollars, captured by Col. Miller, in Upper Peru, and expended by him in paying and provisioning his troops, of which transactions I was not at all cognizant: the sums, however, were no doubt faithfully applied by Col. Miller to the exigencies of the service in which he was engaged; he merely apprising me that he had captured or otherwise collected 32,000 dollars, with which he had given his men two months' pay, and an additional month's gratuity for their gallantry, a transaction no less essential than honourable, but one which the narrow views of the ministry failed to appreciate. No vouchers were, however, remitted to me whilst I remained on the coast, as the following letter from Col. Miller will shew:—

Ica, Aug. 27, 1821.

My Lord,

Inclosed is a memorandum of money received and disbursed to the division under my command. So soon as time will permit, another more detailed and circumstantial account shall be forwarded for your Lordship's approval.

I have written to Major Soler, who is in Lima, to furnish your Lordship with the necessary particulars relative to the capture of the cash.

I have the honour, &c.

Wm. MILLER,

Col. Comm. Southern Division.

I never afterwards saw Col. Miller nor his division in Peru; but the whole that was expended by him in emancipating the country, was charged to me, and thus I was made responsible for the price of his victories, though they did not cost either Government a dollar.

But the most flagrant act of injustice was the deduction from my claims of costs and damages for the detention of neutral vessels seized under the orders of blockade issued by the Chilian Government. The circumstances were as follows:—

The Spanish Government had chartered the *Edward Ellice* and other ships to transport troops from Spain to Peru, but internal divisions in the parent state prevented their despatch. The masters of these vessels thereupon claimed demurrage, which it was not convenient for the Spanish Government to pay—but in lieu thereof licences were granted to carry Spanish goods to Peru. These ships, being thus loaded, proceeded to Gibraltar, where the house of Gibbs & Co. provided them with British papers, in addition to the

Spanish manifests supplied at Cadiz—this fact alone shewing that they considered the speculation illegitimate.

Furnished with these double sets of papers, they came to Peru for the purpose of trading; but as I had advice of this proceeding—and afterwards found the Spanish duplicates in the Peruvian Custom Houses —I seized the vessels on account of the fraudulent papers, they having also on board contraband of war, and was about to send them to Valparaiso for adjudication, when their commanders offered to surrender to me all the anchors, cables, and other illegal cargo, if I would forego this determination, which I did, and applied these articles to the use of the Chilian squadron, which at that time had not a trustworthy anchor in any of the ships.

The course pursued was satisfactory to the masters and supercargoes, and subsequently, on explanation, to Sir Thomas Hardy, whilst it was highly approved by the Chilian Government. After my return to England, actions were brought against me for even the contraband which had been voluntarily surrendered by the masters; but as I was fortunately enabled to produce the Spanish duplicates, they were abandoned, otherwise I should have been involved in utter ruin, for releasing British vessels subject to condemnation, and at the same time *gratuitously providing* for the Chilian ships of war, the essential articles of which they were entirely destitute.

In order to conciliate the English merchants at Valparaiso, the Admiralty Court acquitted various vessels seized under the orders of the Government, charging the costs and damages to my account! and that in the face of its own right to blockade and seizure as expressed to the British Commodore, Sir Thomas Hardy, who, though he insisted on the protection of British ships, disavowed their taking advantage of his protection to supply the enemy with contraband of war, as had been done.

Sir Thomas Hardy's view was this, that if the blockading power was not in a position to render the blockade efficient over the whole coast, it was not recognisable anywhere by the law of nations; but, whilst expressing this erroneous view of blockade, he added, "nor can I resist the right which the " Government of Chili has to establish and maintain " blockade on the same footing as other belligerents."

But even in the extreme views of Sir Thomas Hardy, we were competent to establish and maintain a blockade in its widest extent, and the best proof of the fact is, that the blockade was established. Even Zenteno, the Minister of Marine, pointed out to Sir Thomas Hardy, the ability of the squadron to maintain the blockade which he recognised.

"Our naval forces, perhaps diminished in apparent magnitude by distance, was not believed sufficient to maintain the blockade in all its extent, yet it has had the glory of setting at liberty, and of placing in the hands of the American Independents, all the ports and coasts of Peru, excepting only the port of Callao. Moreover, from the very centre even of that port, and from under the fire of the batteries, the Spanish ship of war, *Esmeralda*, has been cut out by our naval forces, and our strength thereby augmented, whilst that of the enemy is reduced to nothing.

(Signed) "JOSE IGNACIO ZENTENO."

So that, in face of this declaration by the Chilian Minister himself, as to the naval supremacy of the squadron on the coast of Peru, and its consequent right of seizure, the Admiralty Court, for its own sinister purposes, chose to decide that I was liable for seizures of neutral vessels made by my captains, without my knowledge—condemning me in costs and damages for their acts; the result being that I was mulcted in this, and every other charge it saw fit to make in my absence. The injustice of this was the more striking, as San Martin was appointed Commander-in-Chief of the squadron as well as the army, so that, even supposing the decisions of the Admiralty Court to be right, the *onus* lay upon him, not me. Yet he was rewarded, and I was compelled to pay for acts executed under his authority.

In the year 1845, *twenty-three years after* the liberation of Peru, and the annihilation of the Spanish power in the Pacific, the Chilian Government deducted all charges thus unjustly placed to my account, and awarded me the balance of 30,000 dollars (£.6000) for all the services rendered to the country. I have before mentioned that, from the consequence of litigation proceeding from obedience to the orders of the Chilian Government, I was subjected to a loss in England of nearly £.25,000; so that in place of my reaping any reward whatever for my services to Chili and Peru, the liberation of the latter and the completion of independence of the former cost me £.19,000 out of my own pocket!

I would ask the Chilian people and Government whether they do not now see the injurious treatment pursued towards me—arising from the base impositions then practised upon them, though these have been partly compensated by the present enlightened Government, which, as its recent decision has shewn, is composed of men of a far higher stamp than those with whom I was placed in contact, and, as I have every reason to believe, would redeem the stigma left on the national character by their corrupt predecessors of 1820–23, on fully comprehending the treatment to which I was subjected. That explanation is here truthfully laid before them, enabling them to judge for themselves. I will only add that not a single statement has been made in this narrative which is not based on original documents, the more important of which have been incorporated, the whole being about to be photographed and sent out to Chili, so that, comparing them with their official originals, their authenticity shall be beyond question.

I have said that the ministry which paralysed my operations, and by their ill-disguised mercenary practices overthrew the Supreme Director, O'Higgins, was corrupt, though I have thought it beneath the dignity of historical narrative, more particularly to expose their dishonest practices, of which I was well apprised. I feel, however, that in making such a charge, some proof thereof is incumbent on me, I will therefore in conclusion simply adduce a solitary instance of those practices, so damning, that, unless supported by irrefutable testimony, I might well be deemed a malicious libeller for making accusations otherwise utterly incredible.

It has been proved by the narrative—as indeed it has never been disputed—that the vigilance of the blockade before Callao starved the Spanish garrison out of Lima, and ultimately out of the fortress of Callao, this being the main object of the blockade. Whilst I was thus, as the only means within my power, endeavouring to starve out the Spaniards, *the Chilian Ministers were sending corn to be sold, at a thousand per cent. profit, to the blockaded garrison!*

To such an extent was this carried, that even Gen. San Martin, aware of the villainy of his pretended supporters in the Chilian ministry, and dreading the result, put me on my guard by writing to me the following letter:—

Haura, Feb. 21, 1821.

My esteemed Friend,

I am expecting information from you with great anxiety, and sincerely hope that it may be as favourable as that which I received in Ancon when I was in similar uncertainty.

The *Miantinomo* is on her way from Valparaiso, *by permission of the Government, to introduce a cargo of corn into Callao! It is most essential at all risks to avert this mischief, for it would be perfect ruin to admit such a cargo under existing circumstances!* I have officially given you information on this subject.

The day before yesterday the *Andromache* arrived at Huacho; Capt. Sherriff tells me that in a few days he shall return to Callao.

Lady Cochrane is at Huaita, making shift in the best way she can. God give you happiness, my friend. Always count on the sincere esteem of your affectionate

JOSE DE SAN MARTIN.

This testimony from one whose creatures the more influential of the Chilian ministers were, is indisputable, but in the present case their rapacity alarmed even their patron. San Martin is however wrong in attributing the traitorous attempt to the Government collectively—the Supreme Director, O'Higgins, not being capable of such practices as were carried on under his authority—of which this is only one solitary instance. The real perpetrators of these enormities are fresh in the recollection of many Chilenos still living. Yet these were the men who, under the mask of patriotism, originated the most unworthy charges against me, without giving me the slightest credit for having carried on the naval war without national assistance either in money or stores. The present generation of Chilenos are proud of their country, and—as their present excellent President, when awarding me an admiral's pay for the remainder of my life has stated—desire to reward those illustrious foreigners who assisted them in their struggles for independence—but they have great reason to regret the conduct of those ministers who imperilled that independence, and jeopardised the liberties of Chili for private gain.

It is scarcely necessary to add that not a grain of corn in the *Miantinomo*, or other vessels similarly despatched, with the exception of one which arrived during my absence, found its way to the starving garrison of Callao. Yet on their arrival I was implored to permit its landing, and on replying that no such treachery to the people of Chili should be carried on before my face, I was coolly asked to stand off during the night from the blockade, *that I might not see what was going on!* Such was ministerial honesty in the first days of Chilian independence.

The cause of official animosity to me is now apparent. Had I participated in these nefarious practices, or had I accepted the rank, decorations, and estates offered to me by San Martin as the price of my defection from Chili, I should now be rich, however despicable to myself—in place of having long and severely suffered in consequence of my rigorous adherence to the national interests—with the proud consciousness of never having done an act which I desire to conceal.

APPENDIX.

Recent Address of the President of Chili to the Senate and Chamber of Deputies, recognising Lord Dundonald's services, and according to him full pay as Admiral for the remainder of his life.

Fellow Citizens of the Senate and Chamber of Deputies,

Towards the end of 1818, when Chili celebrated the first maritime triumph obtained by our squadron in Talcahuano, the gallant seaman Thomas Lord Cochrane, now Earl of Dundonald, and an admiral in the British service, appeared upon our seas, decided to assist the noble cause of our independence.

The important services of this chief in the British Navy are well known during the European war which ended in 1815.

He was a post captain, not in active service, when the squadron of his country was reduced to the peace establishment, and he accepted the invitation which was made to him in London by the Chilian agent, to enter the service of this country, and came to take the command of our naval forces, bringing in the prestige of his name, his great skill and intelligence, his active and daring spirit, —a powerful contingent to that struggle of such vital importance for our independence, the dominion of the Pacific.

In how far the well-founded hopes in the co-operation of Lord Cochrane were realised by the able direction which he knew how to give to our maritime forces, are facts which have been judged by the world at large and history. Still alive in our memory is the taking of Valdivia, the feats at Callao, the bloody and splendid triumph of the *Esmeralda*, the taking of the Spanish frigates *Prueba* and *Venganza* on the coast of the Ecuador, and the complete annihilation of the power of Spain in these seas executed by our squadron under the command of Lord Cochrane; and this Chief upon leaving the service of Chili in January 1823, and when he delivered over to Government, when there were no longer any enemies to contend with, the triumphant insignia of his rank, he might with justice and truth have said, "I return this into your hands when Chili has "ensured the dominion of the Pacific."

Chili at the same time that she resists unjust and exaggerated pretensions, has always been proud of her desire to reward, in a dignified and honourable manner, the services of illustrious foreigners who have assisted us in the glorious struggle for our independence. This noble and spontaneous sentiment of national gratitude was what dictated the law of 6th October, 1842, incorporating during his life with the full pay of his rank, General D. José San Martin, even when he might reside in foreign parts; and it is the same sentiment which induces me to propose to you at present, and with consent of the Council of State, the following project of law:—

> Sole Article.—Vice-Admiral Thomas Lord Cochrane, now Earl of Dundonald, is to be considered during the term of his life as in active service of the squadron of the Republic, with the full pay of his rank, even although he may reside without the territory of Chili.

Santiago, July 28, 1857.

Manuel Montt.

José Francisco Gana.

Lord Dundonald's reply to the preceding.

To His Excellency the President in Council and Congress of Chili.

Your Excellency magnanimously presented to Congress a brief but lucid enumeration of my services to the State, which being taken into consideration by the enlightened representatives of a judicious and gallant people, "full pay during my life," and an honorary medal, were voted to me, accompanied by the truly gratifying announcement that such estimable gifts were "en "testimonio de gratitud nacional por grandes servicios que prestó a "la Republica durante la guerra de Independencia."

These honours I most thankfully accept, as highly gratifying proofs that, after the lapse of more than thirty years, my zealous, official, extra-official, and successful exertions, to ensure to Chili complete independence, internal peace, and the dominion of the Pacific, are held in grateful remembrance by the Government and People of that highly respected nation. Nevertheless I must be permitted to observe that the grant of full pay, only prospectively, to one who is upwards of eighty years of age, is little more than nominal, as my life, in all human probability, is approaching its close. I had hoped that, as vast benefits have uninterruptedly accrued to the State, ever since the completion of the services so honourably recognised, the grant would have dated from that period, in the same manner that has recently been accorded to me by the Government of Brazil, which has decreed the restitution of arrears of pay from the period that my actual command ceased, and also its continuance during my life.

If my services to Chili be acknowledged to have been great, might I not expect an equal boon from a country which owes the blessings of peace and subsequent tranquillity, and consequent prosperity, to the speedy termination of war? I plead not for myself, most Excellent Sir, for at my advanced age, I have few wants, but for the sake of my children and for the honour of my family. I need only point to the additional examples of Spain and Portugal, where all general officers and admirals of first rank, employed in the struggle for the emancipation and independence of those countries, were rewarded by the subsequent continuance of their pay during their lives; an engagement ever punctually discharged.

I have no doubt that had the recollection of my advanced age been present to the mind of your Excellency when you proposed the project of law in my behalf, and had you remembered that a merely prospective grant would be of little personal benefit to me or to my numerous family, your Excellency would have been happy to have recommended, and the Congress to have conceded, that it should likewise be retrospective, especially as Chili had not (as is the case in my native country) to rear and maintain numerous officers for one found suited to command.

In order to convince your Excellency that I do not desire *full* pay to be granted to me during the long period elapsed since my services were rendered (though from the privations I have suffered and the losses I have sustained, such delay in truth might be deemed an additional title), I therefore beg most respectfully to suggest to the consideration of your Excellency, to that of the Council and National Congress, as well as to the just feeling of the honourable people of Chili, that *one half* of the pay which I received in actual service, be accorded to me retrospectively, in the same manner that a similar boon was granted by the Brazilian nation. This I should accept with deep gratitude, in compensation for the wounds I received this day thirty-six years, in the capture of the *Esmeralda*, for other perilous extra-official services rendered, and the heavy responsibilities incurred, all of which terminated in results most important to the national cause.

Be assured, most Excellent Sir, that it is only my advanced age that prevents me from attempting to re-visit your now peaceful and prosperous country, personally to acknowledge your Excellency's courtesy, and the kind feeling evinced towards me by the Council of State, by the representatives, and people of Chili. It would be with delight that I should see steam vessels now introduced into the national marine, the great railroad from Valparaiso to Quillotta and Santiago, now in progress, and witness the various important improvements accomplished, and advancement in national prosperity effected in the course of the last third of a century. Such happy results testify highly to the merits of the Government and to the character of the Chilian people.

COCHRANE—DUNDONALD.

London, Nov. 5, 1857.

Letter from the Supreme Director of Chili, approving all I had done in Peru. This letter was written in English, in which tongue His Excellency was by no means unversed, having, in early life, had the advantage of a few years spent at Richmond; a circumstance which, in after years, gave to his mind an English tone, elevating him far above the then narrowminded men by whom, unfortunately for Chili, he was surrounded and thwarted.

Most secret and confidential.

Santiago, Nov. 12, 1821.

MY DEAR FRIEND LORD COCHRANE,

Capt. Morgell, the bearer of this, has delivered to me the despatches sent by you in the *Ceransasee*, together with your interesting notes, Nos. 1 to 9, dated 10th to 30th of September last; as also the documents to which they are referred. I have read them with great attention, but have always felt just indignation against the ungrateful course pursued towards Chili, which can only be tempered by the pleasure which I feel in reading the dignity, good judgment, and knowledge with which you knew how to sustain your rights, and those of this Republic.

It was my wish that this reply should not be in writing, but personally, and with embraces of approbation for all that you have said and practised under the difficult circumstances detailed in your private and official letters; but as the great distance in which you are from this deprives me of this pleasure, and as you expect to add new glories to Chili in the seizure of the *Prueba* and *Venganza*, and to bring them to port Bernardo under your orders, I will hastily answer the principal points of your communications.

The party and the words you mention, do not leave any doubt of the small hopes which Chili is to have for its sacrifices; yet there is nothing to fear from such intentions when discovered. Whilst the squadron under your orders commands the Pacific, this Republic is very well covered, and it is in our hands to be the masters of the moral, political, commercial, and even of the physical force of this part of America.

* * * * *

Although the battery placed at Ancon *after* the enemy went away in tranquillity, and the threat (*from San Martin,*) about not paying one *real*, unless Chili should sell the squadron to Peru, made it excusable not to send any mission there; yet I have named my Minister of Finance, in whom I have the greatest confidence, to go to Lima to fix the basis of relations, and to ask compensation for the active debt of Chili against Peru. My Minister has orders to return as soon as possible, let the end of his mission be what it will, and by that time you may have returned to Chili, and then we will accord the ulterior.

It is very painful that the garrison of Callao would not capitulate under your flag! Then you and Chili would have been implored for grants,—then all should have been paid without excuse,—and then you would not have found yourself under the necessity of taking the property retained, to pay and save the squadron. *I would have done the same if I had been there, therefore I say again all has my approbation*, and I give to you, as to the meritorious officers under your orders, my cordial thanks for their fidelity and heroism in favour of Chili, where, in a more glorious and decorous way, the fortune of all will be made in the course of progress which events are preparing for this happy country; whilst it is not known what is to be had in Peru, because, as you observe, the war is only beginning, which will be followed by poverty, discontent, and above all anarchy. They will soon feel the want of you and of the squadron, and those ungrateful officers who separated themselves from you to enter the Peruvian navy will also feel their deceit and punishment. They have been scratched out of the list of the Chilian navy, and I only wait your arrival or an official detail relating to the expedition, to assign lands and premiums to those who have not abandoned you, and in particular to the honourable Captains Crosbie, Wilkinson, Delano, Cobbet, and Simpson, whom you recommend.

Although we live in poverty, and the Exchequer continues in affliction, yet we have sufficient resignation and courage to make convenient sacrifices. All my efforts shall be employed in making the *Rising Star* one of the vessels of our squadron, and then we shall be invincible, and by keeping good relations with Sir Thomas Hardy, and by his means with England, we shall establish fundamental principles to our glories. I am satisfied of the conferences and deliberations you had with this gentleman, and I approve the whole, although the Valparaiso merchants might scream.

I like the precautions you have taken in sending your correspondence directly to me, and not to the ministry. But you must understand that even before I had read your private and official letters, much of their contents was known to the public, no doubt by the private communications of some officers, or by what was verbally communicated in Valparaiso by the officers of the *Aransasu.* On my part, I also recommend you all necessary secresy on the contents of this letter, so that our reserve may not be frustrated, and our best measures disappointed.

I shall claim from the Lima Government satisfaction for putting in prison the First Lieutenant of the *O'Higgins*, and also for imprisoning him of the same class belonging to the *Valdivia,* as also for the threat of the ungrateful Guida, as narrated in your favour of the 29th of September last. I assure you that I will never permit the least insult against the flag of this Republic. I felt the greatest pleasure in the answer you gave to Monteagudo and Guida in your note of the 28th and 29th.

As you have left Callao there is nothing officially to communicate upon your conduct there. You have not submitted to Lima neither directly nor indirectly, and from the moment the independence of that country was declared under the protectoral Government of San Martin ceased the provisional control that he had upon the squadron.

The province of Conception is almost free of enemies, and I hope Chiloe will be so very soon, to accomplish our greatness. There is a nursery for a good navy, and when you can visit that archipelago you will discover advantages and richness, relieved from the care of indolent and despotic Spain.

Believe me, my dear Lord,

Your eternal friend,

O'HIGGINS.

WESTMINSTER:
PRINTED BY THOMAS BRETTELL, RUPERT STREET, HAYMARKET.

For EU product safety concerns, contact us at Calle de José Abascal, 56–1°, 28003 Madrid, Spain or eugpsr@cambridge.org.

www.ingramcontent.com/pod-product-compliance
Ingram Content Group UK Ltd.
Pitfield, Milton Keynes, MK11 3LW, UK
UKHW010349140625
459647UK00010B/949